James Dean Transfigured

James Dean Transfigured

The Many Faces of Rebel Iconography

CLAUDIA SPRINGER

University of Texas Press ❦ Austin

Excerpts from *Crash* by J. G. Ballard. Copyright © 1973 by J. G. Ballard. Reprinted by permission of Farrar, Straus and Giroux, LLC.

Excerpts from *Scene from the Movie Giant* copyright © 1993 by Tino Villanueva. Reprinted with permission of Curbstone Press. Distributed by Consortium.

Excerpts from *Wild Kids* by Chang Ta-chun, edited by Michael Berry. Copyright © 2000 Columbia University Press. Reprinted with permission of the publisher.

Photographs from the David Loehr Collection copyright © David Loehr. Courtesy of David Loehr.

Grateful acknowledgment is made to the following for permission to reproduce material originally appearing in their publications:

"The Seduction of the Surface: From *Alice* to *Crash*," in *Feminist Media Studies* 1, no. 2 (July 2001). *Feminist Media Studies* is published by Taylor and Francis Limited (http://www.tandf.co.uk).

"Playing it Cool in *The Matrix*," in *The Matrix: Cyberpunk Reloaded*, ed. Stacy Gillis (London: Wallflower Press, 2005).

"In the Shadow of *Rebel Without a Cause*: The Postcolonial Rebel," in *Rebel Without a Cause: Approaches to a Maverick Masterwork*, ed. J. David Slocum (Albany: SUNY Press, 2005).

First edition, 2007

Requests for permission to reproduce material from this work should be sent to:
Permissions
University of Texas Press
P.O. Box 7819
Austin, TX 78713-7819
www.utexas.edu/utpress/about/bpermission.html

♾ The paper used in this book meets the minimum requirements of ANSI/NISO z39.48-1992 (R1997) (Permanence of Paper).

Library of Congress Cataloging-in-Publication Data
Springer, Claudia, 1956–
  James Dean transfigured : the many faces of rebel iconography / Claudia Springer. — 1st ed.
    p.   cm.
  Includes bibliographical references and index.
  ISBN-13: 978-0-292-71443-4 (cloth : alk. paper)
  ISBN-10: 0-292-71443-2 (alk. paper)
  ISBN-13: 978-0-292-71444-1 (pbk. : alk. paper)
  ISBN-10: 0-292-71444-0 (alk. paper)
    1. Dean, James, 1931–1955—In mass media. I. Title.
P96.D37S77 2007
791.4302'8092—dc22   2006024668

For Geoff and Jack

Contents

Acknowledgments

Contributions from readers, editors, friends, family, and colleagues have enriched the contents of this book and augmented the writing process. Thanks to Stacy Gillis and J. David Slocum for their editorial virtuosity on individual chapters published separately as articles. Thanks to Kurt Hemmer for generously sharing his impressive expertise on James Dean, and to David Loehr for his assistance with photographs from his superb collection. The Society for Cinema and Media Studies gave me the opportunity to present parts of the work-in-progress as conference papers. I am grateful to Mark Dery for recommending pertinent articles and commenting on an essay of mine that became part of a chapter. Barbara Schapiro also brought relevant material to my attention. Nathan DiMeo was a valuable research assistant whose discoveries early on helped shape the book's form. Kathleen Szantor provided expert translations of French passages, and Virginia Keller was the ideal travel companion during visits to Fairmount.

At the University of Texas Press, Jim Burr, Lynne Chapman, Sue Carter, and Laura Young Bost were consummate professionals and a pleasure to work with. I am also grateful to the Press' anonymous readers for their suggestions.

My colleagues and students at Rhode Island College, where I taught for many years, were a supportive presence during the book's creation.

I received encouragement from family members George Springer, Annemarie Springer, Joel Springer, Yumi Izuyama, Len Springer, Ben Springer, Debbie Springer, Florence Adams, and the late George Adams.

My greatest sources of inspiration were my husband, Geoff Adams, and my son, Jack Adams. They gave me the gifts of time and laughter, and nothing could be better.

James Dean Transfigured

The Rebel Icon

Icons are the most significant and ambivalently, the most unintelligible of images.

— DAVID GERALD ORR
"THE ICON IN THE TIME TUNNEL"

One of the legacies of American films of the fifties is their introduction of an internationally recognizable shorthand for dissent. The angry, alienated teen rebel who sneered at Eisenhower-era complacency from the big screen provided the world with a larger-than-life embodiment of the idea of nonconformity. At the time, there were Americans engaged in protracted struggles against Cold War politics and racial segregation, but their acts of rebellion failed to fire the public's imagination as dramatically as did Hollywood's sullen teens. The teen rebel transcended its origins in iconoclasm—in the rejection of the status quo—and was itself elevated to iconic status, becoming a revered object of devotion. Over the decades that followed, the rebel figure permeated the globe, and its charismatic presence is still felt in the twenty-first century. But the rebel is a particularly ambiguous icon, with meanings that contradict each other and an extraordinary ability to conform to any purpose.

On the one hand, the teen rebel icon is a supremely commercial product used to sell cars and jeans and the complete array of capitalism's flotsam and jetsam; but, on the other hand, it still has the power to surprise when used in innovative, provocative ways. Understanding the parameters of the rebel icon's contradictory appearances can illuminate popular iconography's contemporary functions. Long detached from its original spiritual and religious functions, most iconography is now secular but nonetheless deeply embedded in society. It creates the impression of shared identity by inviting its beholders to join its ranks, not just in admiration but in imitation. As such, it is one of the variables in the array of "lifestyle choices" confronting the contemporary consumer, for whom a "new look" can be just a credit-card purchase away. However, its status as a commodity does not diminish its power to be profoundly meaningful for individuals who incorporate it into their own personal and local contexts. As American pop culture iconography has spread throughout the world, it has displaced local icons and contributed to the erasure of unique cultural memory. And yet there are texts from around the world that defy global homogenization and show that American cultural hegemony can be resisted by turning American iconography against itself.

This is a study of a variety of texts from the United States and abroad that use the teen rebel icon in disparate ways. Included here are films, advertisements, poems, fiction, and Web sites. Films dominate the analysis because the teen rebel achieved its legendary status on screen, and that is where the presence of the rebel icon is most keenly felt. The huge number of texts that use the rebel figure makes it impossible to even come close to being comprehensive. I have sought diversity and have chosen texts that use contrasting strategies. Countless texts use rebel iconography in interesting ways, and it is my hope that the examples I have chosen to analyze will encourage a reevaluation of other examples that can offer up additional complexities and contradictions.

The young rebel figure firmly ingrained in our cultural imagination carries with it traces of Hollywood's screen rebels of the fifties, and none more than James Dean, a point that film scholar Jon Lewis makes when he writes in his study of teen films, *The Road to Romance and Ruin*, that "it is safe to say that after 1955, youth's resort to a kind of mannered anomie—on screen and on the streets—was patterned after James Dean's performance in *Rebel Without a Cause*."[1] The generation that came of age in the early fifties is likely to consider Marlon Brando, whose fame preceded Dean's and who was idolized by him, as the ultimate rebel, but during the following fifty years, before his death in 2004, Brando's image was repeatedly revised (and reviled) as a result of his complicated public and personal life. Most young people are unfamiliar with the tough-talking young biker Brando; it is Dean, by virtue of his early death, who became a legendary figure of inarticulate teenage angst.

Despite its ubiquity, then, the rebel icon is a relatively recent invention with a specific lineage in which James Dean figures prominently. This is not a book about James Dean; it is about the rebel iconography he helped create. There are many books and articles about Dean's mid-twentieth-century life and times, but the rebel icon he contributed to has had a busy life without him for the last fifty years and shows no signs of slowing down. If anything, our mediatized world has heightened the rebel icon's visibility on ever-present screens. Consumer culture obsessively recycles iconic images to suit its many needs, and as consumerism has infiltrated the globe it has been accompanied by its stable of archetypes. Although the rebel icon has spread throughout the world, it has been anything but consistent. On the contrary, both left- and right-wing ideologues, from one extreme end of the political spectrum to the other, use rebel iconography to emblematize their cause. In each case the icon implies a position that has been misjudged and wrongly disparaged by the ruling powers, regardless of the politics involved. Each new manifestation of the icon reorients its constantly shifting allegiances.

Thus the iconic rebel figure—a culturally and commercially mediated, fluid entity—is the focus of this book. My first chapter, "Birth of an Icon," analyzes the formation of the teen rebel icon during the fifties, giving James Dean a central place in its development. I argue that the rebel icon's ambiguities originate in the convergence of a complex host of social and economic phenomena: an emerging consumer culture in an affluent postwar society; a repressive social climate of homophobia, misogyny, racism, and anti-youth rhetoric; the appropriation of a black style by disaffected young white people looking for a defiant stance; the conventions introduced by Hollywood's teen films; and media and studio manipulation of James Dean's public image. The enigmatic nature of the icon made it easy for the advertising industry to grab hold of it as an endlessly malleable and durable marketing tool.

Chapter 2, "Disney's Dean," looks at the Disney studio's 1969 film *The Love Bug* (Robert Stevenson) as an example of the rebel icon's sanitization and decontextualization. Rebel elements flourish in the film, but they are drained of their threatening connotations and rendered tame and innocuous. *The Love Bug*'s treatment of the rebel icon is a microcosm of the Disney studio's typical handling of anything that challenges the status quo. Through a process of Disneyfication, Disney films transform or mock subcultures, oppositional social movements, and racial or ethnic Others. The Disney studio's 1997 television remake of *The Love Bug* (Payton Reed) continues the trend by depoliticizing the sixties and once again homogenizing the rebel icon, and the 2005 theatrical remake, *Herbie: Fully Loaded* (Angela Robinson), is a Hollywood-style "girl-power" film in which being a rebel means hesitantly and apologetically disobeying your father.

Chapter 3, "Rebel Wrecks," contrasts Disney's strategy of eviscerating the rebel icon with British author J. G. Ballard's no-holds-barred novel *Crash*, published in 1973, four years after the release of *The Love Bug*. *Crash* incorporates the rebel icon and is structured around many of the same basic elements as the Disney film, but its treatment of their shared material could not be more radically different. The novel explodes the film's complacency, revealing that pop culture iconography resists fixity, lending itself instead to antithetical appropriations. *Crash* is an acute and disconcerting look at the perverse combination of sexuality, image obsession, celebrity death, and thrill seeking that underlies rebel iconography.

Chapter 4, "The Teen Rebel," argues that despite the descent of much teen rebel iconography into clichés and stereotypes, at least a few texts revitalize the icon in original and meaningful ways. I analyze three films and a novel. Two of the films, *The Doom Generation* (Gregg Araki, 1996) and *Boys Don't Cry* (Kimberly Peirce, 2000), are American and belong to the teen film genre in which the rebel icon has become a mainstay, but instead of recycling the genre's conventions in familiar ways, they make the genre itself their subject matter. Using contrasting cinematic strategies and tones, these films are as much about the shortcomings of the teen film genre as they are about the alarming adversity faced by contemporary young people. I also analyze the Taiwanese novel *Wild Child*, written by Chang Ta-chun in 1996, as an example of the young rebel in literary fiction and as an example of how the rebel icon has been exported from the United States and transplanted into other national contexts. *Wild Child* uses the icon brilliantly in a searing attack on the hypocrisies that followed Taiwan's "economic miracle" of the 1980s, which left in its wake a dispossessed underclass and a generation of young people afloat in a corrupt adult world with only worldwide pop culture detritus to steer them. The teen rebel icon is part of the detritus, and Chang Ta-chun uses it to underscore his young protagonist's dilemmas. In Taiwan as well as in the U.S. and much of the rest of the world, teenagers are viewed as the causes of social problems and perceived as super-predators, when in fact they are victims. I analyze a Swedish film, *Lilya 4-Ever* (Lukas Moodysson, 2003), to show how it opposes the rhetoric of teen predators by using the rebel icon to reveal adult predation on adolescents in the former Soviet Union and Sweden. Teenagers in each of these texts—the two American films, the Taiwanese novel, and the Swedish film—are trapped in hostile environments created by political and social forces beyond their control that prevent them from making their own choices and realizing their aspirations. Rebel iconography seems to offer a refuge, but its limitations become abundantly clear in each case.

Chapter 5, "The Postcolonial Rebel," elaborates on the previous chapter by isolating three texts concerned with a specific aspect of the rebel icon's global dispersion: its role in identity formation among postcolonial subjects. I analyze two films that appropriate rebel iconography to interrogate its relevance to the postcolonial world, *Touki-Bouki*, a 1973 Senegalese film directed by Djibril Diop Mambety, and *La Haine* (*Hate*), a 1995 French film directed by Mathieu Kassovitz. Both films revolve around the powerful attraction of American-style rebel iconography to young people released from colonialism but faced with its legacy both at home and abroad in the former colonial powers. The films are concerned with young people estranged from their communities and struggling to define themselves differently from the norm. In both, young rebels resist the roles thrust on them and move to the margins of their cultures in an attempt to create their own identities. Their attempts, however, are characterized by confusion as they are consistently caught up in political and cultural currents they do not fully comprehend. In an effort to establish a unique identity, they inevitably fall back on American and European pop culture, a ubiquitous presence, and while they find ingenious ways to recontextualize the rebel icon in their own cultural milieus, it ultimately fails to enlighten or assist them in their struggles against Eurocentrism, racism, poverty, and police brutality. In this chapter I also analyze a short story by American fiction writer Robert Ready, "Jimmy the Arab," in which Bachir, the Arab character briefly played by James Dean on Broadway, has grown old and is under house arrest for his gay sexuality in postindependence Algeria. In Ready's story, the rebel icon in the form of the aging Bachir/James Dean challenges colonialism, myths of masculinity, and enforced heterosexuality.

Chapter 6, "The Posthuman Rebel," looks at how rebel iconography has been taken up in another mode, the science fiction genre, and analyzes the hugely popular film *The Matrix* (Wachowski Brothers, 1999) and its two sequels. Behind their flashy special effects and futuristic mise-en-scène, they reenact a familiar scenario that dates back to the fifties: the appropriation of black cool by young white hipsters in search of a rebellious style. Thomas A. Anderson's transformation into the incontrovertibly cool Neo in the *Matrix* trilogy is enacted through the guidance of his hip black teacher Morpheus and the spiritual guide the Oracle, both of whom function in typical Hollywood fashion to promote the success of a white protagonist by imparting to him the benefits of their "special powers." The *Matrix* films revolve around cool and were marketed as cool, but their coolness unselfconsciously reproduces the racial politics at the heart of the rebel icon's emergence in the middle of the twentieth century.

Chapter 7, "The Virtual Rebel," examines the rebel icon's lives on the Internet by analyzing how James Dean continues to live posthumously on Web sites devoted to him and the iconography he inspired. The Internet creates the illusion of immediacy, of proximity to the "real" James Dean, through virtual visits to his hometown or through photographs and memorabilia. Attempts to get close to the "authentic" Dean are doomed to fail, and yet they do provide the valuable experience of community for fans. Web sites dedicated to James Dean originate in all corners of the world, and their diversity reveals the range of meanings associated with him, from the "official" site that presents him as a model of homespun virtues to a multitude of unofficial sites that use him to express a host of extraordinary ideas. Dean's image was so highly manipulated even before his death that it is impossible to uncover the "authentic" James Dean; all we have access to is the way he has been used for contradictory ideological purposes. Authenticity is highly valued now that the media and advertising have largely displaced it, so, ironically, it has become another manufactured commodity.

Cultural studies offers a valuable approach to understanding the teen rebel icon's development. Cultural studies is a form of inquiry that draws on other fields—anthropology, sociology, gender studies, feminism, literary criticism, history, and psychoanalysis, among others—to discuss contemporary cultural practices. Although it draws on other fields, cultural studies also challenges them. Specifically, it challenges what has traditionally been studied and how it has been studied. Cultural studies has sought to transform the objects of study in the humanities to include everything produced within a culture, not just the narrow range of texts traditionally deemed worthy of study—the "great books" in literature departments, for example. Cultural studies opens up textual analysis to all cultural phenomena; television, professional wrestling, the World Wide Web, rap music, grunge clothing, tattoos, popular dance, and fan clubs and their fanzines, to name a few, are all considered texts worthy of serious, rigorous analysis by cultural studies scholars. In anthropology, there has been a corresponding shift from studying "primitive" peoples to studying the organization and rituals of Western industrialized societies. By redefining the object of study, cultural studies has challenged traditionally sacrosanct categories in the humanities. In literary studies, for example, cultural studies takes on the canon: the group of books deemed superior by academic arbiters of literary taste. Instead of singling out a few books on the basis of literary quality, cultural studies "reads" all texts of culture, thereby erasing the line between "high culture" and "low culture." In cultural studies, textual analysis is concerned less with a text's inherent literary value—its "greatness"—and more with its articulation of ideological positions in relation to dominant culture. Cultural studies analyzes texts within the context of their social production, thus challenging the traditional concept of the literary object as autonomous and self-contained.

Cultural studies dates from the 1970s, and its origins include the Birmingham Center for Contemporary Cultural Studies in England, where theorist Stuart Hall wrote some of its classic work, and the French journal *Tel Quel*. The field was founded with a commitment to cultural critique—with exposing the workings of the dominant class and analyzing its use of mass culture as a tool to secure consensus for its dominance. For this endeavor, cultural studies drew heavily on an earlier mode of cultural critique—Marxist theory, in particular the writings of Louis Althusser on ideology and Antonio Gramsci on hegemony. But cultural studies also grew out of a critique of Marxism, out of a sense that traditional Marxist theories were inadequate to explain the complexities of contemporary cultural production and reception. For example, there was dissatisfaction with Marxist economic reductionism, with its emphasis on economic determinants underlying all human experience. For cultural studies theorists, we are not simply constituted by the class we are born into, with all of our thoughts determined by our class identification. Similarly, cultural studies rejected the Marxist Frankfurt School's dismissal of mass culture as debased and corrupt.

Instead, cultural studies scholars trust that there is more than one way to respond to a text, and that people often read texts in creative ways that defy expectation. Many works of cultural studies, then, turn from thinking of texts as pure instruments of cultural control to seeing them as sites of struggle between dominant and oppositional readings. Culture is not uniform and homogenous and defined entirely by class stratification. Rather, it is composed of multiple subordinate groups—subcultures—that often resist falling into line behind a dominant cultural agenda. British scholar Dick Hebdige's 1979 book *Subculture: The Meaning of Style* was an important influence on subsequent work in the field,[2] and his pioneering work was joined by equally insightful studies by scholars Simon Frith, Angela McRobbie, and Iain Chambers, among others, who examined youth subcultures, working-class subcultures, black subcultures, gay and lesbian subcultures, and women's subcultures. Issues of race, gender, and sexuality are central to cultural studies, to some extent replacing the Marxist concept of classes as agents of social transformation with a concept of "identities" as agents of oppositional change.

However, there is little agreement in the field about whether a special subcultural response or reading signifies creative nonconformity. In fact, this question is hotly contested. Standing on one side of the debate is television scholar John Fiske, who grants the audience almost complete autonomy to construct meaning, making the argument that consumers engage in widespread subversive readings of mass culture and actively resist hegemonic dictates.[3] Fiske's position has spawned a slew of cultural studies books that analyze oppositional readings of everything from Madonna videos to slasher films. However, the idea that the consumer freely determines meaning has come under attack from within cultural studies. Fiske has been accused of being simplistic, and his critics have cautioned that by exalting the consumer's unconstrained interpretive abilities, cultural studies can end up celebrating rather than analyzing the status quo. Debates over these issues comprise a lot of writing in the field.

In addition to analyzing consumer reception of mass-culture texts, cultural studies is interested in the possibilities of people creating oppositional cultural work. Subcultural expressions are studied as gestures of resistance to the commercial mainstream; the music of Bif Naked, a struggling Canadian woman punk rocker, for example, can be contrasted with that of the corporate megastar Britney Spears. But there is also a recognition in cultural studies that anything oppositional is likely to be quickly absorbed into the mainstream. The grunge protest against the oppressive fashion industry, for example, was cut short when its baggy flannel shirts appeared on high-paid supermodels on Paris catwalks and the cover of *Elle* magazine. In another twist, though, subcultures often reappropriate what the consumer industries have appropriated from them, creating an interesting cycle of resistance and cooptation. While some argue that corporate plundering of all oppositional forms has made resistance impossible, others, myself included, are interested in tracing the precise workings of appropriation and reappropriation, seeing them as parts of a dialectical process that is never completely resolved.

Cultural studies has grown and changed and branched out since its inception, resulting in many different approaches and methodologies. It has always been eclectic, borrowing its theoretical tools from other fields. The discipline is defined by its openness, and it now includes postmodern cultural studies, black cultural studies, postcolonial cultural studies, Chinese cultural studies, and cognitive cultural studies, among others. Its methodological strengths for the study of rebel iconography are its insistence on the validity of all texts as objects of study and its commitment to contextualization. For example, although *The Love Bug* is far from being a cinematic masterpiece, I have chosen to analyze it at length because it epitomizes the strategy of domesticating the rebel figure and subduing its disruptive connotations. And I devote a whole chapter to an analysis of Web sites even though they vary in quality and in any case would not be considered "art" by traditional mavens of taste. Nonetheless, they are where conflicting interpretations of rebel iconography currently proliferate. My analyses of *The Love Bug* and Web sites, along with the other texts included here, place them in their social and historical contexts, while also noting that their manipulation of the rebel icon is based on a strategy of decontextualization. When figures become iconic, they get wrenched from their original situations and meanings and are opened up to endless reconfiguration, because for the purposes of advertising it is advantageous to abandon origins and earlier contexts in order to invest an image with new and more marketable meanings.

Returning to the rebel icon's original contexts in the fifties means recognizing that not all pop culture emblems of "rebellion" in the decades since have the same derivation. For example, hip hop and rap are often explicitly political and critical, challenging the police force and other American institutions for their racism, and their origins predate fifties teen rebel iconography, drawing instead on the history of the African diaspora and African American cultural forms while also incorporating Hispanic and other musical traditions. Rap is explicitly hybrid and attests to a continuity between the past and present, as American studies scholar Tricia Rose indicates: "These transformations and hybrids reflect the initial spirit of rap and hip hop as an experimental and collective space where contemporary issues and ancestral forces are worked through simultaneously."[4] Rose points out that "hip hop's anger is produced by contemporary racism, gender, and class oppression . . . [and] a great deal of pleasure in hip hop is derived from subverting these forces and affirming Afrodiasporic histories and identities."[5] The styles of insubordination of rap and hip hop have deep historical roots, and these roots contributed to the attitude and appearance of fifties rebel iconography; yet the teen rebel is not a significant antecedent for rap and hip hop. The fifties teen rebel icon is derivative of older styles of resistance and owes them a debt, but the older styles have persisted and evolved independently of it. These styles sometimes overlap, as in the Senegalese film *Touki-Bouki* and the French film *La Haine*, analyzed in Chapter 4, creating hybrid forms typical of a globalized world where multiple influences combine in provocative ways.

It has been half a century since James Dean's death, but the rebel icon persists and is being transfigured. "Transfiguration" is a word that denotes not only metamorphosis but also the attainment of elevated spirituality. The rebel icon is not religious in the traditional sense; its elevation is secular yet imbued with sentiments held in common with religious devotion: mythification, exaltation, ritual, worship. Even though traditional religions do not hold complete sway over twenty-first-century American culture, despite the efforts of the vocal Christian right, religious beliefs and rituals are flourishing in daily practices. Consumer society is organized around assumptions that mirror religious belief systems, uniting its adherents in taken-for-granted modes of behavior. Every religion has its own myths—narratives about its origins and the proper conduct of its believers—and also an overarching myth providing an ideological paradigm for the smaller myths. In our capitalist society, the meta-myth is the American Dream success story, and the sacred ritual of shopping unites the faithful, a point made incisively by professor of religious studies Dell deChant in his article "The Economy as Religion: The Dynamics of Consumer Culture." He writes that "the myth of material success and achievement, gained through mastery of the mysteries of the Economy," is our culture's meta-myth, and he explains that

> religion in postmodern society is that collection of culturally embedded phenomena that mediate individual and collective relationships with the sacred power of the Economy through acquisition-consumption-disposal. It is not enough to simply acquire and consume objects and images. One must do both and one must also dispose of the objects and images for the sacred to be experienced. The entire process must be completed, for only then (in the cyclical manner that is elemental to cosmological systems) can the process begin again. The quicker the process is completed and then begun again, the greater is one's experience of the sacred, and hence the greater one's power in the socio-religious system. For this reason, popular culture venerates the person who is able to keep up with the trends in fashion, who is able to acquire a new car every year (perhaps this explains the recent success of automobile leasing), who buys a new house, replaces appliances on a regular basis, installs a new lawn periodically, acquires the most innovative type of computer, and so on.[6]

Consumerism, seen in this light, is the fundamental belief of contemporary American society, the bedrock upon which most shared customs exist. Its primacy benefits the immensely powerful corporations that have invaded nearly every corner of our public and private space, exhorting us to buy, buy, buy. Unlike members of traditional religions, devotees of the

Economy are subjected to perpetual Sabbath; we can worship at the altar of Wal-Mart seven days a week.

The teen rebel icon has a privileged place in the Economy's sacred cycle of acquisition-consumption-disposal. Just as stories about saints and other holy figures are interpreted differently according to changing cultural attitudes, so the stories that accompany the teen rebel change with the times and with the needs of their tellers. When the advertising industry uses the icon, it invests the already enshrined figure with whatever is necessary to persuade us to buy a product. Recently this has meant using ads that appeal to our desire *not* to participate in the process, to rebel against the pressure to be a consuming drone, but ironically it is necessary to buy the advertised product in order to resist successfully. This nonsensical logic corrals the spirit of the nonbeliever back into the consumer credo and strengthens the Economy's hold. But just as traditional religious figures can be used to pose questions about established religious and cultural norms (think of artist Andres Serrano's *Piss Christ*), so the rebel icon can be used in challenging, critical ways. In this study I am interested in analyzing both ends of the spectrum: the rebel icon as a tool in upholding capitalism's sacred cycle of consumption and as a challenge to that cycle and its accompanying beliefs. It is easy to despair that consumer society's capacity to assimilate all protests against its reign makes it impossible for oppositional ideas to be disseminated. The example of the rebel icon shows not only that iconic figures can be used to feed the cycle of acquisition-consumption-disposal; such figures can be reappropriated, showing that the possibility of opposition persists in the age of corporate dominion.

CHAPTER I

Birth of an Icon

C entral to the creation of the teen rebel icon is James Dean, the immensely popular actor with the tragically short life. Only twenty-four years old when he died, he encapsulated the idea of disaffection, and his presence is still at the heart of rebel iconography. For young Americans in the fifties, Dean embodied a set of concepts that predated his stardom but, after his sudden death, were fused together by his image. He became a posthumous symbol for the constellation of disaffected youth, death by car crash, rebellion, and ambiguous sexuality, crystalizing their combination in an overpowering way that resulted in cultural enshrinement.

James Byron Dean, born on February 8, 1931, was a talented and troubled young man whose early years in the small town of Fairmount, Indiana, were uneventful, characterized by his biographers as a time of closeness to his mother, Mildred Wilson Dean, who joined him in creative games of make-believe and encouraged him to play the violin as well as study tap dance and ballet. His father, Winton Dean, is said to have been remote and emotionally undemonstrative and did not share his wife's love for the arts. The family moved to California for Winton's job as a dental technician when James was six years old, and in later years James recalled that when he started school in Los Angeles he was shy and awkward, and he was mocked for his artistic interests. His life changed irrevocably when he was nine years old; his twenty-nine-year-old mother died of cancer after a sudden decline. Dean's biographers cite the loss of his mother and his subsequent estrangement from his father as the primary causes of his adult moodiness and recklessness. After his mother's death, his father sent him away with his grandmother on the same train that carried his mother's coffin from Los Angeles back to Indiana, where

Main Street in Fairmount, Indiana, during the late 1940s. (The David Loehr Collection)

young Jimmy was then raised by his uncle and aunt, Marcus and Ortense Winslow.

Dean grew up on his uncle's farm in rural Fairmount, where he had a typical small-town Midwestern upbringing that included helping out on the farm, excelling in sports, and speeding around on motorbikes. He also showed an aptitude for acting in his high school drama productions, and he left Indiana after graduating to pursue an acting career in Los Angeles. There he attempted to reunite with his father, who had remarried, but the effort failed in a standoff of uncommunicative antagonism brought about by his father's attempts to steer him away from acting into a more conventional career. James briefly studied theatre arts at UCLA, playing the part of Malcolm in a student production of *Macbeth*. Professional success eluded him, although he did have a part in a Pepsi commercial and an Easter television production in which he played John the Baptist. In 1951 he chose to move to New York, a beacon for those interested in artistic innovation.

Initially overwhelmed and intimidated by the city, Dean made only gradual forays from his room at the Iroquois Hotel. Over time he met other actors as well as artists, dancers, and musicians and even landed a coveted spot at the famed Actors Studio, where his idol Marlon Brando had studied. However, Dean was devastated when legendary acting teacher

Lee Strasberg subjected his first individual class performance to a harsh critique, and after that he rarely attended classes, spending his time soaking up the vibrant urban scene and frequenting diners, bars, and all-night dives. He made an impression on those who knew him for his determination to succeed as an actor and also for his mercurial personality; he could be charming one moment and rude the next. Nonetheless he took a great interest in the variety of people he met and the range of experiences the city offered, and he studied the arts with a passion, playing the bongo drums and taking dance classes in addition to acting in television dramas (he appeared in thirty between 1951 and 1955). His was a bohemian life of poverty and adventure. He had sexual relationships with both men and women, including producer Rogers Brackett, whom he had met while still living in Los Angeles and who continued to be a mentor and lover.

Theatrical success came to James Dean in New York when he was given a prominent role in the play *See the Jaguar*, and this was followed by a major role in the play *The Immoralist*, where his performance came to the attention of Elia Kazan, who was in the process of casting his new project, a film adaptation of John Steinbeck's *East of Eden*. After Dean got the part of Cal Trask in the film and an exclusive contract with Warner Bros., he resigned from the play and flew with Kazan to Los Angeles. *East of Eden* (Elia Kazan, 1955) introduced James Dean to the world and established him as a popular actor and grist for gossip columns. He followed it with the starring role in *Rebel Without a Cause* (Nicholas Ray, 1955) and a central part in *Giant* (George Stevens, 1956), both released posthumously. In the first two films Dean's young characters struggled with antagonistic family relationships, and his performance of estrangement from his on-screen fathers no doubt drew on his alienation from his own father, especially given his Method acting style. *Giant* substituted authority figures for biological fathers, eliciting a similar kind of agonized response from Dean's defiant character.

Dean had a close working relationship with both Kazan and Ray, but experienced tension with George Stevens on the set of *Giant*. Stevens was impatient with Dean's frequent lateness to the set and contempt for direction, while Dean disliked Stevens' old-fashioned dictatorial style and his excessive filming of retakes. By this time Dean was known for being aloof and insolent and for testing his friends' loyalties with his inconsiderate behavior. His romantic life continued to include both men and women, and a relationship with actress Pier Angeli received intense fan-magazine coverage. Fast cars had become a central passion in Dean's life, and in addition to his acting career, he had achieved a degree of success as a race car driver. A lover of daring and speed, he liked to tear through the streets of Los Angeles in his sports cars.

On September 30, 1955, after completing *Giant*, he was on his way to a race in Salinas, about ninety minutes south of San Francisco, when his silver Porsche 550 Spyder collided with a black-and-white Ford sedan on California's Highway 466. Dean sustained massive injuries and died nearly instantly. At the same time, or shortly afterward, James Dean was born—not the twenty-four-year-old man who had died on the highway, but the icon whose image would become instantly recognizable around the world and who would one day be joined by Marilyn Monroe and Elvis Presley to form the holy trinity of doomed pop culture gods. As American fiction writer Robert Ready puts it, James Dean "died and became his name."[1] At the time of his death, only *East of Eden* had been released. His sudden death prompted a flood of mourning and catapulted him into the realm of mythic superstardom.

Almost immediately his name and image became red-hot commercial properties, selling magazines, books, posters, calendars, ashtrays, belt buckles, mugs, fridge magnets, alarm clocks, water globes, key chains, cologne, silk ties, Christmas ornaments, and a huge assortment of other trinkets. The Fairmount Historical Museum in Dean's hometown boasts the "World's Largest Authentic James Dean Memorabilia Collection," and the James Dean Gallery in nearby Gas City, formerly located in Fairmount, has an impressive collection of its own gathered by Dean archivist David Loehr, with nearly every kind of object imaginable on display.[2] In late September of every year, thousands of fans from around the world still descend on Fairmount for its "Museum Days/Remembering James Dean" commemoration of Dean's death, and they file reverently through both museums, where Dean knickknacks sell briskly. Other private collectors in addition to Loehr have amassed enormous quantities of Dean mementos. One, Seita Ohnishi, who lives in Kobe, Japan, has dedicated his life to the memory of Dean, financing a James Dean monument in Cholame, near the site of the fatal accident, as well as a large sculpture in Dean's memory in La Coste in the south of France.[3] James Dean became an industry, like Elvis and Marilyn, whose names got detached from their flesh-and-blood bodies to become instantly recognizable global brand names.

What Dean's name sells is "rebellion," a vague concept that over time has lost any kind of political or social specificity, if it ever had any. Rebels now come in all imaginable styles, and the term is used even by those who conform wholeheartedly to the status quo and, without any sense of irony, label their rejection of oppositional values as an act of rebellious defiance. Even during James Dean's lifetime, "rebellion" was a vague concept, creating an atmosphere in which a moody young actor who had no particular commitment to political activism could come to signify the ultimate rebel.

Although James Dean's name and image still circulate widely, his posthumous presence is felt most clearly in the ubiquitous teen rebel icon, which does not necessarily look like or refer explicitly to him but which carries vestigial traces of his influence.

In the United States before the fifties, young people were understood to be younger versions of their parents who would continue on the same trajectory through life. They dressed more or less like their parents, held their parents' values for the most part, and expected to live their lives much as their parents had. There was little premium placed on defying one's parents, and acts of defiance that did take place were considered personal and individual. But during the fifties, young people became known by the new term "teenagers," and they started to reject their parents' authority and values in such large numbers that adolescent defiance became the norm. The new generational rift caused a cultural crisis and provoked stern government and media attention, especially on its manifestation as juvenile delinquency. Pundits weighed in with their opinions about the origins of the problem and its most efficacious solutions. From the perspective of the young, defiance meant liberation from outmoded beliefs and, besides, it was a lark, much more fun than assuming the burden of adult responsibility. The more they were scrutinized by pedantic authorities and the more criticism was heaped on them, the more estranged adolescents felt from the adult world. They cherished shared symbols of defiance and saw the temperamental young actor James Dean as the exalted exemplar of their sense of alienation. Dean was idolized and imitated, and when he died, he left behind a template for youthful rebelliousness. Torrential adolescent grief followed Dean's death, and after it had subsided, he became archetypal by escaping the specifics of his life and becoming enshrined as a cultural type.

The posthumous James Dean shares with the posthumous Elvis Presley a powerful global presence. An important difference, however, is that the Elvis icon in all of its various manifestations looks more or less like Elvis, although it can evoke different versions of him based on the various stages of his life. Similarly, there are representations of James Dean that resemble the actual James Dean, but Dean also helped inaugurate a concept—the angst-ridden adolescent rebel—that does not necessarily conform to his image. There is a little bit of James Dean in subsequent representations of the lonely, misunderstood teenager, no matter what the teenager looks like (or whether it is a teenager at all, "teenager" having been redefined in recent years as a state of mind). Actor Martin Sheen, whose performance as Charles Starkweather in the film *Badlands* (Terrence Malick, 1973) was heavily influenced by James Dean, concisely pinpointed the difference between the Elvis myth and the James Dean myth when he said, "There were only two people in the '50s. There was Elvis Presley, who changed the music, and James Dean, who really changed our lives."[4] During the late 1950s, "the crucial male figure," according to cultural commentator Jon Savage, who has written several books on pop music and its cultural frameworks, "was not Presley or Brando but James Dean."[5] It can be argued that James Dean became more of an abstract concept—a symbol of the teenage rebel—whereas Elvis Presley's insinuation into the cultural fabric was based more on a cult of personality. While many people may know very little, or nothing at all, about Dean's life, they nonetheless cannot help but be aware of the James Dean–style rebel, which has become firmly ensconced as an iconographic fixture.

None of the countless attempts to explain James Dean's phenomenal impact on American culture has been completely successful, for it is impossible to fully comprehend the convergence of forces at work in the creation of a personality that transcends mere fame and enters the rarified realm of mythic archetype. As much as the entertainment industry tries to analyze the process in order to reproduce it on demand, the precise workings of elevation to iconic status escape comprehension and control. Stars come and go, especially now that fame has become increasingly fleeting and one blink of the eyes is nearly all it takes to miss the swift rise and fall of a new celebrity. Today's stars become "so five minutes ago" before their presence has even registered with many people.

But for a select few stars, fame is merely a stepping stone on the road to enshrinement as an icon, and once inducted into this realm, an icon is worshipped as an entity that has surpassed human limitations. Fans revere icons and establish imaginary relationships with them by projecting onto them their deepest desires. An icon is perceived as "an object of uncritical devotion," providing a form around which fans' inchoate inner lives can cohere, according to Marshall Fishwick, the cofounder of the Popular Culture Association and director of both the American Studies and Popular Culture programs at Virginia Tech.[6] Icons, writes Fishwick in his book *Icons of America*, are "external expressions of internal convictions" and they "help us to decipher, to unlock, the mystery of our attitudes and assumptions."[7] The posthumous James Dean has been particularly adept at reflecting back his fans' projections and embodying a mysteriousness that partakes of the divine; he is a star who possesses "a numinous quality."[8] His aura is the product of some indefinable elements combined with the particular cultural forces at work in the United States during the fifties. The rebel icon he helped forge is the legacy of a decade when centralized social regulation strained against cultural forces impelling people outward into new modes of thought and behavior.

Dean was certainly at the right place at the right time. He lived his short life at a moment when a large segment of the American population perceived his moody personality as expressing their own dissatisfaction with the status quo. His brooding face was beautiful and haunting and inscrutable enough that it could contain whatever sense of bitter disappointment his fans wanted to project onto it. Dean biographer David Dalton writes insightfully that James Dean was "a genuine outsider with a pathetic sense of dislocation" who happened to be positioned effectively to strike a chord with disgruntled adolescents at the time.[9] His refusal to fall into step with the American mainstream appealed to other young people who were less deeply disturbed but who nevertheless could identify with his rebellious detachment. Dalton writes that "through a subtle, tactical act of will and imagination, Jimmy became the personification of the American teen, an instantly recognizable type that his fans would see as the 'real me' latent in their tormented teen souls. It's a sort of standard-issue subversiveness— that oxymoronic entity, the all-American delinquent."[10] Delinquency was just a dream for many disgruntled young people who weren't willing to risk relinquishing suburban safety, but they could play out their fantasy of dereliction through their idol, James Dean.

When the engine of Dean's popularity as a tormented soul was fuel-injected by his sudden death, his fame soared into the stratosphere. His death heightened the perception that he was vulnerable and misunderstood. It was because he already seemed broken before he died, seemed to have a personality in shards, that he held such a powerful attraction to people who identified with him. Andy Warhol's famous line about Dean was, "He's not our hero because he was perfect, but because he perfectly represented the damaged but beautiful soul of our time."[11] Previous generations gazed in awe upon movie stars who appeared to have enviably complete and secure personalities, but James Dean's film persona and the stories circulated about him in the press suggested fragmentation. His splintered persona resonates with the breakdown of categories that characterizes the post–World War II years, which were marked by the disintegration of traditional assumptions about identity, formerly thought to be innate and later perceived as developing in response to cultural influences and given to fluctuation. Social relations also became more fractured as people became increasingly mobile and loosened their ties to family and community. Postwar middle-class affluence sent many Americans scurrying out of densely populated urban centers into suburbs where they had to drive for miles to get anywhere beyond the rows of matching homes. The arts reflected the new atomized spirit with stylistic disjuncture rather than unity, borrowing elements from the past and combining them in jarring ways. Ideological unity was also lost as traditional belief systems no longer held sway over a majority of the population and instead became confined to small clusters of people. The new reigning ideology—consumerism—had a consolidating effect but was based on principles of fragmentation, on carving up the population into demographic units and bombarding them with ubiquitous media messages to buy the products pitched to them.

Cultural commentators have linked the consumerist ethos to increased tolerance, arguing that a late-capitalist economy will sanction nearly anything deemed marketable, but during the fifties, social regulation was still the order of the day. While the old order was falling apart, there was a determined effort by the conservative U.S. government and its institutional allies to enforce adherence to its Cold War agenda. The anti-Communist witch hunts that were launched in Congress in 1947 continued during the fifties, when the Senate started its own hearings, and left some Americans imprisoned or unemployed and blacklisted, their livelihoods snatched from them. Having left-wing political sympathies made a person vulnerable to the charge of being a Communist, and those who had indeed joined the American Communist Party, a legal organization during the thirties, when the economy had collapsed and alternatives to capitalism seemed attractive, were especially susceptible. Labor union activists, professors, teachers, actors, folksingers, and others who advocated progressive social changes were particularly vulnerable.

Although the majority of the population was not directly persecuted, the government inquisition created a climate of distrust that permeated social life. It would be incorrect to assert that all Americans lived in fear, but the targeting of leftists coexisted with a social climate of homophobia, racism, misogyny, and anti-Semitism. Jim Crow segregation laws were enforced in the southern states and white supremacy was implicit in the country as a whole even though it was camouflaged by the "separate but equal" claim. Deviation from narrowly defined roles was scrutinized and could be dangerous. The backlash against working women, a response to women's wartime factory employment, was intense, with some legislators arguing that unmarried women were abnormal and not fit to become schoolteachers, for they would pollute the minds of the nation's children, and others holding that married women should be barred from teaching jobs on the grounds that they belonged at home. The medical profession routinely sedated women with tranquilizers (women's magazines contained an alarming number of tranquilizer ads) and told them that they were mentally ill if they were not satisfied as wives and mothers. Film scholar Joan Mellen refers to the fifties as "an era of nationally orchestrated paranoia,"[12] but one which contained its own unraveling, for "the stress upon conformity . . . only brought to light the lurking presence of the need to form individual judgments."[13]

Advertisers responded to the lurking presence of the need to form individual judgments with ads that created the illusion of fulfillment through consumption. The implicit promise was that product selection was an exercise in individuality, for consumers' individual judgments would lead them to purchase the products uniquely suited to them. In this way desire was channeled into consumption and kept from going in unsanctioned directions. Cultural critic and scholar of consumer society Stuart Ewen describes the process:

> In the years following World War II, the trend toward cultural mobilization reached epic proportion . . . While heralding a world of unprecedented freedom and opportunity, corporations (in concert with the state apparatus) were generating a mode of existence which was increasingly regimented and authoritarian. If consumer culture was a parody of the popular desire for self-determination and meaningful community, its innards revealed the growing standardization of the social terrain and corporate domination over what was to be consumed and experienced.[14]

Consumer culture provided the illusion that Americans' needs were being met, but the repressive social climate indicated otherwise. Corporations and the government were working in each other's best interests and their policies left Americans with limited opportunities to express unorthodox views or engage in nonconformist behavior. Americans were encouraged to reject heterodoxy—or at least to channel any such impulses into acquisition.

It was from this muddle of a decade paradoxically characterized by both centralized social control and the centrifugal forces of the new

James Dean embodies cool in a Warner Bros. promotion shot. (The David Loehr Collection)

consumer society that the rebel icon emerged. Many commentators have observed that the debut of the defiant young rebel figure in films of the fifties was a response to the enforced conformity and outright persecutions of the immediate post–World War II years. At the time, Hollywood was capitulating to the censorious demands of the House Committee on

Un-American Activities, but the film industry was also aware of the growing restlessness of American young people alienated by stultifying social, political, and sexual constraints. Youthful disaffection was the object of considerable scrutiny in the U.S. during the fifties, eliciting numerous books and articles as well as hearings held by the Senate Subcommittee on Juvenile Delinquency in 1954 and 1955, during which Senator Estes Kefauver declared, "I think of delinquency as the scum that rises to the top from the imperfections within our society."[15] Hollywood responded to the national spotlight on juvenile delinquency by releasing a slew of films about American teens running wild, and Marlon Brando and James Dean emerged as the most charismatic and controversial screen embodiments of pent-up teen rage.

It was precisely the deadening aspect of regulated conformity that provoked rebelliousness. Graham McCann, scholar of social and political theory at King's College, Cambridge, argues that American pop culture inevitably got involved in the backlash against conformity: "The 1950s movies reveal the psychic price American culture paid for repression of the right to disagree with social and political policy. This repression led to an outpouring of frustration and rage, depression and confusion, which could not help but surface in popular cultural figures."[16] James Dean held a special place among pop culture figures; he was perceived as a model for those who rejected narrow, hypocritical attitudes, and his look of defiance was compelling. James Dean was cool, and cool was a way to be contrary.

Dean's style did not emerge from a vacuum; rather, it participated in a fifties cultural phenomenon. It was during that decade that black cool found favor with disillusioned white people who appropriated it for their own use, as they were also appropriating blues and jazz music. "One thing is clear," write Dick Pountain and David Robins in their book *Cool Rules*, "by the '50s whites wanted to be Cool too."[17] Cool was an attitude well suited to express rejection of the decade's regimented conformity, and it was taken up by the Beats, bohemians, and other disaffected rebels. But cool was not a new style; it has a history steeped in the black American experience.

Cool's history is multifaceted and has taken different forms in different parts of the world, but the American version is rooted in a charismatic stance brought by West Africans forced into slavery. Art historian Robert Farris Thompson defines the ancient West African Yoruba and Ibo concept of *itutu* as cool. For the Yoruba, "cool philosophy is a strong intellectual attitude, affecting incredibly diverse provinces of artistic happening, yet leavened with humour and a sense of play."[18] For the Yoruba, according to Thompson, *itutu* is associated with physical beauty but also transcends it; a Yoruba elder said, "Beauty is a part of coolness but beauty does not have the force that character has. Beauty comes to an end. Character is forever."[19] Young Americans transfixed by James Dean in the fifties might have agreed that their idol, while certainly beautiful, was also imbued with an indefinable something else, and that it was his enigmatic character that elevated him above the ranks of the merely physically attractive.

Cool was transformed in the New World, where it was used as a subtle attitude by slaves to assert their autonomy and express contempt for slave owners:

> Once transported to America, Africans were forced to surrender their physical integrity and work as plantation slaves, but perhaps they felt that they could protect some part of their spiritual integrity by clinging to Cool, which afforded them a symbolic territory beyond the jurisdiction of their white owners—a secret, shared, black (and at that time almost exclusively male) discourse. All that their white owners were allowed to see were caricatures of subservience, heavy with irony, behind a Cool mask that concealed the contempt and rage that the slaves felt, the frank expression of which would have brought down harsh physical punishment.[20]

Unlike African *itutu*, which was held within the sacred, American cool was a secular attitude

> honed during the early part of the twentieth century by those descendents of Africans (together with some pioneering white colleagues) who played jazz and blues, and who deployed Cool as a body armour against the discrimination, patronization and neglect they experienced from the mostly white-owned entertainment business.[21]

White patrons encountered cool in black jazz clubs during the twenties, and black jazz musicians were at the forefront of cool during the next several decades, with Lester Young and Miles Davis in particular adding their unique touches to the style that the music and cultural critic Nelson George has called "a certain sartorial elegance, smooth charm, and self-possession that . . . suggested a dude that controlled not only himself but his environment."[22] Cool entered the mainstream of white society during the forties through the detective fiction of Dashiell Hammett and Raymond

Chandler and through film noir.[23] White cool in the fifties was defined by the Beats (Jack Kerouac, Allen Ginsberg, and William Burroughs, among others), by Elvis Presley, and, for viewers of American films around the world, by Montgomery Clift, Marlon Brando, and James Dean. Pountain and Robins anoint Dean "Cool's first martyr and saint."[24]

What, then, is cool? Pountain and Robins define this elusive concept as follows:

> Cool is an attitude or personality type that emerged in many different societies, during different historical epochs, and which has served different social functions, but is nevertheless recognizable in all its manifestations as a particular combination of three core personality traits, namely narcissism, ironic detachment and hedonism.[25]

Narcissism is "an exaggerated admiration for oneself, particularly for personal appearance, which gives rise to the feeling that the world revolves around you and shares your moods."[26] Ironic detachment "is a stratagem for concealing one's feelings by suggesting their opposite, for example feigning boredom in the face of danger, or amusement in the face of insult."[27] And cool hedonism is a "pursuit of pleasure" that "tends toward the worldly, adventurous and even orgiastic rather than the pleasant."[28] Biographies of Dean suggest that he met these criteria with a vengeance and that these were the qualities that made him simultaneously intriguing and exasperating to those who knew him.

His imitators over the years span the spectrum of ages, genders, races, ethnicities, and nationalities. Cool, after all, is not specific to any single context; it is not linked categorically to a single political outlook or social stance. Any cause can adopt the accoutrements of cool; even competing movements, such as advertisers of fur coats and anti-fur activists, have been known to latch on to cool to make their case. Cool is now fully compatible with advertising strategies and is helping to prop up the cycle of consumption that drives the economy, while at the same time it is used as a weapon against the powerful consumerist credo.

James Dean was cool, but he was also a commodity. His contract with Warner Bros. meant that the studio could create a public persona for him to meet their needs, and they understood that having a temperamental young actor under contract could be profitable. Marlon Brando had already become a megastar not only because of his acting skills but also because he flouted convention with scornful disdain. Dean worshipped Brando and was touted by Warner Bros. as the next Brando, another surly anti-hero with contempt for propriety. And American culture in the fifties was obsessed with propriety, providing the ideal target for Brando's sneering rebel image. In the words of playwright and screenwriter Paul Rudnick:

> The more cozily bourgeois a culture becomes, the more its citizenry admires the wary iconoclast, the individual with an "attitude problem," the bad boy. Oppressive decency reached its Levittown peak in the 1950s; sex, tight clothing, speed and hair were verboten, or at least constricted. It was an era of panty girdles, placid family barbecues, and straight A's.[29]

Brando and Dean, together with their influential precursor in moody sensitivity, Montgomery Clift, appealed to those who felt trapped by stifling fifties mores. Young people, especially, chafed under rigid social strictures and were defining themselves as a separate category who warily observed society from the alienated sidelines. Film depictions of rebellious frustration resonated forcefully. As Graham McCann writes in his book about three iconic "rebel males": "Clift, Brando, and Dean became central figures in the 'generation gap' debates of the time. They were the first genuinely popular stars with whom young people could easily identify, and the fact that many parents regarded them as 'immoral' and 'indecent' revealed how fragmented the former 'mass' movie audience had become."[30] What set these three rebels apart from other defiant nonconformists of the time was that Clift, Brando, and Dean were glamourized and mythologized by their screen appearances and by the voluminous magazine and newspaper coverage they received.

They enjoyed fame, which is an expression of power. Yet they also lost something; each was subjected to the manipulative Hollywood star machine that shaped their images in a complex system in which the stars were complicit. In his insightful analysis of film stars and society, film scholar Richard Dyer dissects the complicated and contradictory ways that star images are made:

> Stars are produced by the media industries, film stars by Hollywood (or its equivalent in other countries) in the first instance, but then also by other agencies with which Hollywood is connected in varying ways and with varying degrees of influence. Hollywood controlled not only the stars' films but their promotion, the pin-ups and glamour portraits, press releases and to a large extent the fan clubs. In turn, Hollywood's

connections with other media industries meant that what got into the press, who got to interview a star, what clips were released to television was to a large extent decided by Hollywood.[31]

Dyer notes, however, that although the studio bosses liked to think that they could control every aspect of a star's image, there were always unpredictable factors, including warfare between departments, rivalries, and input from unaffiliated media agencies that could produce new facets of a star's image.

Ironically, the rebel movie star was tailor-made for the Hollywood star machine. His adversarial antagonism seemed to threaten the established order; in fact, however, this antagonism was commodified. It was shaped and manipulated for consumption by audiences and fans. The rebel movie star's apparent threat to the system was thus part of the show. His stance resonated powerfully with the deeply ingrained American notion of rugged individualism. And, in fact, the star system as a whole is consistent with this tradition, which depends upon the idea of a unique individual with special qualities. The myth of rugged individualism, then, can be seen as an important aspect of the foundation for contemporary celebrity culture. The star industry must persuade us that the irreducible core of a star—the private self—is knowable to us. Television programs, magazine articles, fanzines, and World Wide Web sites devoted to stars tantalize us with the promise of revealing the "real" person behind the façade.

And the rebel, because uniqueness is so central to his core persona, was perfectly suited to stardom. Richard Dyer observes that "stars articulate these ideas of personhood, in large measure shoring up the notion of the individual but also at times registering the doubts and anxieties attendant on it."[32] Stars function as a mirror in which the viewer can vicariously experience both the pleasure of identifying with the heroism of the iconoclast and the exquisite pain of undergoing the risks attendant on this solitary figure who challenges the status quo. It was these qualities of doubt and anxiety that the rebel figure displayed so effectively in his films, particularly for Clift and Dean. Dean, for one, seemed to be breaking apart, splintering into fragments of insecurity and discomfort, and yet, instead of cracking the star system, Dean's fractured persona actually fortified it, especially after he died, and Warner Bros. Studio received an enormous flood of letters from Dean fans. In July of 1956 alone, Warner Bros. reportedly received seven thousand reverential letters,[33] and one account written in 1996 claims that the studio was still getting an average of five hundred letters related to Dean every week.[34]

Dean gained stardom, but even before he lost his life he had lost the right to self-definition to the Warner Bros. publicity department and the media. By manipulating the media and issuing press releases of its own, the studio manufactured a socially acceptable, sanitized version of Dean. His bisexuality was recast as heterosexuality, his hard work as an actor was reconstituted as effortlessness, his ambitious nature was effaced in descriptions of his reluctance to succeed, and his passion for the arts (dance, music, sculpture, poetry) was deemphasized in favor of his enthusiasm for fast cars and motorcycles. After his death, the fanatical James Dean cult that erupted nearly overnight perpetuated Hollywood's distortions, concentrating particularly on the morbid aspects of the life that appeared to foreshadow his untimely death. His friendship with the black-clad, ghoulish Vampira (whose real name was Maila Nurmi), described by some biographers as a romance, and the photos he posed for stretched out in a coffin were retrospectively interpreted by many fans as foretelling his early demise.

Brando and Dean made their names by spurning "decency" and scoffing at social mores, both in their personal lives and in their onscreen roles. Their iconoclasm suggested an alternative lifestyle, or, at the very least, an alternative hairstyle, for what Paul Rudnick calls "well-fed, restless teens willing to enjoy their parents' largess while spurning their aprons and cardigans . . . Dreamily doodling in their notebook margins, they yearned for a new place to shop, for outfits and anger."[35] But despite youthful readiness for a new, explosive style, Hollywood was intent on creating a socially acceptable, innocuous rebel persona. This was after all the decade of hysterical witch hunts and arranged marriages for embattled gay male stars like Rock Hudson, who was challenged in print by a journalist to prove his heterosexuality. James Dean was celebrated for his rebellious otherness at the same time that his persona was rendered acceptably mainstream. The figure of the young rebel thus emerged as a forceful but empty style, the antithesis of effective political resistance. Teen rebel films have consequently tended to be apolitical, although they have sometimes embraced unexpected political positions, as film scholar Timothy Shary points out in reference to the spate of right-wing patriotic American youth films released between 1984 and 1988 at the height of the Reagan era. Shary writes that "the defiance in these films," exemplified by *Red Dawn* (John Milius, 1984), was "not against mere parents and adults, but against the potential corruption threatened by any alien force; and the conservation of *American* identity, not just youth identity, became the priority."[36]

The mainstreaming of James Dean in the fifties is an early example of corporate capitalism's voracious appetite for marketing oppositional forms after draining them of their subversive power. In an incessant pursuit of the latest trend, the entertainment and fashion conglomerates plunder any original expressions of teenage disaffection and repackage them to suit the prevailing mood. The route from the margins to the market has become increasingly short. Hollywood rebels were drained of political power not only by studio publicity and the media, but also by films with recuperative closures, for even though Marlon Brando and James Dean became known as icons of rebellious anti-authoritarianism, the films that made them popular as alienated rebels were far from revolutionary. Jon Lewis writes:

> Dean's anomic performance—his performance of anomie—which has become the most quintessentially American of youth culture expressions, arose not from the ashes of the adult culture or from the spontaneity of youth subculture, but from the big screen, from the codes inherent to commercial Hollywood family melodrama.[37]

The two most often cited fifties rebel films, *The Wild One* (Laslo Benedek, 1954), starring Brando, and *Rebel Without a Cause*, starring Dean, are in fact both stylistically conservative. *The Wild One*, shot in black and white, shares its unimaginative camera placement and its aggressive musical score with other cautionary films of the period designed to warn viewers about threats to the social order. It is a plea for strict law enforcement and depicts its motorcycle gangs as a dangerous threat to civilization. The original script was more sympathetic to the gangs, but the Production Code Administration, headed by Joseph Breen, demanded script changes promoting law enforcement before it would clear the film for production.[38] *Rebel Without a Cause*, visually novel when it was released for its CinemaScope format and its vivid Technicolor (Nicholas Ray switched to color film stock during production, and it was then that James Dean chose to wear a red jacket), is thoroughly infused by the conventions of Hollywood melodrama. *Rebel* places blame for teenage waywardness on absent parents and aggressive wives who usurp their husbands' authority, in melodramatic fashion attributing personal failings to familial dysfunction. At the end, Jim Stark's (James Dean) rebellious anger melts away as his newly assertive father (Jim Backus) takes control and puts his arm around his son's shoulders. It is easy, however, to ignore both films' warnings and concentrate on their depictions of unrestrained freedom

Warner Bros. presents juvenile delinquency Hollywood-style in *Rebel Without a Cause*. (The David Loehr Collection)

from adult interference. Brando's and Dean's charisma transcends the conservative narratives of the films. In fact, despite the script changes to *The Wild One*, the British censorship board refused to release the film for fifteen years on the grounds that it might promote violence among young people.[39] During the decades that have passed since the films were released, their cautionary messages have been forgotten but their rebel stance has been firmly retained in the public imagination.

In addition to *Rebel Without A Cause*, James Dean's other two films—*East of Eden* and *Giant*—are also dependent on melodramatic conventions and unadventurous visual styles and by the end have contained or discredited the rebel's resistance. *East of Eden*, like *Rebel Without a Cause*, ends by uniting the rebellious son, Cal Trask (played by Dean), with his previously inadequate father, bringing Cal to the bedside of his father Adam (Raymond Massey) for a reconciliation after Adam has suffered a stroke. Cal forgives his father, who has been reduced from a rigid, judgmental patriarch to a helpless invalid, and Adam at last acknowledges Cal's loyalty. *Giant* backs off at the end from endorsing the self-deprecating style of masculinity of Jett Rink (James Dean) over the strict, arrogant style of Bick Benedict (Rock Hudson) by turning Jett into an intolerant and dissolute alcoholic and softening Bick for a reconciliation with his wife, Leslie (Elizabeth Taylor). The film redeems Bick when he renounces his hatred of Mexicans by standing up for an elderly Mexican couple and their daughter who are refused service by Sarge, a racist proprietor of a roadside cafe. Bick defends the rights of the Mexican patrons, including his own daughter-in-law, Juana (Elsa Cardenas), by fighting Sarge, the two of them slamming into each other like angry bulls to the ironic musical accompaniment of "The Yellow Rose of Texas" on the jukebox. Big beefy Sarge wallops Bick and contemptuously asserts his right to refuse service to anyone, but Bick's defeat is a victory of sorts in the film's terms, for it signifies the collapse of the racist walls he had erected around himself and his new acceptance of Juana and her one-year-old son—his own grandson.

Giant's sprawling scope and monumental musical score give it an aura of serious social commentary, and its confused politics have elicited contradictory responses. A collection of poems titled *Scene from the Movie Giant*, by Tino Villanueva, is a brilliant illustration of popular culture's power to humiliate and the ability of those who have been humiliated to restore their own dignity by articulating a response. The film's brawl in the roadside cafe is the collection's defining moment. The twenty poems analyze the devastating effect of Sarge's larger-than-life celluloid racism bearing down on a fourteen-year-old Villanueva sitting in the back row of a movie theatre in the mid-fifties. Villanueva, a young Chicano, stared with disbelief and horror at Sarge's rabid hatred. His poem "On the Subject of Staying Whole" includes the lines,

I am fourteen and the
Muscles come to a stop: From the spell
Of too much make-believe world that is
Real. If I yell, "Nooooo!, nooooo!,"

Would the projectionist stop the last
Reel of the machine? Would the audience
Rise up with me to rip down the screen?
I think now how it went: nothing was

Coming out of me that could choke off
The sentences of Sarge, a world-beater
Released into history I would later turn
Against. A second-skin had come over me

In a shimmer of color and light. I could
Not break free from the event that began
To inhabit me—gone was the way to dream

Outside myself. From inside, a small
Fire began to burn like deep doubt or

A world fallen . . . I held on. I held on.[40]

Villanueva's alienation, his "fallingrief of unpleasure,"[41] is of a different order from that of white suburban adolescents in the fifties, and for him the film leaves a submerged fury that is resurrected years later, in 1973, when *Giant* appears on his TV screen in Boston. While he had once struggled to stay whole when watching the racist cafe scene, because "a child at that age/falls short of endowing dumb misery with speech,"[42] as an adult he responds with the weapon of words:

what I took in that afternoon took root and a
quiet vehemence arose. It arose in language—
the legitimate deduction of the years thought out.
Now I am because I write: I know it in my heart
and know it in the sound iambics of my fist that
mark across the paper with the sun's exacting rays.[43]

For Villanueva, *Giant* is about people "swept up by power and prejudice/ Toward neighbors different from themselves," and he points out that the film's class distinctions remain intact at the end.[44] Despite the softening of Bick's rigid views, nothing much changes; Jett Rink, rather than rebel effectively against the ranchers' snobbish hierarchies, "buried his soul in/ Money and went incoherent with alcohol."[45] Sarge's racism prevails and his arrogant bullying still permeates the Texas atmosphere at the film's end, and, according to an account of contemporary Marfa, Texas, where *Giant* was filmed, it still exists in the twenty-first century. A Mexican American resident of Marfa, Lucy Garcia, is quoted as saying that "a lot of us Mexicans are still pushed around by the gringo like in the time of *Giant* . . . Some things in Texas take a long time to die."[46]

Given the censorious climate of the fifties, the rebel figure was probably unable to take an overtly oppositional political stance in films; it was more effective in expressing an alternative style of masculinity that permanently expanded the range of acceptable masculine traits onscreen.

Most film scholars agree that a number of Hollywood films of the fifties introduced a more introspective and sensitive style of masculinity. Joan Mellen writes:

> In the knowledge that advocacy of dissent would induce a summons before an investigating committee or feed the predatory blackmail indus- try epitomized by *Red Channels* and *Hollywood Confidential*, Hollywood re- placed social dissent with a fascinating and serious examination of *sexual* politics. The assumed definitions of the male sex role were challenged as films discovered the male capable of sensitivity and an open expression of tenderness, feelings which in the forties were ridiculed as effeminate.[47]

New styles of masculinity emerged on screen and on the streets in the fifties as a backlash against the dominant ideal of the corporate cog. The rebel figure was a crucial component in the creation of new masculine styles that revealed vulnerability and confusion and suggested that mas- culinity was a culturally constructed category that arbitrarily imposed its strictures on men who did not easily fit. Although the confused, sen- sitive young males of fifties films began the move away from iron-clad male solidity, there continued to be homophobic limits imposed by the censors. For example, the original screenplay for *Rebel Without A Cause* included more explicit references to the homoerotic tension and attrac- tion between Jim and Plato (Sal Mineo). Among the changes demanded by the Hays Committee in an early *Rebel* screenplay was the removal of a kiss between the two young men. The censor wrote, "It is of course vital that there be no inference of a questionable or homosexual relationship between Plato and Jim." The kiss was cut, as was the word "punk," which was slang for gay.[48]

However, despite the vigilance of Hollywood's censors, there was a perceptible relaxation in the myth of steely-hard masculinity in fifties films. There are significant differences between the mythic James Dean persona and the mythic John Wayne persona established earlier, even though the two myths overlap. John Wayne's characters maintained their aura of invincibility. Ethan Edwards, the vengeful wanderer played by John Wayne in *The Searchers* (John Ford, 1956), starts to tear at the seams and unravel, revealing his racist cruelty, but spectators never see him curl up in a fetal position and tuck a wind-up monkey toy under a newspaper blanket, as does James Dean in *Rebel Without A Cause*. Both characters are tortured by deep-rooted psychological trauma, but Dean's Jim Stark has already crumbled into pieces during *Rebel*'s opening credits. When

James Dean provided an alternative style to "the man in the gray flannel suit."
(The David Loehr Collection)

Wayne's Ethan lets down his guard late in *The Searchers*, it is to suppress
his murderous rage and racism to spare the life of his niece. His act of
compassion does not, however, significantly alter his tough, fortified exterior; the film ends with him wandering back into the desert, still stiffly
resilient and resistant to change.

Unlike John Wayne's rugged version of the alienated, disenfranchised
male, James Dean's rebel persona embodies what Richard Dyer calls "the
sad young man," a gay stereotype prominent in the forties, fifties, and sixties. He describes the sad young man as

a young man, hence not yet really a real man. He is soft; he has not yet achieved assertive masculine hardness. He is also physically less than a man. In many paperback covers he does not hold his head up but hangs it. There is perhaps an echo in the stance of the major source of this imagery, the Judeo-Christian tradition. The sad young man is a martyr figure.[49]

The image of the sad young man circulated in novels and films of the post–World War II period and provided a model for melancholy, unfulfilled gay lives. For Dyer, James Dean's particular version of the figure emerges most clearly when his performance in *Giant* is contrasted with Rock Hudson's in the same film. Rock Hudson's "stillness and settledness as a performer," writes Dyer, "suggests someone at home in the world, securely in his place in society, whereas James Dean's style suggests someone ill at ease in the world, marginal and insecure."[50] It is this quality in Dean's performance in *Rebel Without a Cause* that Jon Savage describes as "so fragmented that he appears as more than an outsider, as a sleepwalker vainly trying to learn the language of an alien dreamscape."[51] For Savage, "In Dean, everything is in flux."[52]

One of the ironies, of course, was that when films contrasted sad young men with "successful, mature adult males," as in *Giant's* opposition between James Dean and Rock Hudson, cultural stereotypes about gay men as nervous and neurotic were upheld and gay male diversity was masked. Thus Hollywood carefully suppressed revelations about Rock Hudson's gayness, and he built a career playing solid, brawny men. According to Dyer, the sadness of Montgomery Clift, Dirk Bogarde, Farley Granger, Sal Mineo, and James Dean was simultaneously exaggerated and capitalized on by the relentless star-forging branch of the film industry.

While *East of Eden* was in production, the Warner Bros. publicity department and Dean's West Coast agent started to design a publicity campaign to introduce him as a romantic lead.[53] Warner Bros. was following the standard fanzine formula of presenting handsome young male actors as heartthrobs and dream dates. David Dalton writes,

> However odd or unlikely the candidate—Sal Mineo, Marlon Brando, Tony Perkins—every rising star had to conform to the prototype. There is something eerie about the Easter Island interchangeability of the classic dreamboats of the fifties: Tab, Bob, Johnny, Pat. Mr. Smoothies with machine-tooled, water-repellent, Turtle Wax-buffed hides. As if molded out of some biosynthetic polymer miracle flesh. That optimistic American obsession with smoothing things out, tidying up, homogenizing

all of life. These are replicants with extruded personalities, your basic pleasure models. Commodity androids planted by the KGB to melt the brains of American teenagers.[54]

An article titled "The Girls in James Dean's Life," published in *TV and Movie Screen* magazine shortly after *East of Eden* was released, exemplifies the glamourization of Dean in breathless fan-magazine style:

> During his first year as a galloping knight on the Hollywood sound stages, Jimmy Dean has been in and out of more romances than you could shake a matchmaker at. He got kicked in the teeth with his ardent courtship of Pier Angeli, but instead of heading despondently for the nearest railroad crossing, he picked himself off the floor, shook the disappointment out of his system, and became one of the most sought after bachelors in fableville's younger set. It almost would take a statistician to keep up with his amours.[55]

Warner Bros., Dean's West Coast agent Dick Clayton, and Dean himself were aware that avoiding heterosexual romantic attachments was professional suicide for a young male actor amid the rampant homophobia of the fifties. After all, this was the McCarthy era, "when it was thought that homosexuals became spies because both led double lives. (It was, of course, entirely fitting that the Inquisitor, Senator McCarthy, was himself bisexual.)"[56]

There are enormous discrepancies in biographical accounts of James Dean's sexuality, even discounting the outlandish claims printed in fan magazines. Early versions from the fifties and sixties represented him as resolutely heterosexual and avoided the issue of homosexuality altogether. During the seventies several biographers revealed that Dean was involved in gay relationships. Film scholar Michael DeAngelis argues persuasively that it would have been impossible for biographies of Dean written in the fifties and early sixties to have described him as gay since homophobic discourses held sway in the public realm. But, writes DeAngelis,

> It is in the early 1970s, with the onset of a more publicly visible gay liberation movement, when homosexuals begin to participate publicly and confrontationally in their own discursive construction—a construction which brings to the forefront issues of "identity" and "place"—that Dean appears in the press as not only an ally to gay rebellion, but also as a potential homosexual himself.[57]

Biographers since the seventies have usually acknowledged the presence of male lovers in Dean's life, but have interpreted their significance in a variety of ways. Paul Alexander, for example, argues that Dean was decidedly gay. Others, including Liz Sheridan, who was Dean's girlfriend in New York for a while, argue that Dean was fundamentally heterosexual but slept with powerful male producers, Rogers Brackett for one, because Hollywood success required it.[58] On the other hand, a male friend of Dean's, John Gilmore, writes about having sex with Dean and describes their relationship as close.[59] His testimony is consistent with other recent biographies that present Dean as bisexual.

Films about Dean's life typically elide references to his male lovers. Robert Altman's 1957 documentary *The James Dean Story* avoids any suggestion that he was anything but heterosexual. Three more recent documentaries also carefully omit the possibility that Dean was gay. *James Dean and Me* (Ben Strout, 1995), makes no mention at all of his sexuality, except obliquely when Liz Sheridan identifies herself as Dean's "friend and [long hesitation] lover." *James Dean: A Portrait* (Gary Legon, 1996), cowritten by Gary Legon and David Dalton, also shies away from Dean's sexuality, except to assert that Pier Angeli and Dean "fell helplessly in love" and she was "the great love of his life." *James Dean: Sense Memories* (Gail Levin, 2005), broadcast on PBS's *American Masters* series, is a collage of interviews with people who knew Dean, all of whom skirt his bisexuality.

Fictional versions of Dean's life on film tend to exaggerate his romance with Pier Angeli, the young star he dated before she married Vic Damone. These accounts make their affair the centerpiece of his life, and interpret everything earlier as leading up to it and everything later as a self-destructive response to its traumatic failure. Thus James Dean's life is transformed into a picture-perfect Hollywood story of doomed romance. The docudrama *James Dean: Live Fast, Die Young* (Mardi Rustam, 1997) gives us a heterosexual Dean who is passionately devoted to Pier Angeli. The film *James Dean* (Mark Rydell, 2001) also makes Dean heterosexual and deeply in love with Pier Angeli, but hints at another side to his sex life by including his famous line—"I'm not going through life with one hand tied behind my back"—when asked by a reporter about his sexuality. Dean in this film also attends a party thrown by Rogers Brackett, who had earlier come on to him, but the door discreetly closes after Dean joins the party. These suggestions of Dean's relationship to men are subtle enough to be overlooked by anyone committed to a heterosexual version of the star.

James Dean's sexuality is uniquely suited to conflicting appropriations, according to Michael DeAngelis, because his short life was characterized by a "fundamental indeterminacy of character" that was intensified by the studio and tabloid emphasis on his destabilized origins (his mother's death, his father's abandonment), his rootlessness (residing in Indiana, then Los Angeles, then Indiana, then Los Angeles, then New York, then Los Angeles again; his frequent changes of address and occasional homelessness when he lived on film sets); and his moody, often abrasive, personality. The three films in which he starred participate in constructing him as indeterminate by portraying his characters as unsettled young men who are ostracized from the mainstream of society, always searching for a place to belong and a stable form to take.[60] When he died, James Dean's life story was left without a satisfying closure, so he was enshrined as an incomplete, amorphous icon. It is this pervasive sense of ambiguity surrounding Dean that allows him to attract fans from the entire spectrum of sexual orientations.

Even though some accounts of Dean's life still strenuously avoid revealing his bisexuality, the gay community has embraced him as a gay icon since the early seventies. The implicit androgyny in the cinematic treatment of Brando and Dean, and before them Montgomery Clift, as well as their own acknowledged bisexuality, have facilitated the rebel figure's association with gay imagery. *The Wild One* and *Rebel Without a Cause* both represent male identity as unfixed and uncertain. *The Wild One* presents Marlon Brando's Johnny as an unsettled young man who vacillates between toughness and vulnerability. Much of the time he struts and swaggers and virtually abstains from speech as he sneers at the world. His aloofness precludes emotional engagement with others, a stance that reduces Kathie (Mary Murphy), the young woman he pursues, to tears. Johnny's detachment is succinctly conveyed in his notorious answer to the question, "What are you rebelling against?" "Whaddya got?" is his sneering response. But, for all his bravado, his tight leather rebel attire, and his ego-fortifying motorcycle, Johnny is a confused kid; he bursts into tears at the cruelty and hypocrisy of the adult world, and he rides out of town battered and bruised by its vindictive bullies. His isolation and outsider status are in part a matter of choice, but they are also the price he pays for being different. He lends himself to a gay reading because, like generations of self-conscious and lonely gay people, he is persecuted by narrow-minded conformists who thrive on the power they feel when they brutalize their victims.

Rebel Without a Cause can be read as a promotion for upholding gender and sexual conventions, and, simultaneously, as undermining those

Marlon Brando as leather-clad rebel Johnny in *The Wild One*. (AllPosters)

conventions. *Rebel* maintains that Jim Stark's mother (Ann Doran) is responsible for his unhappiness because she dominates her submissive husband. "She eats him alive and he takes it," Jim moans. Both Jim's mother and his grandmother are condemned by the film for emasculating his weak-willed father. In this way, *Rebel Without a Cause* is typical of fifties melodramas that function as cautionary tales about maternal power run amok. In his book *The Cinema of Adolescence*, film scholar David Considine devotes an entire chapter to "Movies' Monstrous Moms."[61] And according to film scholar Nina Leibman:

> The character perhaps most important to the 1950's melodrama is the evil, absent, or superfluous mother. These maternal figures exist in both film and television texts in various gradations of malevolence or stupidity, and distinguish the 1950's melodramas from their 1930's and 1940's predecessors, which typically revered the mother-figure. In 1950's films, the mothers are typically portrayed either as judgmental, harsh, undemonstrative, and cold or as smothering, diabolical, and aberrantly attracted to their sons. Mothers not rendered as malicious are depicted as completely out of touch with their children and their children's emotional needs, as physically unavailable (through careerism or even death), or as naïve to the point of mental instability.[62]

Jim's mother in *Rebel* exemplifies the harsh, judgmental screen mothers described by Leibman, and she is entirely out of touch with Jim's emotional needs. She is most concerned with keeping up appearances, in one scene self-righteously reminding Jim and his father that she worked hard all day trying to get the house in order. She demands obedience from her husband, and he dutifully obeys; Jim finds him wearing an apron and kneeling over a tray of food he dropped on his way upstairs to serve her supper in bed. When Jim laughs, his father silences him—Mom must not be disturbed—and hastily cleans up the mess. Jim's mother's obsession with maintaining appearances has meant that the family has moved to a new town every time Jim has gotten into trouble. She is a coward, afraid to face messy situations, but she rules imperiously at home. With Jim she is cloying and manipulative, reminding him that she almost died giving birth to him. The absence of maternal sustenance in Jim's life is symbolically represented by a motif of his gulping milk straight from a milk bottle.

Rebel Without a Cause proposes that Jim would be better off if his father were a belligerent patriarch who took firm control over his wife and son. In fact, it is the sight of his father wearing an apron that most offends Jim, and Jim is chagrined when his father cannot provide a coherent answer to his question, "What can you do when you have to be a man?" In a visual motif throughout the film, Jim is often shown standing over his stooped, cringing father, and when Jim begs him to "stand up for me," he means it literally as well as figuratively. Jim's mother, in contrast, stands ramrod straight throughout the film and in one shot we see her upside down from

Jim's point of view as he lies collapsed on a sofa, bearing down on him like a relentless malevolent force. Because of his "unnatural" family, Jim relies on violence to defend himself and maintain his fragile sense of self.

Despite the film's insistence on the necessity of maintaining conventional gender roles, there are moments when a more sensitive and emotional type of masculinity is validated. When Jim and his new friends Plato and Judy (Natalie Wood) create a substitute family, with Jim assuming the father's role, Judy the mother's, and Plato the son's, Jim and Plato exchange fond looks that suggest male tenderness. With extratextual knowledge that James Dean was bisexual and Sal Mineo was gay, spectators can read their scenes together as contradicting, or at least weakening, the film's surface demand for aggressive, dominating men. In addition, Jim is confused about his identity: he mistakenly starts to enter the women's bathroom on his first day in a new high school, and he plays with a little toy monkey in the police station where he is held for drunkenness. His neediness is emphasized when he desperately sucks down milk from a bottle and when he drunkenly curls up in a fetal position and gently tucks the toy monkey under a crumpled newspaper. For all his toughness, Jim, like Johnny in *The Wild One*, is misunderstood and lonely, and he rejects the hypocrisy of masculine stereotypes.

In the rebel films of the fifties, psychological self-exploration generally excluded women, who were there mostly to illuminate aspects of the young male rebel through their interactions. Rebellion was cinematically represented as a male prerogative; women characters were typically subordinate to the male rebels they accompanied. But the rebel's slouch was easily appropriated and the male monopoly on rebel iconography was short-lived. Biker-chicks and women rock stars have successfully adopted the sneering cynicism of the James Dean stance. The sexual ambiguity of Brando and Dean contributed to the rock-star androgyny of Elvis, Jagger, and Bowie, and the new androgyny could be adopted by anyone, male or female. And not only gay men, but lesbians, too, have borrowed Dean's style, as Deb Schwartz asserts in *Out* magazine when she writes that "Dean is the ultimate ready-to-wear lesbian role model because he's easy for a woman to emulate: He's slight, moves with grace, and his stance and gestures aren't so manly-man that they can't be easily mimicked."[63]

Because of his ambiguous sexuality, James Dean has come to represent every conceivable form of sexuality in the years since his death. The one fairly consistent trait attributed to him is heightened sexuality, whatever form it takes. Ambiguity has been translated into polymorphous sexual super-prowess. James Dean has become a sex god for any occasion, a symbol of surplus sexuality. Michael DeAngelis' explanation of Dean's life story as indeterminate and thus open to multiple appropriations helps account for Dean's sexy legacy. Contributing to the legacy was Dean's ironic detachment, a hallmark of cool. He does not embody predatory masculinity in his film roles. Instead, his characters are the desired ones who passively let other people take the risk. His catlike aloofness invites spectators to long for him and to impose the traits they seek onto him. Also contributing to the legacy was the extraordinary outpouring of fantasies (many of them bizarre and necrophiliac) about him immediately after his death, initiated by his passionate fans and fueled by fan magazines eager for marketable stories. Another factor contributing to his sexy allure was his link with Marlon Brando. Both actors were seen as rebels, and the younger man inherited by association some of the aura of rough and insatiable sexuality attributed to the elder. The young Brando was firmly associated in the public mind with his breakthrough Broadway role, the uncouth and animalistic Stanley Kowalski in *A Streetcar Named Desire*, and the media constantly played up the similarity between Brando and Kowalski with stories of Brando's brooding intensity and wild sexual exploits. Dean and Brando were also linked by their shared disdain for social etiquette as well as their similar acting styles, the so-called Method acting taught at the Actors Studio in New York where they had each studied. Brando's longer life, his weight gain, and his personal tragedies tempered his persona's highly charged sexual aura. Dean was bathed in the same aura, and didn't live long enough to relinquish it.

The hypersexuality of the Dean icon can be seen in the book *Mondo James Dean*, one of a series of anthologies about pop culture superstars published by St. Martin's Griffin, including *Mondo Barbie*, *Mondo Elvis*, and *Mondo Marilyn*. *Mondo James Dean* is a collection of twenty-two short stories and poems written by various authors.[64] What many of the stories and poems in *Mondo James Dean* share is a lurid fascination with James Dean as a phenomenal lover. One story, titled "The Idol," is based on the premise that ever since Dean's death, hundreds of girls in Los Angeles have gone to Griffith Park to lose their virginity in an initiation rite with the tire iron that Dean flung into the bushes in the fight scene outside the observatory in *Rebel Without A Cause*. Brought to a hidden shrine near the observatory by their mothers and other older women, the girls reach orgasm by humping the tire iron and then leave a nude photo of themselves pinned to the wall.[65] In a science fiction story by Lewis Shiner, James Dean is a post-apocalyptic rebel survivor, a violent loner into drugs, women, bikes, cars, and guns who battles space aliens and the gray conformist humans who have sold out the human race.[66] In another story, James Dean rehearses the part of Cal Trask for *East of Eden* with a script editor named Marnie and then transports her back through time to 1917, when the film is set. They act out scenes from the film and, of course, make passionate love.[67] The story "Jimmy Dean: My Kind of Guy" is narrated by a young woman at an artist's colony where James Dean is due to arrive. She vows to seduce him before five gay men at the colony have the opportunity. She and Dean do make love, and when she leaves the colony, he beds the other men and women there as well.[68] In the story "No-Man's Land," a young woman meets someone in Teheran she is certain is the resurrected James Dean, and they travel to the Afghan border together where they make love while waiting in a hotel for a safe crossing. Dean, however, departs with a tall elderly male Swedish diplomat.[69] Another story is about a race car driver named James Dean who wins the 1955 Indianapolis 500 and makes love to reporter Natalie Wood.[70] In an excerpt from the novel *Farewell My Slightly Tarnished Hero*, published in the same collection, Dean seduces a virgin he takes to a bullfight in Mexico, only to lose her to a rival after he refuses to make a commitment. He ends up seduced by a man in drag while watching two lesbians having sex at a New Year's Eve orgy in Los Angeles.[71] A poem by Ai narrated by the dead James Dean describes making love to women in their dreams,

> but when she grabs my hair,
> my head comes off in her hands
> and I take the grave again.
> Maybe I never wanted a woman
> as much as that anyway,
> or even the spice of man on man
> that I encountered once or twice,
> the hole where I shoved myself,
> framed by an aureole of coarse hair.
> By the twilight in '55,
> I had devised a way of living in between
> the rules that other people make.[72]

An excerpt from the play *Come Back to the Five and Dime, Jimmy Dean, Jimmy Dean* is set in a dusty town near Marfa, Texas, where the middle-aged former "Disciples of James Dean" have convened and ponder the identity of a mysterious and elegant woman who seems to know all about them; only later does she reveal that she is their male friend from childhood who has undergone a sex change.[73]

Dean has come to symbolize a full range of sexualities, not unlike the other great American sex god of the twentieth century, Elvis Presley, whose appeal in the fifties hinged in part on his sexual ambiguity. Elvis was in fact a fervent James Dean fan and could quote all of Dean's movie lines. As American studies scholar Erika Doss writes about Elvis' fans: "They recognized that Elvis's body represented new forms of pleasure and that those forms blatantly blurred set postwar images of manliness and femininity, of male and female sexuality."[74] Elvis not only synthesized gender codes, he also presented himself as blatantly erotic and invited a sexual gaze. His style was a significant departure from the velvet-voiced crooners of the previous decade, though he did borrow from them, as just one of the diverse influences he used to fashion his charismatic lure. It has been well documented, for example, that his highly suggestive dancing was appropriated from black performers. The explicitly "feminine" aspects of Elvis' self-presentation—the makeup and ornate clothing— were already being used by black musicians such as Little Richard, who, as Jon Savage puts it, was "triply disadvantaged by prewar standards"; he was "from the South, homosexual, and black."[75] Thus when the squeaky clean, heterosexual, and white Pat Boone recorded a toned-down version of Little Richard's bawdy "Tutti Frutti," it had a "massive, worldwide impact."[76] Elvis' synthesis of black and feminine styles rendered him shocking to straitlaced whites; for teenagers, it gave him an aura of exciting sexual danger in a time of cultural anxiety about race, gender roles, and sexuality.

Dean did not flaunt his body aggressively; rather, his screen persona displayed a softness and a nervous rejection of rough-and-tough masculinity. His characters slouch from self-doubt, but they also invite the camera to adore them, and the spectator's gaze is drawn to them. Dean exuded what Andy Medhurst calls the "passivity of the adored object."[77] Decades later, James Dean's sexuality appeals equally to white-haired grannies, teenage girls, Hell's Angels, overweight suburbanites riding upholstered touring motorcycles, and muscle-shirted gay men. (I have encountered all of these types and more at the Fairmount "Museum Days" celebration.) James Dean's appeal has been explained in many ways, including the lost-little-boy neediness he exuded after the death of his mother and his subsequent distance from his father. Psychologists have in fact identified a link between traumatic childhood loss and adult charisma: "Charisma may sometimes be understood as a displaced or transcendent form of yearning and searching impelled by grievous loss"; Dean's life seems to bear out this connection.[78] Mercedes McCambridge, Dean's co-star in *Giant*, described him as "the runt in the litter of thoroughbreds. You could feel the loneliness beating out of him, and it hit you like a wave."[79] George Stevens, who directed *Giant*, contributes a similar analysis:

> I used to feel that he was a disturbed boy, tremendously dedicated to some intangible beacon of his own, and neither he nor anyone else might ever know what it was. I used to feel this because at times when he fell quiet and thoughtful, as if inner-bidden to dream about something, an odd and unconscious sweetness would light up his countenance. At such times, and because I knew he had been motherless since early childhood and had missed a lot of love that makes boyhood gel, I would come to believe that he was still waiting for some lost tenderness.[80]

In part because of Dean's amorphous, unfixed qualities, the rebel iconography he helped inaugurate has been exceptionally malleable and open to contradictory uses. It has become a common fixture in the discourses of politics, fashion, advertising, sex, and entertainment, but its meaning is ambiguous. Politicians from the entire political spectrum as well as corporate CEOs, rock stars, and other entertainers attempt to prove their bad-boy cachet by donning the rebel's T-shirt, leather jacket, and jeans. There is an implied attitude behind the costume—disaffection, alienation, anger, nonconformity, and the rugged individualism that has been the cornerstone of dominant American ideology since the Revolutionary War.

Rebellion is fashionable and also omnipresent. Corporate CEOs suit up in leather jackets and jump on Harleys, apparently without any sense of incongruity. Detached from any actual accomplishment, rebellion is an easily achieved fashion statement, although not necessarily an inexpensive one. Leather jackets, tongue studs, tattoos, boots, and jeans constitute rebel couture, and they adorn movie stars and high-fashion models as well as high school malcontents. "The fashion world is also hitching a ride," crows the fall 2003 "Men's Fashions of the Times" supplement to the *New York Times*; "Dolce & Gabbana, Junya Watanabe, Martin Margiela and Jil Sander are among the men's-wear designers offering biker jackets for fall."[81] The author goes on to admit that "in a strait-laced culture that has always romanticized a renegade, donning outlaw biker gear requires a lot less commitment than becoming an outlaw biker."[82]

Even the twenty-first-century U.S. military found a way to appropriate the rebel stance in its war in Iraq, advertising its troops not as cogs in a well-oiled fighting machine but as a collection of young rag-tag individualists engaged in rugged self-expression, a calculated move presumably motivated by the desire to erase public awareness of soldiers' boot-camp conformity and regimentation. An emphasis on each soldier's individuality borrows from the hidden side of post–Vietnam War American military culture: the ultra-right-wing paramilitary forces that reject all government authority as too soft and conciliatory and who, despite banding together, still present "the warrior as a lone hero who transcends mass society."[83] Right- and left-wing dissidents converge in their reverence for the rebel icon, and when official organizations like the Defense Department join in, all sense of oppositional value vanishes.

The military's usurpation of rebel cred is not surprising; when every angry gesture from punk to hip hop is appropriated overnight by the mammoth consumer industry, it is difficult to imagine any act of rebellion capable of escaping rampant cooptation. In this age of rebel chic, "Chanel sells $4,800 biker jackets to wear with evening gowns, and teensy leathers are available for newborns to raise hell."[84] Commercial celebration of rebelliousness was perhaps inevitable given the capitalist system's insatiable drive to sustain itself. When the mid-twentieth-century countercultural dissidents grew up, rather than dismantle the economic system, many of them joined it and superficially remade it in their image. A collection titled *Commodify Your Dissent* (comprised of essays originally published in the journal *The Baffler*) identifies and satirizes "the rebel consumer" as well as the defiant hipster corporate executive, arguing that "the countercultural idea has become capitalist orthodoxy, its hunger for transgression now perfectly suited to an economic-cultural regime that runs on ever-faster cyclings of the new."[85] Unlike the fifties ideal of conformity embodied by "the man in the gray flannel suit," the jaded business strategists of today appeal to our desire to be oppositional and different.[86]

A sampling of advertising slogans tells the story. Burger King tells us "Sometimes You Gotta Break the Rules"; WXRT-FM Radio announces, "If You Don't Like the Rules, Change Them"; Arby's states, "This is different. Different is good"; Toyota comes up with, "The Line Has Been Crossed: The Revolutionary New Supra"; and Hugo Boss exhorts us to "Innovate Don't Imitate."[87] A 1999 ad for Adobe software shows a group of men clad in dark suits standing stiffly in a barren landscape with their ties on fire and flaring up into the air. The accompanying text states: "www.smashstatusquo.com."[88] Corporate executives do not concern themselves with the incompatibility between these slogans and the advertisement's intent, for the countercultural idea of dissent has been hitched to consumerism, and all of its formerly oppositional iconography now simply lends pizzazz to advertising campaigns. To drive the point home, Thomas Frank and Dave Mulcahey give us a fictional company called "Consolidated Deviance, Inc." Known as "ConDev," it "is unarguably the nation's leader, if not the sole force, in the fabrication, consultancy, licensing and merchandising of deviant subcultural practice."[89]

James Dean has become the consummate product of commercialism. His name and image have sold hundreds of millions of objects. MDI Entertainment, which licenses pop culture icons for the worldwide lottery industry, trumpets Dean's marketing power on its Web site, saying, "Let a rebel make your instant game a giant," and promising that "just his name on your game makes his fans instant players. James Dean is Now an Immortal Brand—Three great film performances, and a fatal accident in his prime at 24, have immortalized James Dean—making him not only a pop culture icon, but also a powerful brand name."[90] Mark Roesler, whose company CMG Worldwide owns the rights to the James Dean name and image, acknowledges that dead superstars are far more marketable than live ones, and the profitability of Dean and Marilyn Monroe, also represented by Roesler, is clear in the fortunes they bring in, between $3 and $7 million a year, according to one source.[91]

If leather-clad disaffection ever had any precise meaning, it has since been swept away by a tidal wave of consumerism. Now the rebel icon confronts us continually but eludes our interpretive grasp. The contradictions surrounding James Dean in the fifties were written into his legacy and have continued to the present, so that in the summer of 1996 the U.S. Postal Service could choose to immortalize on a postage stamp a young man who some say used drugs[92] and was the subject of a rumor that he was a "human ashtray" with a masochistic predilection for having burning cigarettes stubbed out on his skin.[93] Dean shares with Elvis Presley and Marilyn Monroe the dubious honor of immortalization, and simultaneous mummification, on a United States postage stamp. In 1993 the Elvis Presley commemorative postage stamp was released after months of national debate about whether it should portray the young or the old Elvis. (Not surprisingly, the svelte young Elvis won.) No such choice existed in 1996 when the James Dean commemorative stamp was issued, the second, after Marilyn Monroe, in the Postal Service's "Legends of Hollywood Series." The Dean postage stamp now circles the globe as a form of standardized currency.

It could be argued that Dean's makeover and commemoration on a postage stamp is the death knell for any oppositional power he might have had. Freezing his image and circulating it around the world as a type of American currency would seem to represent its final mainstream appropriation, the culmination of a long process of intensive commodification. While it is natural for some national heroes to parade gloriously around the world symbolizing the American spirit on stamps, there was a forty-one-year process of mainstreaming James Dean to prepare him for his philatelic role.[94]

It is not surprising that the James Dean commemorative postage stamp was the best-selling stamp of 1996, during a time when cool was hot, with 31 million sold.[95] Indeed, the "Legends of Hollywood" series of postage stamps is one facet of the late-capitalist obsession with recycling past styles and stars. Cultural theorist Fredric Jameson writes that we can "diagnose contemporary culture as irredeemably historicist, in the bad sense of an omnipresent and indiscriminate appetite for dead styles and fashions; indeed, for all the styles and fashions of a dead past."[96] A fragment among endless fragments of pop culture circulating in hyperreality, the rebel icon is detached from its origins and exists in a perpetual present as a shorthand signifier of eternal disaffected adolescence.

Even granting that the young rebel may have exuded genuine intensity in the fifties, it is generally agreed that rebel films and the rebel icon itself can no longer emit the same force and have largely become objects of parody.[97] Even so, it is not entirely true that the rebel figure always remains devoid of expressive power. Through a process of counterhegemony, subcultures reappropriate and reinvest overexposed, commercialized material with new, socially marginal meanings. Of course an effective oppositional stance is elusive, if not impossible, in the face of voracious marketing strategies. In an age of depthlessness and pastiche, is there any possibility for an authentic oppositional stance?

Despite the overwhelming presence of rebel clichés, originality still exists. Buried under the international avalanche of rebel imagery, there are some interesting texts that take banal pop culture iconography and invest it with new and provocative life. The following chapters analyze a sampling of films and fiction that revolve around a fascination with the rebel icon whose origins are in the fifties but whose identity is constantly being reinvented. Originally spawned by the conflicts of the fifties and the conventions of Hollywood melodrama, the rebel icon has subsequently assumed extraordinarily diverse shapes. Some of the texts examined here use the rebel figure in highly conventional ways; others attempt to regenerate its power in surprisingly original ways, and still others deconstruct it and question its relevance. Ranging from extreme mainstream sanitization to radical dissent, the various rebel texts span the political spectrum. In much of the industrialized world, the political pendulum has been swinging back and forth between conservative and progressive ideologies for the last hundred years, and this ideological oscillation has been expressed in all kinds of arenas including popular culture, where icons such as the rebel are nothing if not malleable. Marshall Fishwick writes, "Everywhere, in the global mode, people munch on 'icon sandwiches' from the ever-changing menu."[98] The rebel icon is one of the staples on the menu, and it continues to nourish new generations of international fans.

CHAPTER 2

Disney's Dean

1955: James Dean died and Disneyland came into existence.

Demolition derby cars crisscross the screen as the film opens, at first cruising in an orderly pattern through a dirt-track intersection but then starting to career wildly. Accompanied by the lilting strains of Strauss waltzes, they smash into each other with increasing abandon, surrounded by clouds of swirling dust. The choreographed mayhem is rendered light and amusing by Strauss' dance tunes, with each crash comically punctuating the repetitive Viennese rhythm. By the time car 4B collides with a dirt bank and rolls over, viewers have already been assured by the film's playful tone that no harm will come to its driver. And indeed, he crawls out from underneath his overturned car, removes his helmet, and walks away unscathed with nothing more than a comic look of exasperation. The character is Jim Douglas, the actor is Dean Jones, and we have just witnessed the metaphorical resurrection of James Dean in the 1969 Disney film, *The Love Bug* (Robert Stevenson, 1969).

Fourteen years earlier, on September 30, 1955, James Dean did not escape unscathed from the collision of his Porsche Spyder with a Ford sedan. His death triggered fanatical devotion among young people in the middle fifties, for whom he symbolized the consummate doomed rebel, and although he died that day, his spirit lived on in the form of the iconic teen rebel he helped forge. Rebellion was simmering just beneath the hard surface of the fifties, a decade with a shellacked veneer covering seething discontent. When the rebelliousness of the sixties exploded through the nation's surface complacency, the teen rebel icon was poised to represent youthful rage. It did not matter that James Dean had not been concerned with politics, except to express disgust with the narrow-minded intolerance

Jim Douglas crawls out from under the wreckage of his demo derby car in
The Love Bug.

of his hometown.[1] The rebel figure from the fifties and James Dean himself were adopted as countercultural mascots. As biographer Paul Alexander puts it:

> Because Dean symbolized rebelliousness and discontent, radicals from
> the sixties could embrace him. They did too, especially toward the end
> of the decade. Some observers felt Dean probably even inspired *Easy
> Rider,* one of the most influential cultural documents of the sixties. If so,
> it wouldn't be surprising since Dennis Hopper, the picture's director,
> made no qualms about his admiration for Dean.[2]

In January 1971, Elroy Hamilton wrote in the *Chicago Sun-Times* that
the climax of *Rebel Without a Cause,* when the L.A. police shoot Plato
despite Jim Stark's protests, "somehow seems to be an early version of
the deaths of *Easy Rider* and, perhaps, of those at Kent State, though the
intervening years seem to have added the extra ingredient of hatred."[3]
Dean's screen portrayals of wounded fury served as powerful symbols for
sixties countercultural rage, lending an aura of romanticism exploited by
Easy Rider (Dennis Hopper, 1969), *Bonnie and Clyde* (Arthur Penn, 1967),
and other sixties youth films.

But despite the counterculture, the civil rights movement, the black power movement, the gay rights movement, and the women's movement, the nation's most successful film of 1969 was Disney's *The Love Bug*.[4] During the same year as Woodstock and *Easy Rider*, Americans turned out in droves to see a live-action comedy about a lovable Volkswagen Beetle with a mind of its own. A madcap adventure, the film joined other live-action comedies released by the Disney studio during the 1960s following the success of *The Shaggy Dog* in 1959. *The Love Bug* was 1969's highest grossing film; it was so successful that the Disney studio didn't have a bigger hit until it released *Splash* in 1984.[5]

In *The Love Bug* we see the sterilization of dissent, from the opening sequence in which the automobile crash ends not in death or injury, but in the introduction of the uninjured protagonist, who crawls out from under the wreckage. His handsome intensity and passion for racing recall James Dean, but Disney resurrected a "safe" James Dean: Dean Jones. Unlike James Dean, *The Love Bug*'s protagonist—Jim Douglas—played by actor Dean Jones, is inoffensive and nonthreatening. While there is no evidence that anyone associated with the production of *The Love Bug* chose to make the film resonate with James Dean references, it nonetheless can be interpreted as a succinct illustration of the sanitization and evisceration of teen rebel iconography. A close analysis of the film illustrates a consistent strategy of rewriting dissent to assert the victory of social consensus. In *The Love Bug* we see the Disneyfication of the rebel icon, a perfect metaphor for the Disneyfication of the sixties and, subsequently, the Disneyfication of mainstream American culture.

Jim Douglas in *The Love Bug* is an aging driver who refuses to give up racing. Although the character's age is never revealed, Dean Jones was thirty-eight years old at the time. Jones was born in 1931, the same year as James Dean, who would also have been thirty-eight in 1969. Had James Dean not died, he might well have been an aging race driver, since he had an abiding passion for racing, and it is conceivable that he would have gotten the part of the aging race driver in *The Love Bug*.[6] Casting Dean Jones to play Jim Douglas was a logical choice in 1969, since, according to Jones' autobiography, he was a confused and angry young man with a penchant for dangerous motorcycle stunts, and he had been compared to James Dean by British critics, a comparison he reveled in.[7]

During a decade of explosive nonconformity, Jim Douglas' challenge to conventions in *The Love Bug* consists mainly of a stubborn commitment to racing despite a history of losses. His most consistent trait is an obsession with automobiles, and the film is not subtle in presenting an erotic element in a man's passion for his car, what Karal Ann Marling calls the "autoeroticism" of the fifties.[8] While Jim is admiring an expensive European sports car, he asks his love interest, Carole (Michele Lee), "Can you imagine how I'd make it with equipment like this?" Carole wonders, "Is it so important to you?" Jim responds that "without a real car, I'm only half a man." Later, when Jim has begun to appreciate the special qualities of Herbie, the loyal VW Beetle, Carole asks him, "You let that little car get under your skin, didn't you?" Jim responds:

> There's a lot of gloop been written about the bond between a man and his automobile. How he hates it sometimes but mostly how he loves it. Showers gifts on it in the way of accessories. He gets hysterical if someone scratches the paint or makes it lose face on the freeway. Maybe some of those feelings got into the machinery . . . There's something real about that little car. Something that doesn't even have a name. What I don't understand is why out of the millions of people in the world it picked a dog-eared second rater like me?

Carole speculates, "You stood up for it once. It must have thought you were worth belonging to." Earlier in the film, Jim's friend Tennessee Steinmetz (Buddy Hackett) consoles Herbie after Jim has spurned Herbie for a yellow sports car: "He isn't the first guy to lose his head over a bucket seat and a paint job." Tennessee ruefully observes: "Guys give more love to their cars than to their wife and kids."

These thinly veiled sexual references are consistent with the Disney studio's tradition of condensing and displacing sexuality in its films. During the forties, journalists began to write disapprovingly about the new Disney licentiousness.[9] Film scholar Eric Smoodin writes that

> Disney had not so much changed the attitudes in his cartoons toward sexuality as he had changed his representation of it. Instead of anthropomorphic flowers or animals there were now real-life (that is, live-action) women in such films as *Saludos Amigos* and *The Three Caballeros* and drawn women, like Cinderella, who suddenly seemed more human to the critics. Disney's increased realism made the critics notice for the first time how the cartoon producer presented sexuality.[10]

The words used by critics in the forties to describe Disney cartoons included "erotomaniacal" and "orgiastic." The sight of Donald Duck lasciviously pursuing live-action Latin American bombshells in *The Three*

Caballeros "like a berserk bumblebee," as one critic put it, was considered particularly outrageous.[11] Eric Smoodin's point that Disney's cartoons had always presented sexuality, albeit indirectly and with animated figures, is important. Richard Schickel agrees that Disney work "has a strong, though displaced, sexual element."[12] Disney films present the strange fantasies of a puritanical nation obsessed with and yet embarrassed by sex. In the films, though, sexual relations between humans are minimized in favor of peculiar sexual antics between animals or machines, and often involving inter-species or inter-object pairings. In an effort to create an innocent world onscreen by avoiding the representation of adult human sexuality, the films ironically depict a world shot through with displaced sexual references.

Jim Douglas' love for his car in *The Love Bug* may not be "erotomaniacal" or "orgiastic," but it does participate in the techno-erotic aspects of the car mania that swept the nation starting in the late forties and reached fiery intensity during the fifties. Hot rodding and drag racing were notorious outlaw subcultures, the province of defiant bad boys and girls. The chicken run scene in *Rebel Without a Cause*, in which "James Dean drove a customized 1949 Merc, 'channeled' almost beyond recognition,"[13] is built on the fascination with and fear of drag racing in the fifties. Jack Kerouac's devotion to the open road, immortalized in his novel *On the Road*, combined with the Beats' self-conscious sloughing off of conformity, contributed to the mystique of the automobile in the fifties. The end of the Beat era did not signal a decline in drag racing; it is still going strong in urban centers throughout the United States, taken up first by young Hispanics with their low-riders and then by young Asian Americans in Southern California with modified Japanese imports called race rockets. Racing late at night on urban streets is now a multicultural pastime, one increasingly popular among women racers.[14]

Another facet of car mania, demolition derbies got their start in the fifties, although their exact origins are a matter of dispute. Their appeal, according to journalist Andrew Weiner, is in their simplicity: "Stock-car racing is hugely popular in America, and many race fans will freely admit that they come for the chance of seeing a spectacular pile-up. Like a sports-highlight reel, demo (as it's known to its followers) takes the active ingredient of stock-car racing and isolates it to make a more concentrated form of entertainment."[15] Demo is enduringly popular. One demo event from the seventies involved two teams of cars trying to shove a Volkswagen Beetle across some goal lines.[16]

Demo derbies still have the power to attract large and enthusiastic audiences. At the Labor Day stock car races at the Seekonk Speedway in Seekonk, Massachusetts, in 1999, I joined a packed stadium of fans for a medley of racing events that culminated in an eagerly anticipated demo, or what Weiner calls a "carmageddon."[17] Dozens of cars formed a circle around the track, parked with their back ends pointed into the center. When the signal was given, the cars roared into deafening action by backing up and slamming into each other like remote-control toys operated by a demented child. The air was filled with noise and the smell of exhaust, and as the smash-up continued, several cars burst into flames, prompting a fire engine and ambulance to whip into the fray. There were several attempts to continue, but the demo was finally discontinued under a heavy cloud of smoke. Charred vehicles littered the track. The crowd filed out elated.

Vehicles are overdetermined with associations in the United States, and one of their primary connotations is as a rebel's accessory. The ultimate tributes to—and also mockeries of—the rebel's passion for his vehicles are Kenneth Anger's underground films *Scorpio Rising* (1964) and *Kustom Kar Kommandos* (1965), in which the camera slowly and sensuously caresses the sinuous curves of automobiles and motorcycles. *Scorpio Rising* delves into the techno-erotic and homoerotic appeal of biker culture, with its loving attention to the ritual of dressing in leather, buckles, and chains, and its adulation of a rebel leader. The coke-snorting Scorpio (Bruce Byron) is crosscut with other objects of worship—Jesus (of the Hollywood film variety), Marlon Brando, and Nazi swastikas—as well as objects suggesting the lurking presence of death. *Kustom Kar Kommandos* showcases a young man's love for his customized car, which he strokes adoringly with a powder puff to the seductive song "Dream Lover."

James Dean loved his cars and, like Jim Douglas in *The Love Bug*, did not hide the fact. After he bought a new car, he wrote to a friend: "A new addition has been added to the Dean family . . . a red '53 MG. My sex pours itself into fast curves, broadslides and broodings, drags, etc. . . . I have been sleeping with my MG. We made it together."[18] Graham McCann notes that during the fifties, "American culture had the accumulated associations of virile sportsters, libidinous limousines, back-seat petting and mobilized amorality."[19] *The Love Bug* presents a tame, Disneyfied version of these associations when Jim Douglas drives Carole to lover's lane, called Seabreeze Point, where she taunts him about his reputation by saying, "I've heard it said that Jim Douglas is only interested in fast cars

James Dean with his Porsche Speedster. (The David Loehr Collection)

and easy money." "Not true," says Jim, and kisses her for the first time to prove it. Their parked interlude, however, remains short and chaste.

The objects of James Dean's techno-erotic desire were not pudgy little Beetles. Dean's love for his red '53 MG was later displaced by a prefer-ence for Porsches, culminating in the silver Porsche 550 Spyder in which he took his last ride. He bought the Spyder only two days after hearing about it from his mechanic, Rolf Weutherich, who was his only passenger and who survived the crash. The Porsche 550 Spyder had "gathered class

A replica of Dean's Porsche Spyder at Fairmount's "Museum Days/Remembering James Dean" festival.

wins at Avus, Le Mans, Sebring and the Mille Miglia" and was being sold in the United States in very limited numbers.[20] Dean biographer Donald Spoto describes the car:

> A sleek convertible with only a token windscreen a few inches high, the Spyder was eggshell-thin and pitched low to the ground. Some might have described it as not much bigger than a tropical turtle, or as an outsize roller-skate.[21]

During the week after he bought it, Dean "washed and rewashed it: it was his great new toy, and—a young man of his time and place—he cherished it as he had no previous possession."[22] He had it customized by George Barris, customizer extraordinaire, who years later would create Herbie for *The Love Bug*. Dean not only cherished his new Porsche, he identified with it; in addition to having Barris paint his racing number (130) on the hood and doors, he had the words "Little Bastard" painted across the back, words that have prompted much curiosity and various explanations from his fans. Donald Spoto speculates that Dean was aware that he was conceived before his parents were married and that the words "Little Bastard" on the Porsche may have been a reference to himself meant to shock the straitlaced. According to Spoto, "The distinction between himself and his car, once referred to as a lover and now the instrument of his ultimate competition, was at last forever blurred."[23]

James Dean and Jim Douglas were not alone in their adoration of cars. In one account, originally published in 1973 in *The Journal of Forensic Sciences*, a forty-year-old airline pilot who was married and the father of two young children was found dead after he had bound himself nude to his 1968 Beetle using a custom-made ten-foot chain harness fastened to the car's bumper.[24] Police investigators trying to reconstruct events leading up to his death determined that he had set the car up so it would drive slowly in concentric circles around the end of an isolated road while he jogged behind it, nude and attached by the chain. They believe that when he tried to stop the car, it drove over his chain, which then began to twist around the back axle and gradually drew him closer and closer until, struggling, he was crushed against the rear of the car. The report, accompanied by graphic photographs, is reproduced in literature and film scholar Mikita Brottman's anthology, *Car Crash Culture*; Brottman points out that such cases "all emphasize how little we really know about people's relationships with their vehicles."[25]

Passion for chrome has given rise to a discourse of lascivious men drooling over feminized automobiles. A particularly flagrant example, replete with misogynistic clichés, is John Keats' 1958 book *The Insolent Chariots*, which begins,

Once upon a time, the American met the automobile and fell in love. Unfortunately this led him into matrimony, and so he did not live happily ever after. Cooler heads could have told him the affair was doomed from the start, for in the beginning, the American was poorly prepared to make judgments in such matters. He was merely a rustic Merry Andrew with a cowlick and an adolescent tightening in the groin. In his libidinous innocence, he saw the automobile only as curious, exciting—and obviously willing. Wherefore, he joyfully leaped upon her, and she responded to his caresses by bolting about the landscape in what can only be called a succession of bumps and grinds.

This Arcadian idyll did not persist, of course. Had he loved her and left her, all would have been well. Had he restrained himself, and viewed her as a possible hired woman to be trained for work about the farm and otherwise left strictly alone, all would have been better. But he was innocent; she handed him a likely story and led him to the preacher. Then, before they were fairly out of the churchyard, she began to demonstrate less enchanting aspects of her character. The American, it seems, was trapped by a schemer . . . As the frightful marriage wore on, the automobile's original appeal shrank in inverse proportion to the growth of her demands. She grew sow-fat while demanding bigger, wider, smoother roads . . . And, of course, her every whim was more costly than the last.[26]

American culture's techno-erotic attachment to cars is present in *The Love Bug* in an antiseptic, sanitized form. Although at first Jim yearns to "make it" with sleek sports cars, he discovers that what he really loves is his trusty little VW, Herbie. What the film neglects to mention is that the Volkswagen Beetle and the Porsche have a shared ancestry. The Beetle was invented by Professor Ferdinand Porsche in 1936 with direct involvement from Adolf Hitler, who had called for the creation of a "people's car" (*Volkswagen*) made to resemble the streamlined proportions of a beetle (*ein Maikäfer*).[27] Twelve years later, in 1948, Porsche's son used the Beetle as the inspiration for the car given the Porsche family name.[28] By choosing to construct the film around a Beetle rather than a Porsche, Disney in effect downplayed the sexual element in techno-eroticism by incorporating a benign and antiseptic domesticity stripped of its Third Reich origins but still, ironically, evoking Nazi ideology's celebration of all things *volkisch*—ordinary and unpretentious as opposed to haughtily aristocratic. Modest little Herbie perfectly embodies Hitler's *volkisch* ideal, down to his antagonistic relationship to the stiff, upper-class English car dealer, Peter Thorndyke (David Tomlinson).

Disney could get away with representing a Beetle as amiable because of the successful marketing campaign of the Doyle Dane Bernbach agency, which got the Volkswagen account in 1959 and created a series of ads designed to make Americans forget about Volkswagen's Nazi connotations. Those connotations were well known and made VW cars anathema to Americans during the fifties, but DDB's campaign was so effective that by the late sixties the Beetle and the microbus were the counterculture's favorite vehicles, signifying anti-authoritarian ideals in direct opposition to Nazi totalitarianism. Ironically, the head of the agency and several members of the creative staff who designed the VW campaign were Jewish.[29]

Jim's love for Herbie is decidedly romantic, but not explicitly sexual. In one of the film's climactic moments, Herbie flees alone in the night after destroying Jim's sultry new red Lamborghini in a jealous rage. Jim dashes into the dark to find Herbie, running frantically through the fog-shrouded

Jim Douglas tries to prevent Herbie from leaping off the Golden Gate Bridge in *The Love Bug*.

San Francisco streets shouting "Herbie! Herbie!" The night, fog, and lush orchestral music bathe the scene with romantic connotations. Jim's friend Tennessee has stayed behind, observing wisely that "this is a private thing between you and Herbie." When Jim catches up to Herbie, the car is on the Golden Gate Bridge, lunging over the side in a desperate suicide attempt. Jim tries to stop Herbie and ends up dangling from the car's front bumper over the abyss in a wacky Disney reinvention of the fatal chicken run scene in *Rebel Without a Cause*. Disney provides a safe resolution, with Herbie saving Jim's life and his own by carefully returning to the bridge. From this point on, Jim stops indulging his fondness for dazzling sports cars and remains loyal to plump little Herbie, while for his part Herbie rescues Jim from self-destruction, preventing him from becoming the Disney version of the bad-boy outsider. Tennessee explains to Carole that things were bad before Herbie arrived: "Jim was defeated. It was murder. He couldn't get a job. He got into trouble. Everybody was on his back. Then Herbie came into his life . . . Jim started winning races again. He got his self-respect back."

The romantic implications of Herbie's suicide attempt were not lost on the director or star. Dean Jones writes in his autobiography that the scene of Jim Douglas trying to dissuade Herbie from committing suicide was the first one they filmed, and "early on a Monday morning, it was difficult to keep from laughing." Director Robert Stevenson "was very patient. 'Herbie loves you very much,' he explained with a wistful British accent. 'Being very hurt that you have fallen in love with Michele Lee, he's trying to kill himself.' 'Got it, Robert,' I said, and then broke up again."[30]

Of course there is something perverse about a film in which a man learns to value monogamy with a Volkswagen car. There is also something perverse about a film implying that a car has a sex and romantic inclinations. But Disney diminishes the perversity by giving Herbie a mission: to domesticate Jim's boyish masculinity and replace Tennessee with Carole as his closest companion. Jim and Tennessee are roommates and best friends in a domestic arrangement that hints at married life, but at the end Jim marries Carole. His transformation asserts the primacy of what sociologist Bob Connell calls "hegemonic masculinity," the style of masculinity that upholds the tenets of a particular era's dominant ideology. Connell defines the term as "the configuration of gender practice which embodies the currently acceptable answer to the problem of the legitimacy of patriarchy, which guarantees (or is taken to guarantee) the dominant position of men and the subordination of women."[31] The hegemonic masculinity embodied by Jim Douglas at the end of *The Love Bug* involves heterosexuality, monogamy, and marriage: he has abandoned his romantic pursuit of sexy cars, has replaced Tennessee with Carole as his partner, and departs on a honeymoon that appears to be conventional in every way except that he and Carole sit together in the back seat while Herbie drives himself.

In accordance with Connell's definition of hegemonic masculinity, Jim's new masculinity upholds the legitimacy of patriarchy in the film: Carole is a pawn in the power struggle between Jim and the film's villain, Thorndyke. She is the prize in a male game, and the winner—Jim—"possesses" her through marriage at the end. A social structure based on competition between men has been called "homosociality" by Eve Sedgwick;[32] Steven Cohan elaborates on its workings:

> Homosociality has as much to do with power (*over* women as well as other men) as it does with desire (*for* other men as well as women), which is why it so readily takes the form of one man's domination of another, emphasizing independence, competition, and aggression as the hallmark features of virility, and usually going even further to manifest fear of alternate male behavior—such as effeminacy—in homophobic violence.[33]

Jim and Thorndyke in *The Love Bug* take their rivalry to infantile extremes. They compete for racing trophies and for possession of Herbie, the little car that miraculously wins every race. When Thorndyke is thwarted in his attempts to claim Herbie, he does his best to sabotage the car, disabling it in all kinds of nefarious ways. Herbie is the disputed object of desire for the two men, but it is an unconventional desire, one that involves more than a hint of techno- and homoeroticism. To offset their infatuation with an automobile, the film also has them try to prove their virility through ownership of Carole. Our first introduction to Carole in the film emphasizes her status as object: she consists of a pair of shapely legs seen by Jim through the window of a car dealership as she struggles to hang the bottom part of a sign, the top of which states "May We Direct Your Attention To These . . ." With the sign covering her head and most of her body, her disembodied legs have a fetishized life of their own. Although she has the spunky nature of many of Disney's live-action women characters, she nevertheless performs the function of a pair of legs throughout the film.

Her legs and Jim's growing relationship with her at Herbie's insistence disavow Jim's implicit gayness. From the beginning, Herbie conspires to bring Jim and Carole together, locking his doors so that Carole is trapped inside with Jim and even driving them to lover's lane when they are together in the car for the first time and arguing angrily. Jim's pairing with Carole also shifts attention from Jim's close relationship with Tennessee. The two men share a house with a workroom on the ground level and living quarters up above. When the police arrive early one morning to arrest Jim for car theft, Jim and Tennessee appear dressed in their pajamas in two open windows of the second floor, and Tennessee is shaving. His role throughout the film is to worry about Jim and dispense sage advice. Although there is no overt romantic relationship between Jim and Tennessee, their living together and mutual dependence suggest a close, emotionally intimate friendship between men.

The suggestion of a homoerotic bond between Tennessee and Jim is repressed in the film. In fact, Tennessee becomes the most enthusiastic proponent of Carole, his replacement in Jim's affections. Herbie and Tennessee both actively disavow their intimacy with Jim by pushing Jim and Carole together, becoming confidants and fussing over Jim and each other, with Tennessee serving as an amateur mechanic for Herbie although his actual vocation is welding metal sculptures. Thus the film enacts a pattern of repeatedly displacing its implied homoeroticism (between Jim and Tennessee, and between Jim and Herbie) to reach a conventional heterosexual resolution when Jim marries Carole and they motor off together in Herbie for their honeymoon.

By ending with Jim's marriage to Carole and repudiating his closeness to Tennessee and Herbie, *The Love Bug* perpetuates the homophobia of the fifties, when James Dean and other gay and bisexual actors were required to strenuously hide, or disguise, their sexuality. The film's nostalgic version of fifties gender roles ignores the decade's actual variations in masculinity. Most importantly, the film rejects the sensitive and sexually ambiguous personae introduced to the big screen in the fifties by James Dean, Marlon Brando, and Montgomery Clift. The characters they played in films were characterized by emotional turmoil and self-doubt, qualities that were condemned by John Wayne in a 1960 interview when he expressed disgust with "the psychotic weaklings depicted as heroes in modern down-beat movies." He went on to say that "ten or 15 years ago audiences went to pictures to see men behaving like men . . . Today there are too many neurotic roles."[34]

Dean, Brando, and Clift threatened Wayne's—and traditional American culture's—complacent belief in the hegemonic manly man. Each of the three "rebel males" played characters that were racked by insecurities and that diverged from the heterosexual norm. Hollywood's publicity machine strenuously worked to hide Clift's, Brando's, and Dean's gay involvements—there was a powerful taboo against openly gay actors—but the stars were not entirely in the closet. Dean, as mentioned in the previous chapter, responded to a question about his sexuality by saying, "I'm not going through life with one hand tied behind my back," and Brando referred to himself as "trisexual."[35] Clift, Brando, and Dean destabilized gender categories, but their methods had to remain cloaked and indirect during a decade that would not have tolerated outright insurrection.[36]

The Love Bug brings fifties intolerance into the late sixties, when traditional codes of iron-clad masculinity were being openly challenged by the counterculture's adoption of androgynous styles. A prominent aspect of the sixties generation gap was a battle over styles of masculinity, with young men openly flouting gray flannel suits and flaunting long hair, beards, loose colorful clothing, and sandals, brazenly "letting it all hang out." Counterculture youth rejected the clean-cut he-man style for its association with their parents' smug values and American aggression in Vietnam. Androgyny served both to express individual identity in opposition to the cookie-cutter sameness of buzz cuts and suits and to provoke the ire of straitlaced authority figures. Clothing and hairstyles were still powerful semiotic codes in the sixties: a long-haired young man wearing bell-bottom jeans, a flowing shirt, sandals, and beads was sending a message about his left-wing political alignment.

But despite their androgynous appearance, most countercultural young men were, ironically, as homophobic as their parents. Film and literary scholar David Savran writes that "despite the New Left's commendable concern with broad cultural issues in addition to political ones, the vast majority of political radicals did not question the structures of heteronormativity."[37] Indeed, the sexual revolution for the most part meant heterosexual freedom, reproducing the unprogressive sexual politics of the status quo. As Stuart Hall puts it, "The tiny 'family man' is still hiding away in the heads of many of our most illustrious 'street-fighting' militants."[38] The older generation nonetheless perceived a threat to heteronormativity; conservatives who made up the "moral majority" were offended by feminized young men with long hair who adorned themselves with jewelry and wore brightly colored "sissy" clothing.

The Love Bug looks backward to a time when gender and sexual codes were more strictly controlled. Perhaps Herbie's racing number—53—is a subconscious reference to a year when androgyny was not yet pervasive and the United States was actively repressing and persecuting its gay population. Herbie's number 53 also evokes James Dean's '53 MG, the car with which he claimed to have "made it." (One author asserts that the film's producer and writer, Bill Walsh, chose the number 53 because it was Dodger pitcher Don Drysdale's number.[39]) A racing official in the film expresses the film's underlying desire to return to the hypermasculine past when he announces, "Instead of all this technical namby pamby there's so much of today, we're putting the emphasis on speed, endurance, and courage: the way things used to be." Joined with Herbie's red, white, and blue racing stripes, the number 53 takes on the connotations of a nostalgic yearning for a mythical America populated by square-jawed men with crew cuts married to women who found satisfaction as brisk and efficient housewives.

The Love Bug succinctly captures the Disney studio's nostalgic ethos during the late sixties. Richard Schickel describes Disney's sixties live-action films as "little time capsules of 1950s bourgeois life, when it was thought that the worst thing that could happen to an individual was to be singled out, separated from the crowd."[40] Walt Disney died in 1966, three years before *The Love Bug* was released, in the middle of a decade that must have been perplexing to a man who clung to the simple ideals of rural America. Historian Steven Watts writes in *The Magic Kingdom: Walt Disney and the American Way of Life* that Disney's postwar work emphasized "sentimentalism, wholesomeness, innocence, and virtue," endearing him to families across the country who longed for homespun virtues.[41] By the fifties Walt Disney had become a trusted figure to traditional-minded Americans determined to uphold their rosy version of the past. Uncle Walt was a reassuring presence to those swept up by Cold War fears. For instance, he solemnly gave his advice in newspaper stories on how to combat juvenile delinquency, and promised that he would "make movies that showed the good side of teenagers."[42] He signified conservative values and offered strong yet gentle guidance for Americans searching for a safe haven from threats thought to be lurking on all sides.

Walt Disney himself vacillated on social issues, and in this he embodied one of the major contradictions of his era: a love for tradition and a simultaneous urge to supersede it. Watts explains:

> Standing midway between the country and the city, both emotionally and historically trapped between the demands of his father's moral code and the attractive new creed of consumer America, Disney spent much of his life struggling with his conflicting feelings about his personal history. Like other influential architects of modern America who used their money to clutch at a vision of the past—Henry Ford and Dearborn Village, for instance, or John D. Rockefeller and Williamsburg, Virginia—Disney came to cherish the traditional values and structures that he had helped to destroy.[43]

It certainly is ironic that Disneyland and Disney World, as well as many Disney films, celebrate small-town virtues and local entrepreneurship, while the Disney Empire established by Walt has been at the crest of a tidal wave of mass consumerism that has all but crushed those very virtues.

The Disney Corporation has ingenious ways of disguising this contradiction, as author and journalist Carl Hiaasen points out in his study of Disney World titled *Team Rodent: How Disney Devours the World*: "Disney will devour the world the same way it devoured this country, starting first with the youth. Disney theme parks have drawn more than one billion visitors, mostly kids. Snag the children and everybody else follows—parents, politicians, even the press. *Especially* the press. We're all suckers for a good cartoon."[44] Disney's whitewashed public relations are also on display in its corporate-owned town in Florida, aptly named Celebration, where the plan was for neat lawns and white picket fences to recall the small-town simplicity that existed before corporate behemoths like Disney made mass consumption one of the nation's top priorities. Not surprisingly, the reality of life in Disney's town has not matched this idealistic vision.[45] But paradox is not new to the Disney Corporation. Steven Watts describes how Walt Disney managed to embody both nostalgia and futurism during the Cold War era:

> This staunch defender of national and domestic security became a source of strength in an era of tremendous ideological pressures. Yet Disney's powerful evocation of Americanism during the Cold War included another important element of modern life. Consumerism, the buoyant cultural outgrowth of a dynamic capitalist economy, became increasingly critical to the postwar American economy of abundance. It also became central to Walt Disney's appeal.[46]

Walt Disney's embodiment of contradictory values is a microcosm of the paradoxical nature of advertising starting in the sixties. During that decade of social rebellion against "mindless conformity," American business itself underwent a shift, one that rejected the advertising strategies of the past in favor of a "hip consumerism" documented by Thomas Frank in *The Conquest of Cool*.[47] Frank argues that advertisers did not so much cynically co-opt the rebelliousness of the sixties as perceive it as a welcome antidote to the rigid and increasingly ineffective strategies of earlier decades. What appealed to advertising executives in the sixties was the counterculture's rejection of "the old values of caution, deference, and hierarchy" in favor of "creativity" and "flexibility."[48] The younger generation of advertisers recognized the advantages of a countercultural preference for rapidly changing tastes, for seeking out the newest thing as opposed to settling for the tried and true. The hippies' emphasis on oppositional styles to distinguish themselves from their square parents was entirely compatible with the needs of corporate capitalism, and advertisers began to push the notion of consumption as a means to rebel against conformity. "Rebel consumers" are encouraged to participate in the latest, hippest trend by purchasing objects with the appropriately rebellious connotations and demonstrating that they reject consumerism even as they join in.

By the nineties it had become commonplace for advertisers to appeal to people's distrust of advertising to sell products. Oppositional cultural practices, such as grunge or hip hop clothing, were quickly and easily absorbed into the fashion mainstream, where they remain. "Seattle-born grunge look is back as a backlash to glamour" is the headline of a fall 2003 newspaper article. We learn that "grunge has been a recurrent theme in fashion since the early '90s, when rockers like Cobain transformed kilts, moth-eaten sweaters and lumberjack plaids into the insignia of yuppie revolt." In grunge's early twenty-first century reappearance, Marc Jacobs, "who notoriously created a grunge collection for Perry Ellis a decade ago," has built his new collection "on an amalgam of rainbow-colored layers, a sprightly version of the style that was once embraced by disaffected high schoolers and the protagonists of *Wayne's World*," and Jean Touitou's "grunge-inspired fall collection . . . evocatively christened Smells like Seattle . . . is full of lumberjack shirts in plaid polyester, beefy cardigans, striped leggings and kilts."[49] The line separating rejection of the status quo from its endorsement has been thoroughly breached. William Burroughs appeared in a Nike commercial and the Velvet Underground's song "Venus in Furs" accompanied a commercial for Goodyear tires. Iggy Pop's nasty punk-rock anthem "Lust for Life" has been used in a television advertisement for Royal Caribbean Cruise Lines, and the Rolling Stones' "Jumpin' Jack Flash" has hawked Corvettes. Contradictions have become a mainstay of the language of advertising.

The Disney studio is one of the corporations that early on understood the value of mining cultural references, sanitizing them, and using them for commercial purposes. For example, Disneyland, which opened its doors in 1955, is a major money-making cog in a gigantic corporate machine. It exists, in the words of Richard Schickel, "to keep everyone in a spending mood without ever once overtly suggesting that Disneyland is, in the last analysis, hardly a charitable enterprise."[50] Walt Disney himself is characterized by Schickel as a puritan who feared man and nature[51] and who was obsessed with cleanliness and sanitation at Disneyland.[52] His legacy is a sanitized culture unwilling to acknowledge and seriously address its social problems, preferring instead to escape into mass-produced fantasies.[53] Disneyland and Disney World are advertised as places that deliver not only fun and excitement (guests at Disney World can stay at a hotel with a Herbie the Love Bug theme), but also the more profound experiences of family unity and personal fulfillment. What is suppressed is that they are first and foremost money-making endeavors engaged in reaping mammoth profits.[54]

As early as 1958, screenwriter Julian Halevy, writing in *The Nation*, observed that in Disneyland,

as in the Disney movies, the whole world, the universe, and all man's striving for dominion over self and nature, have been reduced to a sickening blend of cheap formulas packaged to sell. Romance, Adventure, Fantasy, Science are ballyhooed and marketed: life is bright colored, clean, cute, titivating, safe, mediocre, inoffensive to the lowest common denominator, and somehow poignantly inhuman.[55]

The adjectives used by Halevy in the fifties apply also to Disney's live-action films of the sixties, in particular *The Love Bug*, which is "bright colored, clean, cute, titivating, safe, mediocre, inoffensive to the lowest common denominator, and somehow poignantly inhuman." As Richard Schickel notes, live-action films from Disney were "too cozy, too bland, too comfortable and comforting."[56] The films tended to use stock characters and settings[57] and to cast stars who "are utterly interchangeable with others of their type."[58] Dean Jones in *The Love Bug*, for example, may have the lithe, slender body and boyish good looks of James Dean, but the film presents him as unmemorable and nonthreatening. He avoids appearing "sensitive and spooky," qualities that *Look* magazine attributed to James Dean in a 1958 article.[59] Art historian Richard Meyer refers to James Dean's "method actor angst and performative volatility."[60] Dean Jones, however, is not known for having an explosive screen presence.

Walt Disney had established a practice of avoiding casting big stars in his live-action films, in part because he didn't want to pay the inflated salaries they commanded.[61] Similarly, he avoided hiring directors with a strong signature style, preferring those who would conform to his house style.[62] Few people watching *The Love Bug* would be able to identify it as a film directed by Robert Stevenson, the Cambridge-educated British director who had been prominent in England before being brought to Hollywood by David O. Selznick in 1939. He started working for the Disney studio in 1956 and stayed there for the rest of his career, directing films such as *Old Yeller* (1957), *Mary Poppins* (1964), and *That Darn Cat* (1965). These films and others directed by Stevenson for Disney are generally known only as Disney films, for the studio's house style tended to obliterate most directors' idiosyncrasies. Richard Schickel reports that at the Disney studio, "even the most adventurous writers and directors came to understand implicitly that challenging the studio's conventionalities of content and style was a waste of energy, that the essence of their task was always to seek the formulaic solution."[63]

Disney's live-action narrative formula of the sixties included replacing genuine nonconformity with good-natured and harmless mischief. *Mary Poppins*, writes Richard Schickel, was "acceptably nonconformist."[64] Typically the films associate their villains, who are often pompous bankers, with narrow-minded propriety, and it is the mischievous protagonists in league with lovable children, animals, or inanimate objects who inject a welcome note of lightness and frivolity into the community. In *The Love Bug*'s final race, the El Dorado, Jim, Tennessee, Carole and Herbie are the fun-loving foursome who take on the greedy and conniving British snob, Thorndyke. This villainous car dealer is an elitist prig who is repulsed by Jim's and Tennessee's uncouth ways and repeatedly races against Jim in an effort to put him in his place and win back Carole's loyalty. After learning that Herbie is a consistent winner, Thorndyke tries to cripple the little car and, when that fails, to win it in a wager. He is finally vanquished when Jim and Herbie win the El Dorado despite all odds, and despite Herbie having been severed into two halves.

The antagonism between working-class Jim Douglas and wealthy Peter Thorndyke is a class struggle, but its socioeconomic implications are repressed and superseded by an emphasis on their individual characteristics. Thorndyke, in typical Disney fashion, is so thoroughly unpleasant that any opposition to him is unquestionably justified. An upper-class twit, he joins the film's other targets of mockery. Hippies are characterized as confused, laughable clowns in funny wigs and outrageously goofy clothes. Early in the film Jim is trying to prove to the disbelieving Carole that Herbie is unlike other cars, when two hippies in a hot rod pull up beside them and challenge Jim to a drag race. Herbie does a wheelie and flies past them. Their inane response—"groovy!"—elicits a grimace from Jim and Carole, whom the film presents as the sensible ones. Hippies are again associated with drug-induced derangement in the film when a cop, having seen Herbie rescue Jim, says, "Boy, was he lucky. This little car saved his life . . ." The other cop responds derisively, "I think you've been up on that Haight Ashbury beat too long." In another example, Herbie takes Jim and Carole to a drive-in diner and, when Carole tries to flee, locks his doors. Carole pounds on the window and screams, "I'm a prisoner in here! Help!!" Two hippies in a psychedelically painted van parked beside Herbie watch her with vacant expressions, and one intones, "We all prisoners, chickie baby. We all locked in." When Carole continues to struggle, the hippie comments to his friend, "A couple of weirdos, Guinevere." The joke, of course, is that in their big wigs and mismatched brightly colored hippie gear, they are the actual "weirdos." (An inside joke is that one of the hippies was played by Dean Jones, unrecognizable under the makeup and big hair.)[65]

These goofy hippies are impossible to take seriously, and that is precisely the point. Nonconformists are marginalized and mocked by the film, and any values they might represent are marginalized along with them, so that the counterculture comes across as a silly endeavor attractive only to oddballs and misfits. Packaged as innocent family fun, *The Love Bug* actually conveys strong ideological support for the status quo, consistent with the Disney tradition described by cultural studies scholar Henry Giroux:

> Insidiously, Disney uses its much-touted commitment to wholesome entertainment to market toys, clothes, and gadgets to children. Beneath Disney's self-proclaimed role as an icon of American culture lies a powerful educational apparatus that provides ideologically loaded fantasies.[66]

By obscuring and mocking the counterculture's oppositional social views in *The Love Bug*, Disney participated in depoliticizing it and turning it into an empty fashion statement. By the time a sixties revival swept the nation during the early nineties, the counterculture had been thoroughly reduced to a fashion accessory, and anyone could become a "sixties person" by donning fringes, bell bottoms, peace-sign necklaces, and sandals; the counterculture had become a merchandising gimmick.

At the same time that *The Love Bug* drains the counterculture of significance, the film also adopts some of the movement's signifiers to gain hip currency. The notion of a "love bug" is a reference to the counterculture's "love, not war" ethos that Robert Indiana celebrated in his large "LOVE" painting in 1968. Even the film's musical score borrows a countercultural motif by using a humming flute, the sound associated with Ian Anderson of Jethro Tull. Herbie's red, white, and blue patriotism is compatible with these countercultural motifs in the same way that consumerism is compatible with rebellion in this postparadoxical age. As Phil Patton points out, even though "for Disney, *The Love Bug* offered a sort of vaccination against counter-culture infection," it was also "Disney's bid for hipness."[67]

Hippies are not the only group used for comic relief in *The Love Bug*. Chinese Americans, too, are represented as a homogenous and peculiar lot, in keeping with the Disney practice of featuring groups of zany ethnics in both its animated and live-action films. Herbie flees after being captured by Thorndyke and hides under a dragon in a Chinese New Year parade in San Francisco's Chinatown, and then drives into a shop to escape detection and leaves it in a shambles. The Chinese shopkeeper, Mr. Wu (Benson Fong), shouts furiously in Chinese and later finds Herbie impounded at the police station with telltale strips of dried squid on him. Although Mr. Wu is a businessman who wears a Western-style black suit, he pulls out an abacus with which to total the damages to his shop. The punch line to the film's joke about Mr. Wu is that after Tennessee speaks loudly and slowly to him in exaggerated Chinese, Mr. Wu responds in perfect English. After this Mr. Wu becomes increasingly allied with Jim and Herbie against Thorndyke, and during the El Dorado cross-country race there is a comic interlude at what the film calls "Chinese Camp." When Herbie is unable to proceed because Thorndyke has sabotaged his gasoline reserves, a group of young Chinese men in running suits appear mysteriously and carry Herbie on their shoulders to the camp. The film's musical score emphasizes their mincing steps with clichéd cartoon-Chinese music.

Another sequence shows a race in Mexico and introduces a crowd of stereotypically comic Mexicans accompanied by clichéd Mexican brass band music. Michele Lee remarks in her audio commentary for the Special Edition DVD that "the role played by the Mexicans wouldn't be tolerated today."[68] In the Disney lexicon, ethnicity is farcical when it is not white, Anglo-Saxon, and American. The center is defined as WASP; all other ethnicities are placed on the fringes, where they are objects of laughter and a condescending gaze.

What *The Love Bug* and other Disney live-action films of the sixties consistently do is decontextualize their references. The counterculture is detached from its social context, Chinese Americans and Mexicans are detached from their history and culture, and Thorndyke is detached from his English cultural context. Even Herbie, the lovable little VW, is detached from his origins in the Third Reich, when Hitler started the Volkswagen company to build affordable cars for "the people" and then decreed that its cars would be built by slave laborers, many of them from Eastern Europe. Not until 2001 did the German parliament approve the release of billions of dollars of restitution to surviving enslaved workers, including those who had worked for Volkswagen, where "90 percent of the workforce by the end of the war was foreigners laboring under horrific conditions."[69] (Ironically, the German origins of James Dean's Porsche Spyder may not have been overlooked after the fatal accident in 1955. Philippe Defechereux and Jean Graton contend that the driver who was responsible for the accident, Donald Turnupseed, was acquitted in part because "Jimmy was driving a foreign-German-racing vehicle." Turnupseed was driving "an all-American car, a Ford Custom.")[70]

Decontextualization of this kind is one of the ways that the advertising industry has been able to incorporate contradictions without getting swamped by paradox. Images and words devoid of context are more easily juxtaposed in contradictory ways than are fully contextualized ones. Successful marketing depends upon the confusion between appearance and reality to support its bloated claims for the benefits of nonstop accumulation. *The Love Bug*'s decontextualizations thus not only reinforce its regressive politics, but also engage in the late-capitalist economy's primary marketing strategy of mystification.

And yet the film's visual style asserts the opposite of mystification with the claim that everything on-screen is simply self-evident. The Disney live-action film aesthetic of the sixties is on full display in *The Love Bug*. Unlike the French New Wave's practice of shooting on location with a handheld camera and editing elliptically, a style that was taken up enthusiastically by young American directors in the sixties, *The Love Bug*'s aesthetic emphasizes clarity, with bright, saturated colors, obviously constructed sets, rear-projection during many of the racing scenes, and a clear cause-and-effect narrative logic. The musical score is jaunty and brisk, and frequently engages in mickey-mousing. Perhaps the most striking aspect of the film's aesthetic is its framing. Objects and characters are consistently placed centrally; there is very little off-center framing. The film's emphasis on clarity and centrality contributes to its attempt to define itself as ideologically reasonable and rational. The reliably centralized framing is an aesthetic corollary to what the film wants the viewer to believe is a reliable social stance. From this solid vantage point, the film implies, we can determine the location of the ideological center and from there locate the lunatics on the fringe.

Avoiding the New Wave aesthetic that was associated with youth culture in the sixties, *The Love Bug* displays a dated style consistent with its nostalgic yearning for the fifties. In some ways the film's style resembles the highly exaggerated melodramatic aesthetic of Douglas Sirk, whose films from the fifties were drenched in saturated Technicolor and who placed objects centrally in the frame to emphasize their symbolic significance; yet *The Love Bug* is entirely devoid of Sirk's sophisticated social commentary. While Sirk's films put American customs on display in order to scrutinize their hypocrisies, *The Love Bug* enacts them in order to normalize and celebrate them.

However, the comparison to Sirk's fifties melodramas reveals an important aspect of *The Love Bug*'s reception during the sixties. The observation that *The Love Bug* was the nation's most successful film in 1969 does not take into consideration the ways that audiences at the time might have responded to this cinematic throwback. For children, it was no doubt an unproblematic fun-filled adventure, one that allowed them to indulge their tendency to anthropomorphize inanimate objects. But adults, especially young adults, might easily have responded to the film as camp. Instead of engaging with the film on its terms, young people in 1969 could have found it unintentionally hilarious for its sexual innuendos, its fifties aesthetic, its exaggerations, and its naiveté. Their laughter would have mirrored Dean Jones' own while trying to film his passionate intervention in Herbie's suicide attempt. The Disney studio, and Uncle Walt in particular, had become objects of derision in sixties' youth culture, and in the spirit of countercultural mockery of the Establishment, *The Love Bug* would have been a likely target of laughter. Especially when juxtaposed with *Easy Rider*, which was released during the same year and took itself far too seriously, *The Love Bug* could have provided some welcome comic relief in ways probably not intended by the Disney studio. Additionally, the film's close relationships between Jim Douglas, Tennessee, and Herbie lend themselves to a queer reading that emphasizes their intimacy. Ironically, the Disney studio's homoeroticism and countercultural references unleash readings that remain valid despite the film's conservative, heterosexual closure. It is possible, for example, that someone might have read the sequence of Herbie being cut in half during the final race as his being torn in two by the conflicting demands placed on him: his desire to continue his romance with Jim, and the requirement that he pair Jim with Carole.

The Love Bug was followed by three sequels, none as successful as the original: *Herbie Rides Again* (Robert Stevenson, 1974), *Herbie Goes to Monte Carlo* (Vincent McEveety, 1977), and *Herbie Goes Bananas* (Vincent McEveety, 1980). In 1997, the Disney Studio remade *The Love Bug* for television, directed by Payton Reed. Its version of the rebel icon is even tamer than the 1969 version, and, like the original, it functions to sterilize the sixties and a hodgepodge of social and political issues dating back to World War II and the Beetle's origins.

The remake, like the original, is steeped in nostalgia, but while the original fondly recalls the fifties, the remake, set in the nineties, nostalgically evokes the sixties, which it renders sweet and cuddly. This is apparent in the documentary mode of the opening sequence, showing archival footage from the sixties of hippies surrounded by flowers and sunlight, "make love, not war" signs, and a voice-over narration that intones: "Love was everywhere, in our homes, streets, and especially in our cars." The film provides clips from the original *The Love Bug* and praises Herbie, the little car who was "willing to try almost anything, all for the love of his owner." With this opening, the film replicates the nostalgic tone of the original, which is heightened by its casting of sixties' actors: Mickey Dolenz of The Monkees fame plays the role of a stock-car race promoter, Clarence Williams III from *The Mod Squad* plays the owner of Chuck's Garage, and Dean Jones makes a guest appearance as the older Jim Douglas.

Their casting is consistent with the nineties' phenomenon of resurrecting actors from the sixties, seventies, and eighties in a manic recycling of the past. When confronted with actors known for their past work, viewers are encouraged to step outside the diegesis and notice the actors as actors, not as characters. This is most obvious in *The Love Bug* remake when Herbie's new young crew bids farewell to Jim Douglas, who departs after having provided wisdom and encouragement, and the camera lingers on his receding figure and their expressions of admiration. It is the elderly Dean Jones, not Jim Douglas, whom the film is worshipping, momentarily elevating him to the status of an icon, and James Dean, whom he originally evoked, seems much farther away, frozen in his youth, whereas Dean Jones has comfortably aged. Had he lived, James Dean would have been sixty-six, the same age as Dean Jones, in 1997; but instead, the elderly Dean Jones looks as though he could be James Dean's kindly grandfather.

By worshipping Dean Jones and nearly putting a halo around his head, the new *Love Bug* is also evoking the actor's religious conversion: Jones is a "born-again" Christian who converted during the seventies. His autobiography, *Under Running Laughter*, is a heartfelt account of his dissolute early years and his subsequent spiritual awakening. He currently writes an online column twice monthly for Christianity.com, speculating in one on whether Walt Disney had found the Savior before his death, in another asking "Why Hollywood Makes Dirty Movies,"[71] and in another excoriating the separation of church and state: "Would the polarized anger and strife we are experiencing today be possible if our Congress were publishing Bibles, our Supreme Court taking Communion, our Senators calling for public thankfulness to God?"[72] Dean Jones has, ironically, become a rebel, but rather than challenge dominant American culture, he advocates expanding its powers and imposing a single belief system onto everyone.

The Love Bug remake's opening also unleashes the diverse implications of "love" between a man and his car. In the remake, Hank Cooper (Bruce Campbell), a Formula One racing has-been who is now a mechanic at Chuck's Garage, plays the Jim Douglas part of a reluctant suitor to Herbie. Bruce Campbell is big and hulky and resembles Rock Hudson during the fifties: tall, square-jawed, and solid. Hank is pushed to express his affection for Herbie by Roddy (Kevin J. O'Connor), in the Tennessee Steinmetz role, an installation artist working in Chuck's Garage who does "vehiculart" installations. The original sexual dynamics between two men and a car are duplicated in the relationship between Hank, Roddy, and Herbie. Roddy has a special bond with Herbie and encourages Hank to appreciate the little car's uniqueness. Roddy, like Tennessee, is goofy looking, and he first feels an affinity for Herbie when Herbie is being passed over by drivers choosing stock cars, causing Roddy to recall that he was always picked last in grade school when sides were chosen for kickball. The sensitive Roddy later consoles Herbie after Hank spurns the car, saying, "He doesn't mean it; he'll come around." For his part, the hunky Hank takes note of Roddy's growing attachment to Herbie, asking, "Since when did you start liking cars?" "I like this one," Roddy responds.

These sexual innuendos evoke techno- and homoeroticism, and, just as in the original, they are disavowed by the presence of a woman—Alex Woodburn (Alexandra Wentworth)—a reporter for a car and track magazine who once dated Hank. Hank and Alex revive their relationship with the encouragement of Herbie's matchmaking and divert attention from Hank's attachments to Roddy and Herbie. Even so, the film cannot entirely deny its implied gay relationships. During one of his dates with Alex, Hank takes the opportunity to vent some steam about Roddy, confiding in her, "Sure Roddy's one of my best friends. But sometimes he really bugs me." Alex is momentarily Hank's confidant, rather than his love interest, as he tries to work through his conflicted feelings toward Roddy. Roddy, for his part, never becomes romantically involved with a woman (like Tennessee in the original), although at the end of the film, when a bride tosses a bouquet, Roddy catches it and shouts, "Herbie, looks like I'm next!" while everyone laughs. That Roddy may become a bride seems plausible given his close relationship with Hank, and the implication that Herbie might be the groom is not that far-fetched either.

As in the original, Herbie is the object of the two men's affections. Roddy quickly becomes Herbie's ally and is the first to believe that Herbie has a consciousness and can speak (with comically exaggerated honks of his horn) and drive himself. He displays Herbie in an installation on the opening night of the "Vehiculart" group exhibit. The "Vehiculart" exhibit can be read as a tame Disney version of British author J. G. Ballard's collection of stories titled *The Atrocity Exhibition*, in which he started to work through the themes of sex, death, and car wrecks he would again draw on for his 1973 novel *Crash*, analyzed in the next chapter. In 1969, the same year as the original *The Love Bug*, Ballard did actually stage an exhibition of crashed cars after having recently finished writing *The Atrocity Exhibition*, in which a character stages an exhibition of crashed cars. Ballard says:

> I knew this American girl, Pam, she was in charge of the gallery at the New Art Lab when it moved from Drury Lane to this former pharmaceutical warehouse. Anyway, I said to Pam, "I'd like to put on an exhibition. I'll put on an exhibition of crashed cars." Which I did: crashed Pontiac, crashed Mini, crashed Morris Oxford. It had the most raucous opening night party.[73]

Ballard goes on to say that he had a closed-circuit TV system and a naked young woman interviewing guests at the exhibition, all in an attempt to provoke the audience: "The whole thing was a psychological experiment—to see if my basic hunch about the latent, hidden psychology, the depth-psychology, of the car crash, was on the right track. Whether my hypothesis was accurate. It was a test. I was lab testing *Crash*."[74]

The motivation behind the Vehiculart exhibit in the 1997 remake of *The Love Bug* is unclear, although the film appears to be sending up the excesses and oddities of the art world. (Vehiculart is advertised on a poster in the film as "an artistic happening.") The clean shiny cars on display in Vehiculart are much too intact to suggest the morbid fascination of Ballard's show. But even though the techno-eroticism in *The Love Bug* remake is subtle, it is there. The romantically charged sequence in the original when Jim Douglas runs out into the rain-soaked night shouting "Herbie! Herbie!" is present in the remake when Hank belatedly realizes what Herbie means to him and announces, "I've got to find him," and dashes through the streets shouting his name. The sequence begins in bright daylight, but dissolves into night, heightening the aura of romantic desperation. As in the original, however, the film ends with heterosexual coupling, in this case Hank with Alex.

The remake's most bizarre sequence attempts to explain Herbie's origins, and it mixes a Disney version of politics and sexuality in a strange brew. The film's villain, a wealthy young Scotsman named Simon Moore III (John Hannah), is determined to destroy Herbie, and discovers that under Herbie's hood is a metal plaque with the engraved words *Herbie der Volkswagen von Dr. Gustav Stumpfel in 1963 gebaut* (Herbie the Volkswagen, built by Dr. Gustav Stumpfel in 1963). Simon finds Dr. Stumpfel, now an elderly, rumpled, white-haired scientist, living nearby and asks him to explain how he built Herbie. Dr. Stumpfel explains that "I was employed by my government to make a simple car, a people's car . . . After the war, the American military asked me to come over here." Dr. Stumpfel never acknowledges that he, like the actual Ferdinand Porsche, worked for the Nazis, and that he must have had Nazi sympathies, too, to be a top-ranking car designer during the Third Reich. Instead, his government and the Volkswagen are made out to be entirely innocent while the Americans are villainous. A black-and-white flashback sequence, shot with severe German Expressionist low angles, shows an American military officer chomping on a cigar—doing a dead-on imitation of the psychotic General Jack D. Ripper in *Dr. Strangelove* (Stanley Kubrick, 1964)—and browbeating the young Dr. Stumpfel, who is cowering in a chair, to build the same type of car for the Americans.

Dr. Stumpfel's tale evokes the German scientists who were brought to the U.S. to work for the Defense Department after World War II at a time when the U.S. military's highest priority was to produce a hydrogen bomb. In *The Love Bug* remake, Simon hires Dr. Stumpfel to build another car, one that will be capable of destroying Herbie once and for all (not unlike an H-bomb). Dr. Stumpfel explains that it may be impossible, because when he created Herbie, a framed photo of his "beloved Ilse" fell into the mix, and his powerful feelings for her transformed the little car into a sentient being. Simon provides a framed photo of himself, and Dr. Stumpfel proceeds to build Horace, a sleek, black, and very malevolent VW Beetle. (Phil Patton likens this bad Beetle to Charles Manson's fleet of dune buggies made from refurbished Beetles.)[75]

Soon after, Horace beats up Herbie in a dark alley, where Herbie's battered remains are found by Hank, who embraces and caresses Herbie's metal fender, saying, "Hang in there, buddy." Simon also loves his car; his hand is shown in close-up slowly caressing its dark shiny surface. The film's climax is a road race between Hank and Simon, pitting the rebuilt Herbie against the hostile Horace. After once again getting severed in half, Herbie wins, and Horace plunges over a cliff into the arid earth, leaving a large crater from which an enormous fireball explodes into the air. Horace's death by massive explosion recalls the H-bomb tests in Bikini Atoll and heightens the comparison between the bomb and the Beetle already established in the film by Herbie's postwar creation.

Horace is evocative not only of the H-bomb, but also of urban thugs, and when he beats up Herbie in a dark alley, the color coding smacks of racism. While the original film singles out hippies, upper-class Englishmen, Chinese Americans, and Mexicans for derision, the remake's target is urban youth, represented by Horace and also by two tough-looking Hispanic young men coded as *cholos*, whose low-rider convertible is stopped at an intersection next to Herbie. The low-rider and Herbie engage in a contest of one-upmanship, with the nimble Herbie triumphing over the humiliated convertible, leaving the two young men in the low-rider amazed by Herbie's athletic display. With Herbie's ancestral origins in the Third Reich, as established by the film, it is disconcerting to see the "Aryan" Herbie with his two white passengers—Hank and Alex—emerge victorious.

With this scene, the Disney studio continues its traditional practice of pushing to the margins and mocking its stereotyped groups of people. The targets of derision have changed, but the practice of mockery continues. Although hippies are present only in the prologue's documentary footage, where they are completely depoliticized and fondly recalled for having symbolized "love," the remake does retain the original's class antagonism: the upper-class English Thorndyke has become the upper-class Scotsman Simon, whose hatred for Hank is explicitly expressed as disdain for the working class. Hank, like Jim Douglas, represents "the little guy," and his victory over the arrogant Simon is complete when Simon is led away in handcuffs. Herbie is still adorned with his red, white, and blue racing stripes (as well as the number 53), representing the U.S.A. against the world.

Herbie's relevance to the nineties became even more obvious in 1998, a year after the remake of *The Love Bug* was broadcast, when VW introduced its New Beetle. The redesigned Beetle received a great deal of attention and sold well, and also revived interest in the old Beetle (which was still in production for the South American market until 2003), prompting comparisons and debates about which one was superior. Here was Herbie for the nineties—rounder, less angular, and in designer colors—joining the glut of fifties and sixties paraphernalia being revived and marketed for a new generation. The New Beetle is just another indicator that consumer society in the late twentieth century looped back on itself to devour the products of the century's middle, keeping Herbie and rebel iconography, among other mid-century creations, alive and thriving into the twenty-first century.

Also in 1997, a new biographical James Dean film was released. Originally titled *James Dean: Race with Destiny* for a limited theatrical release, the film was rereleased on video as *James Dean: Live Fast, Die Young*, directed by Mardi Rustam and starring Casper van Dien as James Dean. The film is a fictional version of a short period in Dean's life, starting when he was at work on *East of Eden* and ending with his death, and it is almost exclusively concerned with Dean's relationship with Pier Angeli (Carrie Mitchum), who is presented as the love of his life. Dean obsessively pursues her, and when she marries Vic Damone to please her overbearing mother, Dean descends into a spiral of heartbroken despair, culminating in his death.

The major motif in the film is Dean's love of vehicles and speed, referred to in several car racing sequences, in scenes showing him careen through the streets of L.A. on a motorcycle, and in a scene in which he shows off his new Porsche Spyder to his father. A running joke throughout the film is that soon after arriving in Hollywood to make *East of Eden*, Dean offends Jack Warner by roaring onto the Warner Bros. lot on a motorcycle and nearly smashing into him. Warner takes to calling Dean "the little bastard," and this is the film's tidy explanation for the "little bastard" inscription on the back of Dean's Porsche.

After its thoroughly sanitized presentation of Dean's brief time in Los Angeles, the film ends with a surprisingly lurid sequence of the fatal car crash. The collision between the miniscule Porsche and the lumbering Ford is shown from many angles, and ends with high-angle shots of Dean's body pinned inside the Porsche, his neck broken and his head thrown back, and copious quantities of bright red blood running down his face and soaking his white T-shirt. After this shot, the film cuts to black and written text providing information about Pier Angeli's subsequent life and death by barbiturate overdose in 1971. By ending with the crash and a piercing gaze from above onto Dean's mangled body, the film not only underscores the tragedy of living fast and dying young, but also heightens James Dean's association with celebrity, technology, sadomasochistic desire, and apocalyptic death. We live in a crash culture, and our fictions are filled with wrecks. The 1999 film *Jesus' Son* (Alison Maclean), for example, sustains a car crash motif throughout, and also indirectly evokes James Dean in Billy Crudup's performance of a young misfit loner, as well as in the casting of Dennis Hopper.

Disney remade *The Love Bug* in 2005, this time for theatrical release, and gave the updated film an updated title, *Herbie: Fully Loaded*. The film was directed by Angela Robinson, a young black lesbian woman who made her mark with a film titled *D.E.B.S.* (2004), a lesbian love story and teen action movie parody. Her helming of the *Love Bug* remake prompted speculation about possible gay themes, and in a *New York Times* article before the film's release, Robinson said that although there are no gay characters in the film, she considers it a coming-out story: Maggie (Lindsay

Lohan), a recent college graduate, hides from her father (Michael Keaton) that she wants to race cars, for he is a former stock car racer who, after her mother's death, has forbidden her to race.[76] To engage in her secret passion, she dresses like a man and successfully races Herbie, the lovable little Beetle who, despite being a rusty junkyard wreck, can still defeat top-of-the-line NASCAR cars at immense speeds. For director Robinson, Maggie's public revelation of her identity in her father's presence is a coming-out metaphor: "She literally has to take her mask off in front of her dad so that he can come to terms with who she really is and what she really wants to do. And then he has to come around."[77]

Despite Robinson's enthusiasm for the film as a metaphor, *Herbie: Fully Loaded* is no different from the scads of other films about teenagers who hide their true interests from their parents. If anything, it displays obsessive heterosexuality with its male garage-mechanic love interest (Justin Long) for Maggie, a blonde woman for Maggie's father, and a "female" yellow New Beetle that arouses Herbie's interest (and stiffens his antenna). The original *Love Bug* actually resonates more strongly with homoeroticism for anyone who cares to look for it. Robinson joins all of the other Disney directors whose signature styles and themes are overridden by the studio's house style.

Herbie: Fully Loaded confines its rebel theme to Maggie's racing ambitions, but it succeeds in bringing to the *Love Bug* enterprise a woman protagonist and a "girl power" message. Maggie has progressed beyond Carole's subservient role in the original; while Carole served the purpose of provoking two male drivers' rivalry, Maggie steps into the driver's seat and leaves her male competitors in the dust. Feminist progress is diminished, however, by Maggie's midriff-baring wardrobe and tight jeans, giving her an objectified screen presence reminiscent of Carole's eroticized and disembodied legs. Maggie conforms to the Disney paradigm for women characters with her cute spunkiness, and her rebellion is mild and easily overcome when her father relents and becomes an enthusiastic proponent of her racing career. Meanwhile, this Herbie-for-the-new-century is more Disneyesque than the original: staunchly heterosexual—unleashing his passion for the flirtatious "female" Beetle—and more anthropomorphized; he "speaks" with perky little sound effects that reveal his thoughts and emotions with cloying obviousness.

The original *Love Bug* films are given an exalted place in *Herbie: Fully Loaded;* they now function as history, replacing actual historical events and creating a self-contained *Love Bug* universe detached from the real world. While the television remake began with a nostalgic montage of iconic sixties scenes, *Herbie: Fully Loaded* opens with a montage of clips from the original *Love Bug* films, most of them showing Herbie racing. Media fictions are so dominant in the twenty-first century that nostalgia now refers back to previous films; they supersede actual events and constitute our shared past. Following the example set by the television remake, a cameo with Dean Jones was shot for *Herbie: Fully Loaded*, but it was omitted from the finished film. What made it into the film was product placement; advertisements cover the NASCAR drivers, cars, and speedway and give the film the feel of an extended television commercial. Herbie is dwarfed beneath the profusion of ads, and his racing dexterity threatens to recede into the background. In this film, cars are meant for pitching products as much as for racing.

Cars are woven into American history and the mythic version of American progress despite their propensity to kill. Their high body count does not prevent them from being cherished by popular culture and having an intimate alignment with rebel iconography. James Dean's violent death by car crash is imprinted in the rebel icon's DNA. *The Love Bug*'s rebels, in the original and its remakes, have been rendered wholesome and nonthreatening by the Disney treatment. To see what happens when rebel iconography and the car crash motif are not sanitized, it is necessary to look elsewhere.

CHAPTER 3

Rebel Wrecks

With *The Love Bug*, the Disney studio trawled the cultural waters for hip and trendy references, decontextualized those references, and returned them to the culture in nonthreatening ways. The original and its remakes exemplify the strategy of defanging the rebel icon and using it to uphold the status quo. They illustrate one representational strategy, but there have been other, less complacent, approaches to the same material. An approach that stands at the opposite end of the safe-to-scary spectrum from *The Love Bug* is J. G. Ballard's 1973 novel *Crash*. Published just four years after the release of 1969's *The Love Bug*, *Crash* also takes as its raw material auto-eroticism, techno-fetishism, homoeroticism, and rebel iconography, but in *Crash*, the material remains raw. Not intended for children, the novel is an allegory for western industrial culture's obsession with technology, which Ballard presents as having utterly transformed human psychosexuality. In *Crash*, friendship with a car is not the cuddly affair of Jim Douglas and Herbie; it is not even romantic; it is an explicitly sexual entanglement fueled by a desire for all-out apocalyptic and orgasmic death by car crash, what Ballard calls "this coming autogeddon."[1] The novel hearkens toward the "end of the world by automobile,"[2] and *The Love Bug*'s chaste romance between Jim Douglas and Herbie can be read as an early, subtle portent.

Crash's English protagonists become fascinated by car crashes and sexually aroused by gruesome injuries, scars, and jagged metal. James Ballard, the novel's forty-year-old main character and narrator, is injured in a two-car collision that kills one of the other car's occupants and injures the dead man's wife, and his own life is utterly transformed by the crash. He has an affair with the survivor of the crash, Dr. Helen Remington, and the two lovers can only perform sexually in Ballard's car. The crash also revives Ballard's sexual relationship with his wife, Catherine; Ballard relates that "I could bring myself to orgasm simply by thinking of the car in which Dr. Helen Remington and I performed our sexual acts."[3] Ballard's and the two women's desires are bound up with the vinyl and chrome contours of cars and the violent possibilities of metal gashing through skin.

But the most dramatic transformation of Ballard's life after his crash results from his encounter and subsequent relationship with Dr. Robert Vaughan, the "nightmare angel of the expressways,"[4] a man who obsessively seeks out car wrecks and photographs the dead or injured occupants. Vaughan becomes Ballard's mentor in the pursuit of techno-erotic thrills, and together they cruise the highways around London searching for accidents. Sex and cars, chrome and skin, shattered glass and sex organs are indistinguishable components of their dreams and desires. They pick up young women prostitutes in Vaughan's "ten-year-old model of a Lincoln Continental, the same make of vehicle as the open limousine in which President Kennedy had died,"[5] and while Ballard drives, Vaughan has sex with them in the backseat. Ballard finds that he can choreograph Vaughan's backseat moves with his driving and observes that Vaughan's gaze at the prostitutes is identical to his own gaze at battered accident victims; sex and car wrecks evoke the same response.

Arousal in *Crash* derives from human intimacy with technology, especially in the violent interpenetrations of metal, glass, and skin. When Ballard describes his growing attraction to Vaughan, he explains that he is aroused by the image of Vaughan in his car, not by Vaughan alone:

> Vaughan excited some latent homosexual impulse only within the cabin
> of his car or driving along the highway. His attraction lay not so much
> in a complex of familiar anatomical triggers—but in the stylization
> of posture achieved between Vaughan and the car. Detached from
> the automobile, particularly his own emblem-filled highway cruiser,
> Vaughan ceased to hold any interest.[6]

When Ballard and Vaughan do have sex, it is in Vaughan's car, and Vaughan opens his leather jacket to reveal his damaged body, a body that is, in Ballard's words, an "ugly golden creature, made beautiful by its scars and wounds."[7] And after they have sex:

> Together we showed our wounds to each other, exposing the scars on
> our chests and hands to the beckoning injury sites on the interior of
> the car, to the pointed sills of the chromium ashtrays, to the lights of
> a distant intersection. In our wounds we celebrated the re-birth of the

traffic-slain dead, the deaths and injuries of those we had seen dying by the roadside and the imaginary wounds and postures of the millions yet to die.[8]

The intimacy of Ballard, Vaughan, and Vaughan's car enacts a scenario that *The Love Bug* only hints at in its threesome of Jim Douglas, Tennessee, and Herbie.

Crash depicts technology superseding the dimensions of nature and human life in suburban London, described as an "endless landscape of concrete and structural steel" where "the human inhabitants of this technological landscape no longer provided its sharpest pointers, its keys to the borderzones of identity."[9] Identity has expanded to encompass technology; humans in *Crash* are no longer unique, separate entities, but ones whose parameters fuse with machines and whose fantasies are fueled by them. The narrator, James Ballard, is endlessly excited and exhilarated as he moves through glistening streets and notices the reflections cast by sunlit chrome on his skin.[10]

James Ballard's overstimulation guides his narration, but he maintains a dispassionate tone, one that duplicates the cold, hard, sterile façade of technology and the industrial landscape. Humans in *Crash* have abandoned affect as a result of their techno-transformation. Ballard's descriptions of sex acts are precise and clinical; sex is detached from its conventional cultural trappings of courtship and romance and revealed to be a numb exercise. It is the type of sex described by Jean Baudrillard in his ruminations on postmodern culture's surface aesthetic, in which electronic networks have supplanted human couplings. He writes,

> Obscenity is not confined to sexuality, because today there is a pornography of information and communication, a pornography of circuits and networks, of functions and objects in their legibility, availability, regulation, forced signification, capacity to perform, connection, polyvalence, their free expression . . . It is no longer the obscenity of the hidden, the repressed, the obscure, but that of the visible, the all-too-visible, the more-visible-than-visible; it is the obscenity of that which no longer contains a secret and is entirely soluble in information and communication.[11]

Sex in the world described by Baudrillard is nonhuman and purely functional, and not surprisingly he turns to cars when he wants to provide an example of the absence of emotion in people's postmodern relationship to objects. He paraphrases Roland Barthes' observation about "a logic of driving" that leads to "the transformation of the subject himself into a driving computer"[12] and asserts that

> one can conceive of a subsequent stage to this one, where the car is still a performative instrument, the stage at which it becomes an informing network. That is, the car which speaks to you, which informs you spontaneously of its general state and yours (eventually refusing to function if you are not functioning well), the advising, the deliberating car, a partner in a general negotiation on lifestyles; something (or some*one*, since at this stage there is no more difference) to which you are *wired*, the communication with the car becoming the fundamental stake, a perpetual test of the presence of the subject vis-à-vis his objects—an uninterrupted interface.[13]

One can easily conceive of this stage if one has seen *The Love Bug*, and one wonders whether Baudrillard may have had Herbie in mind as he worked out his line of reasoning. Baudrillard's oeuvre in fact leads from this perhaps unintentional reference to Herbie to praise for the novel *Crash* as the ultimate expression of the hyperreal's seductive surface. He writes that "the technology of *Crash* is glistening and seductive, or unpolished and innocent. Seductive because it has been stripped of meaning, a simple mirror of torn bodies."[14] Baudrillard exults in being released by the novel from the responsibility of making moral judgments, since the novel resists any attempts to impose morality: "The moral gaze—the critical judgmentalism that is still a part of the old world's functionality—cannot touch it."[15]

While Baudrillard's celebration of *Crash*'s amorality has been roundly criticized, his stance is given an incisive reading by Bradley Butterfield, who analyzes both *Crash* and Baudrillard's theories in the context of the post-Nietzschean eclipse of the ethical realm by the aesthetic. For the theorists of postmodernism who have elaborated Nietzsche's insights, it is impossible to defend any single all-encompassing theory, for such theories are always based on transient socially constructed beliefs masquerading as universal truths, and thus ethics, with its inevitable belief in some changeless truth, is just another insupportable discourse among others. In Butterfield's reading, both Baudrillard and Ballard explore ways to reintegrate death into life without resorting to untenable moral absolutes. Their shared project stands in opposition to the market economy's attempt to "abolish death through accumulation," and in fact subversively rejects consumer society's cheerful promises from within its own surface aesthetics.[16] Butterfield is intrigued by Baudrillard's blurring of the line between literary theory and literature, apparent in his adoption of the same "what if" approach as Ballard's in *Crash*, suggesting possibilities that should not be taken absolutely literally but are an "imagining of a world that is perhaps right around the corner."[17]

At the center of *Crash*'s "what if" strategy is Vaughan, the man who is leading the way into the new techno-sexual future with a devoted following of men and women who are drawn to his obsessions. Vaughan is the mysterious enigma at the center of *Crash*, and the novel revolves around him. Vaughan can be interpreted as Ballard's version of the rebel icon, made from the features bequeathed by the fifties and molded into an altogether sinister character. Rebel iconography's violent core is exposed in *Crash* and is found to be hideously attractive. The novel is told in a flashback after Vaughan's death in a fiery crash, with Ballard elegiacally describing Vaughan's magnetism:

> Now that Vaughan has died, we will leave with the others who gathered around him, like a crowd drawn to an injured cripple whose deformed postures reveal the secret formulas of their minds and lives. All of us who knew Vaughan accept the perverse eroticism of the car-crash, as painful as the drawing of an exposed organ through the aperture of a surgical wound.[18]

Although Vaughan remains enigmatic throughout the novel, there are aspects of his life and personality that are reminiscent of James Dean, just as Jim Douglas in *The Love Bug* resonates with Dean references. Both texts in fact begin with car wrecks: Jim Douglas' demolition derby smash-up, and Vaughan's fatal drive over the rails of the London Airport flyover into a bus filled with passengers. Vaughan missed the target of his suicidal plunge: a limousine carrying the actress Elizabeth Taylor, whom Vaughan had wanted to kill in a dramatic crash that would join their bodies in a twisted embrace.[19] But unlike Jim Douglas in *The Love Bug*, Vaughan is a bad-boy rebel with a razor-sharp edge:

> As one of the first of the new-style TV scientists, Vaughan had combined a high degree of personal glamour—heavy black hair over a scarred face, an American combat jacket—with an aggressive lecture-theatre manner and complete conviction of his subject matter, the application of computerized techniques to the control of all international traffic systems. In the first programmes of his series three years earlier Vaughan

had projected a potent image, almost that of the scientist as hoodlum, driving about from laboratory to television centre on a high-powered motorcycle. Literate, ambitious and adept at self-publicity, he was saved from being no more than a pushy careerist with a Ph.D. by a strain of naive idealism, his strange vision of the automobile and its real role in our lives.[20]

He is a hoodlum in an American combat jacket, riding a high-powered motorcycle, adept at self-publicity, and with an obsessive interest in cars; he is James Dean with a Ph.D. Ballard explains that Vaughan's career had ended after he was seriously injured in a motorcycle crash that permanently damaged and scarred his face:

> His features looked as if they had been displaced laterally, reassembled after the crash from a collection of faded publicity photographs. The scars on his mouth and forehead, the self-cut hair and two missing upper canine gave him a neglected and hostile appearance. The bony knuckles of his wrists projected like manacles from the frayed cuffs of his leather jacket.[21]

James Dean too had missing teeth; as a teenager in Fairmount he had knocked out his four front teeth while swinging on a rope, and when he was a star he enjoyed shocking people by casually dropping his false teeth into a glass while drinking. Dean liked to embellish the circumstances of his accident, claiming that he had lost his teeth in a motorcycle accident,[22] and Vaughan makes good on what for Dean was only a wished-for explanation for his lost teeth. Also like Vaughan, Dean reportedly was unkempt; his lack of personal hygiene disgusted some of those who came into contact with him, and he was often rude to friends as well as professional acquaintances and the press. According to the novelist Maurice Zolotov, Dean was "surly, ill-tempered, brutal without any element of kindness, sensitivity, consideration for others, or romantic passion. He was physically dirty. He hated to bathe, have his hair cut, shave, or put on clean clothes. He smelled so rankly that actresses working in close contact with him found him unbearable."[23] One biographer reports that Dean was once thrown out of the house of Leonard Spiegelglass, a story editor at MGM, who is quoted as saying, "His manners were terrible. He flicked ashes on the rug and behaved like an animal. The boy was absolute poison."[24] Dean himself sometimes concurred: "I wouldn't like me if I had to be around me."[25]

In Vaughan, unlike Dean, the facial features are ragged, not beautiful, and the hostility lingering just below the surface of many James Dean photos is readily apparent. Vaughan embodies the dangerous, unstable side of Dean, and his post-accident face is like a badly pieced together version of Dean's. After Dean's accident, the hundreds of photographs that circulated immortalized not his shattered body but his publicity-photo face. A photographer friend of Dean's, Sanford Roth, was in a car following Dean's to the race in Salinas at the time of the fatal crash; he snapped photos of the mangled car and the ambulance crew at work, and there have been persistent rumors that he photographed Dean's dead body. According to his biographers, Dean liked being photographed, had a stable of photographers as friends, and often arranged to have his life photographically documented. When he returned to Fairmount in February of 1955, Dean brought along photographer Dennis Stock to document the visit, and the photographs were published in a *Life* magazine profile of Dean on March 7, 1955.

Vaughan, too, likes to be photographed. He exposes the posturing side of rebel iconography, its concern with appearances—with looking cool—over accomplishments: "Vaughan was dramatizing himself for the benefit of these anonymous passers-by, holding his position in the spotlight as if waiting for invisible television cameras to frame him. The frustrated actor was evident in all his impulsive movements."[26] The reference to publicity photos in the description of Vaughan's face is significant, for *Crash* is about photographs almost as much as it is about car wrecks. James Ballard, the narrator, works for a film studio producing television commercials, and Vaughan takes and collects photographs of accidents, their victims, and all of the various medical personnel who are marshaled into action after a crash. Films, television commercials, and photographs are paradigmatic products of a consumer society obsessed with surface appearances. Our world is bombarded by photographic images that take on a life of their own; they are the essential features of the postmodern age, with its collapse of distinctions between actuality and representation. Citizens of consumer society are pelted by rapid images in which "the surface is all,"[27] and the "instant read icon," according to film scholar Wheeler Winston Dixon, is presented "just long enough to make a psychic imprint on the viewer's consciousness,"[28] preventing any readings beyond those confined to a very narrow range. Images converge and collide around us, and we find ourselves wandering disoriented amid the wreck of their collisions.

In the novel *Crash*, accident casualties and movie stars commingle in the swirl of photographs handled by Ballard and Vaughan. Vaughan's obsessive desire to die in a flaming embrace with Elizabeth Taylor is a logical culmination of his fascination with movie star publicity images and accident photos. Vaughan dramatizes the ultimate indistinguishability of one type of photograph from the other in his obsession with both; they all are used, after all, to titillate and seduce their viewers. Celebrity culture is an image culture; it is through the massive circulation of celebrity pictures in films, television, the Internet, magazines, newspapers, and billboards that stars gain the exposure that makes them instantly recognizable. The image of a star's face has moved beyond itself and become a stylized pattern infused with significance onto which are projected a constantly shifting network of meanings, some of which are determined by ad agencies and film studios, and some of which are projected by the public. Part of the public's fascination with star photographs is the knowledge that a real and imperfect person exists somewhere behind the glossy surface of the image, and so there is a strong urge to discover a blemish behind the perfection. Hence the extraordinary fascination with stories that purport to "tell all" about a star, with star scandals, and, most intensely, with star deaths.

Celebrity culture holds a special, elevated place for its stars' deaths, and James Dean's death is one of the most revered. Not surprisingly, Vaughan, in *Crash*, worships the accidents that have killed stars and fantasizes elaborately about crashes destroying living stars:

> Vaughan dreamed endlessly of the deaths of the famous, inventing imaginary crashes for them. Around the deaths of James Dean and Albert Camus, Jayne Mansfield and John Kennedy he had woven elaborate fantasies. His imagination was a target gallery of screen actresses, politicians, business tycoons and television executives. Vaughan followed them everywhere with his camera, zoom lens watching from the observation platform of the Oceanic Terminal at the airport, from hotel mezzanine balconies and studio car-parks. For each of them Vaughan devised an optimum auto-death.[29]

In Vaughan's psyche are fused the twisted obsessions of our celebrity-worshipping and voyeuristic culture: his activities integrate photographs, stars, and death by car crash. *Crash* makes clear that Vaughan is simply a heightened version of forces already present in postmodern culture, and that his interests are shared by many others in our "crash culture."[30]

This becomes apparent in the novel when Ballard takes Helen Remington to the stock car races. One of the featured events is "The Recreation of a Spectacular Road Accident" in which stunt drivers simulate dramatic smash-ups.[31] Ballard and the rest of the crowd watch the re-creation of a

The wreckage of James Dean's Porsche Spyder was put on public display as a warning. (The David Loehr Collection)

five-car pile-up in which seven people had died. Not long after, the driver who drove the main car in the re-creation, and who had suffered a concussion as a result, is the stunt double for Elizabeth Taylor in a film under production at the studio where Ballard works. He is Colin Seagrave, a former racing driver and a burnt-out case; a walking zombie, he is what Jim Douglas could become in a nightmare sequel to *The Love Bug*. He is heavily made up and dressed to look like Taylor as he prepares for the scene in which he will drive a Citroën into a collision. For another scene, Elizabeth Taylor herself, made up with simulated wounds, is in the crashed Citroën, sitting "like a deity occupying a shrine readied for her in the blood of a minor member of her congregation."[32] Continuing "these potent confusions of fiction and reality,"[33] the novel presents an "Open Day at the Road Research Laboratory," where excited onlookers watch the fiery collision of a car holding a family of four mannequins with a motorcycle ridden by a mannequin named Elvis. Spectators are enthralled by the spectacle—Vaughan masturbates himself to orgasm as he watches—and then crowd around to see it replayed in excruciating slow motion on videotape.

Crash captures the distorted logic of a culture obsessed with voyeurism, simulations, and celebrity deaths, the logic analyzed by English professor and cultural studies scholar Mark Seltzer in his article "Wound Culture: Trauma in the Pathological Public Sphere." He writes that the obsession with spectacles of violent death "has come to make up a wound culture: the public fascination with torn and opened bodies and torn and opened persons, a collective gathering around shock, trauma, and the wound."[34] In Seltzer's analysis, as in *Crash*, eroticism is the most obvious articulation of the public's morbid fascination. Vaughan's orgasmic anticipation of an "autogeddon" is just an overt expression of a pathology already deeply embedded in contemporary high-tech culture, for sexuality, the fiercest expression of human desire, is inevitably caught up in the current human craving for faster and more exhilarating technological thrills.

In the 1996 film adaptation of *Crash*, directed by David Cronenberg, the re-creation of a spectacular road accident is James Dean's accident, and Colin Seagrave suffers a concussion while playing the part of Dean. The novel and the film both proved to be frighteningly prophetic, for the 1997 death of Diana, Princess of Wales, vividly and hideously illustrated their themes. In both the fictional texts and the death of Diana, the cults of technology, celebrity, and sex intersect and lead inexorably to death. As Salman Rushdie writes in an essay making the analogy between *Crash* and Diana's death, "In Diana's fatal crash, the Camera (as both Reporter and Lover) is joined to the Automobile and the Star, and the Cocktail of death and desire becomes even more powerful than the one in Ballard's book."[35] Rushdie interprets Diana's death as a warning about our culture's obsessive pursuit of photographic images. He writes, "The battle is for control; for a form of power. She did not wish to give the photographers power over her—to be merely their (our) Object. In escaping from the pursuing lenses, she was asserting her determination, perhaps her right, to be something altogether more dignified: that is, to be a Subject. Fleeing from Object to Subject, from commodity toward humanity, she met her death."[36]

Rushdie was not the only one to make the connection between *Crash* and Princess Diana's death. In an interview with novelist Iain Sinclair, Ballard reports that he was sought out at the time:

Well, a lot of people were ringing me up after Di's death, more or less accusing me of stage-managing the whole thing . . . I didn't say anything at the time, because I think there's no doubting the fact that she died in a crashed car, pursued by the furies—like Orestes. A classical death, if there is one. The fact that she died in a car crash *probably* is a validating—in imaginative terms—signature. To die in a car crash is a unique twentieth-century finale. It's part of the twentieth-century milieu. The deaths of car crash victims have a resonance that you don't find in the deaths of hotel fire victims, or plane crash victims.[37]

The kind of logic that tries to hold Ballard responsible for the death of Princess Diana is articulated by Iain Sinclair with obvious irony: "Had he activated a demonic psychopathology that could only be appeased by regular sacrifices? Was this the curse of prophecy? Does the visionary/ paranoid writer, in the heat of composition, somehow fix the future?"[38] Of course, rather than fix the future, Ballard had perceptively read the same cultural signs that would still be in place when Princess Diana died and provoked a massive international deluge of grief and morbid fascination.

Salman Rushdie's analysis of the link between crash culture and image culture is relevant to the life of a real-life Vaughan in Providence, Rhode Island. A newspaper article in July 2000 about the death of a local free-lance photographer named Ira S. Nasberg reports that "until recently, Nasberg lived on the fringes of society, working at a pawn shop and convenience store while hawking videotapes and photographs of late-night car accidents, fires and crimes to area television stations and newspapers."[39] Nasberg

> had been attracted to the horrific, listening on a scanner for the latest tragedy and then rushing to photograph it. His car, with antennas sprouting from the trunk and a license plate reading "TV 134," exemplified his passion for capturing the lurid. So did his Web site, "Ira's Spot News in Motion: Infamous Pictures of Death Scenes." On the Web site, Nasberg posted photographs and video stills of car accidents and murders. One photograph depicted a "headless drunk driver." Another showed the victim of a carjacking "with a bullet-riddled head." "If it ever happens to you and you carry a weapon LEGALLY like I do . . . blow the bastards away!" Nasberg wrote on his Web site.[40]

Nasberg's "passion for capturing the lurid" recalls the fictional Vaughan's obsessions, and both are eruptions of latent cultural forces that, when blended, produce what Rushdie calls a "cocktail of death and desire." This cocktail is symptomatic of an emotional numbness in contemporary western life—captured by the lack of affect in *Crash*—that compels people to seek out photographic evidence of cataclysmic events to elicit an emotional response. The horror of seeing a photo of a "headless drunk driver" or a "bullet-riddled head" provides temporary relief from massive boredom. The desire for this momentary "pleasure" is decisively sexual; in the novel *Crash*, the men and women who congregate around Vaughan are drawn to his new form of automotive sexuality as a way to revitalize their humdrum sex lives.

A wish to escape boredom also motivates the search for "authenticity," for something that insists on its own brutal reality in a culture dominated by fictions, and photographs of crashes serve this purpose. In an analysis of the film version of *Crash*, film studies and cultural theory scholars Fred Botting and Scott Wilson write that "crashes become, for the hypermodern subject, simulations of the traumatic (missed) encounter with the real. Which is why they must be photographed. The photograph functions as a scar in time, freezing the moment when the mortal being becomes Other, fully transforming into pure image."[41] Fueling, so to speak, the fascination with images of large-scale destruction, Hollywood action films have become more and more formulaic, leaving us, in the words of Wheeler Winston Dixon, "with disaster created solely for consumption, the celebrity of violence and death."[42]

J. G. Ballard has written one of the most concise and perceptive analyses of his own novel, identifying before Baudrillard wrote his theories of postmodernism the slippage between reality and fiction as a major characteristic of our age:

> I feel that the balance between fiction and reality has changed significantly in the past decade. Increasingly their roles are reversed. We live in a world ruled by fictions of every kind—mass merchandising, advertising, politics conducted as a branch of advertising, the instant translation of science and technology into popular imagery, the increasing blurring and intermingling of identities within the realm of consumer goods, the preempting of any free or original imaginative response to experience by the television screen. We live inside an enormous novel. For the writer in particular it is less and less necessary for him to invent the fictional content of his novel. The fiction is already there. The writer's task is to invent the reality.[43]

In a world governed by fictions, in which the media has preempted emotional expression, the public hungers for authentic experiences, and in a twisted equation, "authenticity" is delivered photographically via the media. Ironically, television purports to provide access to the very "real" that it has superseded, hence the recent emphasis on reality TV. That these programs are heavily mediated only increases the irony that they represent "the real" in our society of simulation. Ballard, whose essay on *Crash* was written in 1974, explains that "throughout *Crash* I have used the car not only as a sexual image, but as a total metaphor for man's life in today's society . . . Needless to say, the ultimate role of *Crash* is cautionary, a warning against that brutal, erotic and overlit realm that beckons more and more persuasively to us from the margins of the technological land-scape."[44] Seen from Ballard's vantage point, western history demonstrates an inexorable and frightening march toward ever more sophisticated technological methods of incinerating and mangling human bodies.

In the twenty-first century, after a century of advanced technological mayhem and some colossal new carnage, *Crash* seems astonishingly prophetic, and the gap separating its themes from those of *The Love Bug* appears quite small. Their shared interest in crashes and "autosex"[45] are expressed in different degrees of explicitness, but both extrapolate from the same cultural currents. The two texts experienced a cultural convergence during the middle 1990s when they were both used as the basis for new films: *Crash* was adapted for film by David Cronenberg and released in 1996, and Disney released its made-for-television *The Love Bug* in 1997. Their joint reappearance at the end of the twentieth century indicates a continuing interest in their shared themes, although neither of the nineties texts was as successful as the original.

Cronenberg's *Crash* is an intelligent effort to realize the novel visually, but some of its choices render it less incisive, and it fails to add anything new to our understanding of rebel iconography. Most significantly, the book's interest in tracing the features of a new posthuman sexuality is translated by the film into the familiar conventions of softcore pornography. The book revolves around the fetishization of scars and wounds to explore its new sexuality, but its tone is cold and clinical. As the book's narrator tells us at one point, "the erotic dimension was absent."[46] Elsewhere, narrator James Ballard tells Catherine, "It isn't sex that Vaughan is interested in, but technology."[47] Indeed, throughout the book, sex acts are devoid of heat and intensity. The film, however, is steeped in the erotic dimension. Scars, bruises, and wounds are signified with Frederick's of Hollywood–style lingerie. Gabrielle (Rosanna Arquette), the most disfigured character, wears a tight black lace bodysuit, leather straps, and metal prosthetic contraptions that imply softcore bondage. The film's glossy, elegant lighting also heightens its stylish allure. By heating up the book's icy tone, the film transforms an unsettling new paradigm into a familiar and trite scenario.

The film's softcore erotica intersects with horror film conventions in its narration. Unlike the book's first-person narrator, the film gives us an omniscient narration represented by a moving camera that consistently tracks toward events from a distance, its slow, deliberate movements evoking conventional horror film cinematography that lurks on the periphery of events and pursues characters in long, suspenseful track-ins. Although the book's narrator—Ballard—is also the main character in the film (played by James Spader), his point of view does not control the camera's stealthy gaze. He and the camera are, however, both intimately involved with the same character: his wife, Catherine (Deborah Unger). She is the film's erotic centerpiece, and she is presented in an entirely conventional way: mannequin-like, she is a smooth, shining female object of desire with a hard lacquered surface and a stunned, vacant demeanor. The camera's obsessive stare heightens her association with a high-fashion model posing for photographs.

As if Catherine's subjectivity weren't already sufficiently absent, the film undertakes the job of eliminating its last remnants. An analysis of the film's opening and closing sequences reveals an attempt to destroy her control over her own sexuality. In the opening sequence, the camera tracks through an airplane hangar to find her caressing a plane's smooth surface with her breast and then encouraging her flight instructor's sexual advances. She is the one in control of the encounter, choreographing a dance of desire involving herself, a man, and a machine. In contrast, the film's final sequence shows her husband, Ballard, driving the big phallic 1963 Lincoln that Vaughan drove to his death; he pursues his wife's small sports car. On a rain-slicked highway, Ballard forces Catherine to drive over an embankment and crash, followed by his climbing down the embankment to her wrecked car and finding her injured body sprawled on the ground. When she says she thinks she's all right, he whispers, "Maybe the next one, darling," evoking his earlier use of these words when she told him that she hadn't come during her interlude with the flight instructor in the hangar. Then Ballard has sex with Catherine as she lies bruised and broken on the ground, and the film ends.

Ballard and Catherine are attempting to kill themselves in this crash, to reach an unprecedented orgasmic intensity through death, and by "maybe the next one," he means that they might succeed in their next attempt. What we see, however, is a woman who has lost the more active role she originally had in a sexual encounter with a human being and a machine. In the context of the film's use of horror conventions, she is its victim, a standard horror-film formula that falls far short of introducing the new posthuman forms of sexuality proposed by the book. As Barbara Creed, scholar of film and feminist theory, argues, "the potentially radical nature of Cronenberg's representation of desire is undercut by an unadventurous approach to questions of sexual difference and sexual choice."[48] It is the film's safe gender politics that prevent it from successfully consider- ing "the nature of desire in the postindustrial, postmodern age,"[49] for "Crash . . . speaks male, not female, desire . . . If, as Vaughan argues, the crash is a truly liberating, or fertilizing event, then ideally it should be liberating for both sexes."[50]

Interestingly, J. G. Ballard strongly defends the film, denying that its representation of sex is conventional. In response to cultural critic Mark Dery's comment that "Cronenberg reads Crash as softcore porn in the Helmut Newton mode," Ballard responds that for him, "book and film are far too cool and self-aware to be erotic."[51] Ballard also defends his friend Helmut Newton, saying, "I don't see Helmut Newton as a pur- veyor of softcore porn but as the creator of a unique imaginative world not too far from Crash—he loved Cronenberg's film, and I told him in London recently that if he ever made a film it might be like Cronenberg's Crash; he didn't disagree."[52] One man's softcore porn is another man's unique imaginative world when it comes to interpreting images. In a sad irony, Helmut Newton, a photographer known for nude high-heeled women and sadomasochistic themes in his photographs, died in 2004 in a crash of his Cadillac against a wall as he was driving out of the Chateau Marmont Hotel on Hollywood's Sunset Boulevard. His death evoked Ballard's Crash perhaps even more powerfully than the film he admired.

The film elicited mixed responses from reviewers, some of whom complimented its languorous style and its ability to evoke a world where everything resides on the surface and emotions are absent. Iain Sinclair, in his impressively detailed book on the film, proffers much praise, but ends by acknowledging that the film strips away too many of Ballard's cultural references, which give the novel its rich associations and its pre- science. Sinclair writes that Cronenberg "depoliticises Ballard's frenzied satire. He makes the pornography safe and elegant. He finds a place, a stoical nowhere, where savage rituals can be enacted without pain."[53] It was Ballard's ability to distill the components of contemporary celeb- rity culture to their disturbing core elements that made his novel so profoundly effective. Without the novel's specific cultural milieu, the film is a stylish fantasy operating at the level of a subdued murmur instead of a piercing shriek.

Disney's 1969 film *The Love Bug*, J. G. Ballard's 1973 novel *Crash*, David Cronenberg's 1996 film adaptation of *Crash*, Disney remakes of *The Love Bug* in 1997 and 2005, and 1997's docudrama *James Dean: Live Fast, Die Young* all spin around the intersection of cars and rebel iconography. Although their differences are obvious to contemporary observers, it is likely that future generations will look back and perceive them as remarkably similar, as belonging to a peculiar age of auto-eroticism when millions worshipped a doomed young star whose meaning was contested but whose posthumous presence undeniably saturated the period's fictions. "We're living in a time when the machines of mythology are more powerful and pervasive than ever," says Art Simon, author of the book *Dangerous Knowledge: The JFK Assassination in Art and Film*.[54] Since Dean's death, celebrity worship has thoroughly permeated the culture and is no longer confined to adolescents or treated with bemused curiosity by the media. Now the mainstream media are in the business of manufacturing obsessive interest in stars with around-the-clock television coverage of celebrity lives and a cessation of other news coverage whenever a particularly prominent star dies, especially when death is sudden and the circumstances are violent. It is one of the ironies of our media age that any event that pulls massive numbers of viewers to their televisions and keeps them there for days is good for the television industry, giving a boost to individual networks' and stations' ratings and benefiting advertisers. Tragedies can be packaged and spat out even as events are still unfolding, and most media coverage conforms to familiar pacing and instantly recognizable sequences of requisite moments. Television viewers become armchair Vaughans every time the camera turns on another tragic and gruesome celebrity death.

For celebrities who die young and suddenly and are rewarded with enduring superstardom, posthumous fame far surpasses anything experienced by those who survive into old age and are honored with lifetime achievement awards and standing ovations. Stars who die young are perceived as having unlimited possibilities ahead of them, unlike aging celebrities, whose lives have taken their course and precluded alternative trajectories. Early death precludes any life trajectory, but in the realms of fantasy and representation, detached from the star's actual existence, anything is possible. Stars who die young are "a receptacle for a lot of fantasies . . . And that may be the perfect definition of the ultimate celebrity."[55] James Dean continues to be a receptacle for a lot of fantasies, and the fantasies tell us a great deal more about ourselves than they tell us about the opaque young man from Indiana. Dean's life fades further and further into history, but the rebel iconography he helped create stays young and filled with promise for each new generation.

Celebrity culture is also a capitalist culture, as film and cultural studies scholars Mikita Brottman and Christopher Sharrett point out, for "celebrity is possible only within the framework of a consumer culture, which provides the economic forces necessary for the formation of the public relations and the motion picture industries."[56] While the ethos of consumerism encourages a compulsive fascination with celebrities, who appear to live more vividly, more energetically, than their adoring fans, celebrity death introduces a jarring dissonance, a rip in the seamlessness of the powerful institutions that support celebrity fame. The ultimate breakdown of barriers between the celestial celebrity and the ordinary fan is the car crash, for, according to Brottman and Sharrett, "If the obsession with celebrity is a by-product of capitalism, then the obsession with celebrity car crash is a fantasy of literalization: the final and much longed-for union between the celebrity and members of their audience."[57]

Ironically, while a car crash death exposes a star's mere mortality and diminishes the distance between stardom and regular existence, the star's posthumous fame can enter a realm so inconceivably elevated and rarefied that a new and wider gap is established separating fans from their dead idols. The mundane elements of the fatal crash—the car, the clothes worn by the celebrity, the site, other participants and witnesses—become emblems of intense fascination that bridge the divide between the ordinary and the mythic, not unlike a saint's relics. They can evoke deep sorrow and, at the same time, *schadenfreude*. All of the pleasures combined with the frustrations of living amid the false promises of consumer culture are stirred up by violent celebrity deaths. In the case of James Dean, his youth at the time of his death intensified the emotional impact, his unfulfilled potential undercutting the official U.S. rhetorical promise of unlimited possibilities for each and every citizen. The crash that took his life took everything that he might have become, and it also gave the lie to the American Dream. A revised dream was left for succeeding generations, the one that lives on in rebel iconography, a dream of success in the form of quick fame cut short by sudden violent death followed by immeasurable stardom and immortality. It is simultaneously the ultimate dream and the worst nightmare our culture offers, and it is a legacy of the fifties for every subsequent generation.

CHAPTER 4

The Teen Rebel

"Teenagers" were a relatively recent phenomenon in the fifties, having emerged as a separate and unique sector as recently as the middle forties at the dawn of the postwar age. The postwar economic boom made it possible for many young people in the U.S. to prolong their youth and avoid entering their parents' serious world of work and responsibility for as long as possible. Adolescent leisure time fit in well with the needs of the burgeoning corporate empire in the U.S., for teenagers were a lucrative new market. James Dean came along at just the right time for a segment of the population whose members were still in the process of defining themselves and eager to latch on to shared symbols to distinguish themselves from their parents. With the release of *Rebel Without a Cause*, "the Teen Dream was born, and Jimmy was speaking for all of us."[1] *Rebel*'s Jim Stark was wracked with pain over the adult idiocy surrounding him, and his misery spoke for every cringing, unhappy teenager. Becoming a James Dean fan allowed teens to symbolically escape from their parents and create a new extended family for themselves, just as Jim, Judy, and Plato briefly form a substitute family in *Rebel Without a Cause*. But even better than becoming a James Dean fan was becoming James Dean. With the right jacket and a sullen demeanor, countless teenagers attempted to do just that. In a 1958 poem-like essay published in *Esquire* magazine, John Dos Passos took note of the phenomenon and contemplated teen veneration of Dean:

> There is nothing much deader than a dead motion picture actor,
>   and yet,
> even after James Dean had been some years dead,
> when they filed out of the close darkness and the breathedout

air of the second and third and fourth run motion picture theatres
where they'd been seeing James Dean's old films, they still lined up:
   the boys in the jackboots and the leather jackets, the boys in
the skin-tight jeans, the boys in broad motorbike belts,
    before the mirrors in the restroom
    to look at themselves
    and see
    James Dean;
    the resentful hair,
    the deep eyes floating in lonesomeness,
    the bitter beat look,
    the scorn on the lip.

    Their pocket combs were out; they tousled up their hair
and patted it down just so;
    made big eyes at their eyes in the mirror
    pouted their lips in a sneer,
    the lost cats in love with themselves,
    just like James Dean.[2]

Dos Passos beautifully captures the imitators' masquerade, with their reliance on mirrors to externalize their deep-felt wounds.

But postwar anxiety was more than just a pose; it was easy to become disillusioned in the U.S. in the fifties, when the air itself seemed saturated with hypocrisy. The Eisenhower era brought a self-congratulatory mood to those benefiting from upward mobility and affluence, while shocks to the system—the not-so-distant Depression, World War II and Nazi atrocities, the ongoing anti-Communist inquisition, racist injustice and segregation, the Korean War, and the threat of nuclear annihilation—were mostly repressed. Social drinking was a way for suburban Moms and Dads to anaesthetize themselves and avoid confronting the emptiness at the heart of materialism. Teen disillusionment was a logical response to the insincere platitudes and paranoid ramblings of politicians in the sanctimonious social order of the American fifties. "Perhaps there has *not* been a failure of communication," wrote Paul Goodman, author of *Growing Up Absurd: Problems of Youth in the Organized System*, in 1960. "Perhaps the social message has been communicated clearly . . . and is unacceptable."[3] James Dean's sneer, his every gesture and mannerism expressing the utmost scorn for phoniness, and his early death—interpreted as a decision to opt out—crystalized widespread disillusionment into one symbolic image: the rebel icon.

In the half-century since the emergence of rebel iconography, it has become clear that teenagers have more serious concerns than simply donning an outfit and affecting an attitude. With the difficulties they face and their lousy reputation, teens are living in tense times. They have become scapegoats for many social ills, blamed for urban violence, crime, drug abuse, drunkenness, out-of-wedlock pregnancies, and the spread of AIDS. Anti-youth rhetoric, however, fails to acknowledge that adolescents are victims of staggeringly high rates of poverty, and that policy makers choose to excoriate young people as immoral and irresponsible rather than try to solve the systemic problems that oppress them. In his book *The Scapegoat Generation*, sociologist Mike Males, author of many articles and several books on youth issues, writes that there is "a war against children and adolescents" in the U.S. He cites statistics showing that in California, elderly poverty dropped significantly between 1970 and 1995, while child poverty soared.[4] However, he writes, "the unwillingness of American institutions to face the serious impacts of poverty, abuse, and adult behaviors on teenagers has crippled realistic policies."[5] Adolescents are consistently blamed for social ills rather than recognized as their victims. Politicians and citizens groups find it easier to accuse the media—in particular heavy metal and rap music—of causing adolescents to become violent and suicidal than to address social issues.

The spring 1999 shooting spree at Columbine High School in Littleton, Colorado, intensified the attacks on musicians, particularly Marilyn Manson, who was demonized as a pernicious influence. Suddenly any student dressed in Goth attire was perceived as a diabolical threat, and schools began enforcing dress codes, as if clothing itself made kids go bad. Anti-youth rhetoric became increasingly hysterical, evoking the vehement denunciations of "juvenile delinquents" in the fifties but with heightened animosity. The media and many politicians are eager to denounce young people because it is easier than responding insightfully to actual social complexities, and "few contemplate just what it means when a society's most affluent generations of elders choose to enhance our own well-being at the expense of attrition against our young."[6]

The demonization of American youth is on shrill display in the diatribes of criminologist John J. Di Iulio (a professor of political science at the University of Pennsylvania who served as the first director of the White House Office of Faith-Based and Community Initiatives under President George W. Bush). Di Iulio warned in 1996 of "juvenile super-predators— radically impulsive, brutally remorseless youngsters, including ever more pre-teenage boys, who murder, assault, rape, rob, burglarize, deal deadly drugs, join gun-toting gangs, and create serious communal disorders.

They do not fear the stigma of arrest, the pains of imprisonment, or the pangs of conscience."[7] Di Iulio's rhetoric dehumanizes adolescent boys and feeds fears that they are spiraling out of control. By contributing to a culture of fear, anti-youth discourse hampers efforts to improve conditions in which adolescents have to live. Cultural critic Mark Dery speculates convincingly that the rampant condemnation of teenagers springs from the aging counterculture generation's fixation on retaining its youth: "The Boomer love-hate relationship with today's teenagers is deeply rooted in their jarring sense of obsolescence and their proprietary attitude toward adolescence"; he observes that "just in time for its midlife crisis, the counterculture has exchanged its founding myth—Oedipus slaying his father and laying his mother—for the story of Kronos eating his own kids." Despite studies showing that adolescents are no more violent now than they were twenty years ago, "today's teens must be sacrificed (metaphorically, at least), lest they displace the eternal adolescent every Boomer sees in the mirror—especially when he or she is zipped into leathers for a rumble with the other weekend Hell's Angels from the office."[8]

When teen spirit is monopolized by middle-aged wannabes, it is tempting to agree with Thomas Hine that the term "teenager" has outlived its usefulness. Hine notes that the term, first found in print in 1941, has functioned to infantilize young adults, reducing expectations for them and consigning them to the dysfunctional holding pen of high school. According to Hine, "Teenagers have this license to be irresponsible and then they are blamed for being irresponsible."[9] For Hine, identifying young men and women as teenagers hinders their attainment of adulthood. Among his recommendations are more work-related options for young people and smaller high schools with greater individualized attention to each student. "He is hoping," writes Kathleen Megan, "people will stop dismissing young people as hormone-crazed teenagers and instead see them not as 'fundamentally different from adults,' but as inexperienced and therefore in need of extra patience and attention. He suggests we call them 'beginners.'"[10] Although his term smacks of condescension, Hine is correct in asserting that large, impersonal high schools and widespread denunciation of adolescents have made it difficult for young adults to grow up gracefully with a sense that they can contribute to defining their own particular version of adulthood.

Seen globally, young people are thrust into painfully grim roles beyond their choosing. Poverty and war wreak havoc on young lives. The concept of a "teenage" period of fun and freedom from worry is horribly inappropriate and an impossible dream in many parts of the world. The existence of child soldiers in Sierra Leone, the Democratic Republic of Congo, Uganda, and Colombia, for example, reveals the gap between dream and reality. In Congo, "the warlords have killed even childhood," reports Somini Sengupta from the Congolese town of Bunia, writing that "as militia groups battle for control of this provincial town, Bunia's young are paying a high price. The war has shuttered their schools, left them lame and hungry, killed their parents before their eyes. It has turned children into merciless killers and haunted them with memories of mayhem unfitting for the most hard-bitten grown-ups. Girls have been raped, toddlers have been butchered, babies left crying among dead bodies." One boy, "a daily fixture on this main road, carries his deadly cache [of hand grenades] in a bright yellow cartoon-print backpack."[11]

In Myanmar (Burma), rent by civil strife for the last fifty years, the insurgent group God's Army recently had as its leaders twin twelve-year-old boys Johnny and Luther Htoo, who chain-smoke and profess to have special powers that protect them from deadly weaponry. We learn that "the Htoo twins rallied their village in 1997 to avenge a government offensive in which—as in many similar reported incidents—the soldiers raped women, killed men in front of their families and set fire to homes."[12] Young people in war-ravaged countries are deprived of their youth by adult violence, denied an education, and given no buffer from the full onslaught of pain and grief. And as Marie Smyth, founder of the Ulster-based Institute for Conflict Research, points out in her study of young combatants in Northern Ireland, the Middle East, and South Africa, "despite their role in hostilities . . . young people are rarely involved in peace negotiations," often leaving them disenfranchised and vulnerable to postwar criminal activities.[13] In much of the world, the teen rebel is struggling for survival, and the concept of idle years between childhood and adulthood is preposterous.

Despite the horrors of adolescence in much of the world, Hollywood's youth films remain committed to anachronistic formulas inadequate to the task of addressing contemporary complexities. The films exist in a golden vacuous bubble in which outdated notions of teen existence are preserved. Film scholar Jon Lewis criticizes Hollywood for failing to keep up with drastic changes in adolescent existence, relying instead on images and narratives recycled from the fifties, when today's most prominent filmmakers were young and whose fond but anachronistic memories fuel their creativity. These aging filmmakers are key figures in perpetuating the postmodern nostalgia mode analyzed by Fredric Jameson, a mode that has suffused contemporary western culture in the vacuous styles of the past.[14] Lewis cautions that

> the dark side of such a nostalgic project is that teenagers today are denied the very community these films insist once existed. For this generation of teenagers, the present is dominated by images and narratives of their parents' youth. These largely reassuring journeys into the past are plenty diverting, but may well leave today's youth wholly unprepared to think seriously about the future in any terms other than those they've already seen on the big screen.[15]

The difficulty, if not impossibility, of thinking seriously about the future is a major theme in youth films that are not sunk in rose-tinted nostalgia. This type of film relinquishes the conservative moral lessons of the fifties youth films, the anti-authoritarian challenge of the sixties and seventies youth films, and the nostalgia of the eighties and early nineties youth films, and instead depict hopeless, self-destructive teenagers awash in cynicism and mind-numbing boredom. While some of these films are sensitive in their treatment of young people deprived of optimism for the future, others sensationalize bleakness and contribute to the anti-youth hysteria pervading the U.S. Most notably, *Kids* (Larry Clark, 1995) depicts urban teenagers as immoral monsters who pose a terrifying threat to social order. It is a film that, while perceived at the time of its release as unconventional and edgy, is in fact thoroughly conventional in upholding the most vicious stereotypes disseminated by right-wing youth-haters. Mike Males asserts rightly that "the danger of a movie like *Kids* is that it reinforces a building 1990s adult belief that we are justified in casting such a hopeless mass of vicious brats adrift." He points out that three months after the release of *Kids*, its theme was "re-issued in book form by the Carnegie Corporation, whose Council on Adolescent Development embodied like escapism in its report declaring half of America's 10–14-year-olds 'at risk' due to their bad behaviors. It is a well-worn theme not original to either film or academic exercise. It is a common fiction of adult self-flattery that underlies the public policies that endanger America's future."[16]

Well-worn themes have dominated youth films, and despite their differences, nostalgic teen films and suicidally bleak teen films all refer back to the archetypal rebels Marlon Brando and James Dean. (Sometimes the reference is explicit; for example in *Heathers* [Michael Lehmann, 1989], the bad-boy rebel is named Jason Dean and referred to as J.D.) Nowhere is James Dean's influence more apparent than in the trajectory of youth films that followed his death. Young people had already been identified by Hollywood studios as a significant audience before his death, but the massive youth cult that sprang up around him posthumously ensured his place as an enduring cinematic prototype, and the three films he starred in became models for the hundreds of teen films to follow. By the late nineties, youth films had become so thoroughly conventionalized that new, innovative treatment seemed impossible. Even films that promised novelty often fell back on the same tired clichés, as is the case with *Better Luck Tomorrow* (Justin Lin, 2003), set in a Southern California suburb, only this time with Asian American academic high achievers who flirt with danger. Despite its new ethnic milieu, the film recycles tired cinematic conventions for depicting teen angst, sexuality, and gender dynamics.

However, three films—*The Doom Generation* (Gregg Araki, 1996), *Boys Don't Cry* (Kimberly Peirce, 2000), and *Lilya 4-Ever* (Lukas Moodysson, 2003), along with a novel, *Wild Child*, written by Chang Ta-chun in 1996—were surprisingly successful at injecting vitality into a moribund form and providing a fresh perspective on rebel iconography. Instead of recycling the genre's conventions in familiar ways, they made the genre itself their subject matter. Using entirely different strategies and tones, these texts are as much about the shortcomings of youth films and iconic rebel imagery as they are about the alarming adversity faced by young people. *The Doom Generation* evokes the clichéd conventions of youth films and their rebel figures only to deconstruct them in highly ironic ways and suggest that any sincere adolescent expression has been precluded by the media's packaged imagery. *Boys Don't Cry* evokes clichés with less irony, but the film engages in deconstruction by subjecting the genre's gender codes to minute scrutiny and illuminating the sexual ambiguity in iconic rebel imagery. Both films identify the codes of youth films as major influences on adolescents' cultivations of identity. After fifty years of youth films, these films tell us, their conventions have come to dominate the formation of adolescent subjectivity. The disaffected Taiwanese adolescents in the novel *Wild Child* rely on rebel clichés to try to find meaning in their lives on the fringes of the affluent Taiwanese society that has abandoned them. And in the Swedish film *Lilya 4-Ever*, a Russian teenager is discarded by her mother and clings to her pop culture dreams as long as she can despite the damage inflicted by corrupt and predatory adults.

The Doom Generation, the second film in director Gregg Araki's "teen apocalypse trilogy," pulls out all the stops in a campy, overblown descent into slacker nihilism and millennial despair. Its colors are vivid and oversaturated, its characterizations are exaggerated, and its black comedy crosses over into the grotesque. It is a road movie for the end of the century, and along the way it wickedly satirizes youth films, mixing them up with a pastiche of film noir and gangster conventions. The three rebels in *The Doom Generation* are the nihilistic descendents of James Dean depicted as products of a pointless, superficial society and pop culture influences that have left them virtually brain dead.

The Doom Generation derives from *They Live by Night* (Nicholas Ray, 1949), *Bonnie and Clyde* (Arthur Penn, 1967), *Badlands* (Terrence Malick, 1973), *Wild at Heart* (David Lynch, 1990), *Natural Born Killers* (Oliver Stone, 1994), and every other film about rebels on the run. *Doom*'s rebels—Amy (Rose McGowan), Jordan (James Duval), and Xavier (Johnathon Schaech)—fall passively and unintentionally into their murder spree, however; they are hardly even aware that they are murderous fugitives on the run. The closest they get to confronting their situation is when Amy interrupts Jordan as he is playing a video game to say: "Would you kindly pull your head out of your rectal region. We're accessories to two homicides. Doesn't that concern you in the fuckin' least?" Jordan merely looks confused. Unlike their young and reckless predecessors Bonnie and Clyde, Amy, Jordan, and Xavier derive no satisfaction from their outlaw status. The murders they commit are always in self-defense, and they gain nothing except escaping with their lives and unpaid-for fast food. In fact, it is only Xavier who kills throughout most of the film, and only to protect the slacker couple, Amy and Jordan, from raving lunatics. Amy and Jordan drift through life, their affect remaining unchanged; a day of bloody carnage is no different from a day at the video arcade. These are teens whose minds are too numb to grasp that they have been thrust into the dramatically charged role of teen rebel.

Their rebellious roles are foisted on them by a culture that has already deprived them of authenticity. Jordan and Amy, the teenage couple, are joined by the mysterious Xavier, who literally falls out of the sky onto their car's windshield at an abandoned drive-in movie theatre populated at night by teens hanging out and riding skateboards. Jordan and Amy have left a red-tinted punk-music club called "Hell," and after a failed attempt at sex, they comment on their condition. Their dialogue satirizes the anguished laments typical of teen films. Amy says, "I think sometimes the city is sucking away at my soul," and tells how she was stuck in a traffic jam and just couldn't wait to get by the dead bodies on the asphalt so she could move again. Jordan agrees: "I know. I feel like a gerbil [inaudible] in Richard Gere's butthole." Amy sums it up: "There just isn't a place for us in this world." Their dialogue voices the clichéd cynicism of youth films, and Jordan contributes a repulsively graphic pop culture metaphor that suggests the limited range of metaphorical associations provided by a media-driven world. Throughout the film, the three friends' bored inarticulateness comments on the postmodern unavailability of original language. Every possible conversation has already been scripted and disseminated in pop culture texts; there is little if any space for authentic expression.

In the film, violence inhabits the most mundane exemplars of consumer society, especially drive-ins and convenience stores: a Korean Quickie Mart manager, a young male cashier working at a fast-food drive-through window, and a pool-playing woman named Brandy in a huge blond wig and heart-shaped rose-tinted glasses all inexplicably turn on the three young protagonists. To be a teenager, the film implies, is to be feared and hated. Amy and Jordan are repeatedly threatened by seemingly ordinary people who suddenly become violent weapon-toting psychotics, and Xavier comes to their rescue. People continually mistake Amy for a former lover and attempt to kill her when she denies knowing them. These misrecognitions are also a symptom of the postmodern absence of authenticity, for Amy displays a pastiche of recycled styles: punk, film noir femme fatale, and fifties' suburban teenager. Her frequent style changes leave her open to people's fantasies; she becomes a type, embodies a "look," and cannot escape people's delirious impressions that she is somebody they have known.

The film follows the three outlaws' path of sex, carnage, and fast food throughout Southern California. They are presented by the film as products of a vacuous society drained of significance except for absurd coincidences and frequent references to the end of civilization. Throughout the film, the landscape emits prophetic messages: "The Rapture Is Coming," reads a giant billboard alongside the highway; "Prepare for the Apocalypse," warns a banner in a secondhand clothing store. Tawdry religious symbols and omens of death abound. These teenagers are adrift in a world that reminds them at every turn that they have no future. Amy and Jordan leave "Hell," their punk-music hangout, for "heaven," an abandoned drive-in movie theatre. A Jesus figurine dangles from their car's rearview mirror. Amy and Jordan smoke cigarettes from a black package decorated with a white skull and crossbones. Their cigarette lighter is shaped like a skull. Everything they purchase costs them the same satanic amount, $6.66, and federal authorities learn in a terse briefing that Amy's less-than-impressive cumulative SAT score was also 666. After their first murder, the three friends spend the night in an all-red room at the "Headless Horseman 666 Motel." Xavier has a tattoo of Jesus on his penis ("so people when I'm bonin' them can say, I've got Jesus inside me").

Trapped in a meaningless world headed for annihilation, Amy and Jordan are for the most part lethargic, but they occasionally respond to their predicament. A tender moment between them gets expressed in apocalyptic hyperbole, when Jordan murmurs, "I hope we die simultaneously, like in a fiery car wreck, a nuclear bomb blast or something." Amy smiles and responds, "You are so romantic." In a culture pervaded by media disseminations of death, destruction, and sex, the logical conclusion is to romanticize car wrecks and mass death. But Amy and Jordan are not always able to turn despair into desire, and near the end of the film, existential meaninglessness bears down on them. "The world sucks," sneers Amy. "Life is lonely, boring, and dumb," she concludes. Jordan, who for most of the film has been utterly vacuous, suddenly starts to ponder the big picture. "Hey X," he asks, "do you ever wonder what the meaning of our existence is?" "Huh?" responds Xavier. "Do you ever wonder why we exist?" repeats Jordan. "What for?" asks Xavier. "No reason," says Jordan. A few minutes later, during sex with Amy, Jordan asks the same question again. "You gotta be kidding," she answers. "No really, don't you ever think about it?" presses Jordan. "Christ, I was about to come. Can't we talk about this later?" says Amy. "I guess," says a dejected Jordan.

Shortly afterward, Jordan loses his life during the final attack on the trio launched by a group of neo-Nazi thugs who first see them in a music store. The thugs' leader, George (Dewey Weber), starts to harass Xavier and then sees Amy, whom he claims is his long-lost love Bambi. Later, the thugs find the three friends at night in an abandoned warehouse. Chanting homophobic hatred, they attack Xavier and Jordan just as the two are on the verge of making love. George, adorned with a blood-red swastika painted on his chest, rapes Amy on an American flag while listening to the national anthem and reciting the Pledge of Allegiance. George goes berserk when Jordan insults his mother, an exaggerated version of the tensions surrounding mothers in most teen films. In retaliation, George kills Jordan by cutting off his penis with large garden shears. Blood spatters everywhere in a strobing scene of extreme carnage as Amy grabs the shears and bludgeons George repeatedly. The film ends after an ellipsis to the daytime with a two-shot showing Amy driving her car with Xavier in the passenger seat formerly occupied by Jordan. The dashboard is littered with disposable plastic junk, and a little plastic skeleton dangles from the rearview mirror. Amy and Xavier both wear black sunglasses and are silent, gazing impassively at the camera. In a daze indistinguishable from the daze that enveloped them before Jordan's demise, they reach for the oral gratification that has fueled them throughout the film. With Amy smoking and Xavier munching on Doritos, the car races off in a high-angle shot down a deserted beachside road.

All of the adult authority figures in the film are as hopelessly incapable of making sense of the world as the three teen rebels, but the authorities are more pompous and play their occupational roles with absurd seriousness. Although the FBI agents attending a briefing about the crime spree in California are propped up by the trappings of respectability, they are just as demented as the lunatics who misrecognize and attack Amy. The FBI agents are gray-suited male bureaucrats sitting across the table from their identical doubles, who mirror their every move. The official in charge speaks in a terse voice about "the suspects: a paramilitary brigade of three youths [who] appear to be on a freewheeling crime spree heading north." He gives Amy's vital statistics, including her cumulative SAT score, and says she should be considered armed and dangerous, concluding, "Gentlemen, I want you to find her, and, if necessary, kill her." His words are precisely those used by the spurned lunatics who mistake Amy for their dream lovers and resolve to find her and kill her.

Equally inane are two television newscasters who report on the murder of the Quickie Mart proprietor. Their puffed-up sense of importance combines with ignorance to capture the pretentious self-inflation of TV news. After showing graphic video footage of the proprietor's still-talking severed head and the bloody corpses of his wife and three children, who died in a "ritualistic murder/suicide," the male newscaster interrupts the female to ask, "Wait just a second there: *disemboweling* them?" "Yes," responds the woman cheerfully. The only clue, she goes on, is a skull earring, "the type sold most frequently in rock 'n' roll paraphernalia shops, often worn by homosexuals, Satanists, and members of other dangerous cult groups." The male newscaster interrupts again: "Hold it, Sandy. Correct me if I'm wrong, but don't a lot of people, especially teenagers following the latest fad, kids who are otherwise perfectly normal, don't they sometimes wear earrings similar to the one shown here?" "Yes . . .," she admits. The newscasters engage in a pathetic attempt to make sense of adolescent behavior and hide their obliviousness behind well-modulated authority. The woman's vilification of gay people as comparable to satanists and other "dangerous cult groups" indicts the media's underlying homophobia. It also satirizes through exaggeration the hysterical tone of adults in countless youth films. We learn soon after that the skull earring belongs to Jordan and was a gift from his mother when he "finally passed

Algebra/Trig." "It's got sentimental value," he explains. Jordan's reality does not match the media's sensationalized version of it.

The Doom Generation, like *Rebel Without a Cause*, revolves around a trio of rebels comprised of two young men and a young woman. In reviving *Rebel's* threesome in the post–Production Code era (and released without a rating), *The Doom Generation* makes very explicit the sexual tensions that remain submerged in *Rebel*. In *Doom*, the sexual triangle—Jordan and Xavier both have sex with Amy—is complicated by the fact that Xavier is more interested in Jordan and spends the entire film trying to seduce him. The film highlights its twist on conventions with an opening title that introduces it as "A Heterosexual Movie." But it is not so much a heterosexual movie as it is an ironic riff on the latent homoeroticism in the teen film genre.

The film makes explicit its revision of the original fifties rebel figure for the nihilistic nineties by turning Xavier into James Dean. He emerges from a secondhand clothing store wearing an outfit straight from Dean's wardrobe in *Giant*: a white cowboy hat, western-style shirt, tight jeans, and cowboy boots. Johnathon Schaech, who plays the role of Xavier, strikingly resembles Dean in this getup, especially when he turns his head in profile with a cigarette stuck between his lips, recalling the famous publicity still from *Giant* of Dean lying back languidly with his cowboy hat pulled down over his eyes. The shot is known by many who have never seen *Giant*; it was the inspiration for an advertisement for Levi's Jeans in the eighties, an example of postmodern decontextualization of an image to turn it into a floating emblem of cool. In *The Doom Generation*, the pièce de résistance of Xavier's tribute to James Dean is a cheesy belt buckle showing a cowboy on a bucking bronco that bucks when it is wiggled. Xavier wiggles the buckle provocatively for Jordan, who, wide-eyed and innocent, says, "Wow! Can I?" Jordan then wiggles the belt buckle close to Xavier's crotch in an erotic close-up, followed by a shot of Xavier's cigarette rising in a symbolic erection.

Xavier is a James Dean who knows what he wants, whose desires have superseded those of Cal Trask, Jim Stark, and Jett Rink. Unlike Cal and Jim, Xavier doesn't yearn for his parents' approval or guidance. The three young friends in *The Doom Generation* have become violently unmoored from their families. The dysfunctional families introduced in *Rebel*, the paradigmatic teen film, are exaggerated to the point of absurdity here, where the concept of family is sordid. Amy reveals that her Mom has been a heroin addict and is now a Scientologist. Amy's father is dead and she's not sorry because he was "an alcoholic pig always trying to molest me."

Jordan (left) enjoys wiggling the bucking bronco belt buckle Xavier (right) wears in *The Doom Generation*.

Xavier explains that his Mom shot his Dad and then killed herself when he was twelve. Jordan's admission that his parents live in Encino is met with a long sympathetic silence. Later, he phones home from a phone booth, saying, "Hi, Mom, Dad. It's me. I'm sorta taking a little vacation with Amy right now and, uh, . . . Fuckin' machine hung up on me!" Amy and Xavier have come through family tragedies, but Jordan, with suburban parents and a malfunctioning answering machine, is the most pitiable.

Like the three friends in *Rebel*, the *Doom* trio create their own surrogate family, but in *Doom*, the ties that bind them are overtly sexual. The tensions implicit in a sexual triangle, those that are latent in the relationship between Cal, Aron, and Abra in *East of Eden*; Jim, Judy, and Plato in *Rebel*; and Bick, Leslie, and Jett in *Giant*, are altered for the slacker nineties in *Doom*. Rather than burn with jealousy when he learns that Amy has had sex with Xavier, Jordan shrugs and says, "whatever, Amy." When Amy expresses the desire to ditch Xavier, it is Jordan who stands up for him: "He's not so bad. I mean, he's sorta like us, lost, and he doesn't fit in." Jordan later watches through a window while Xavier and Amy have sex, and instead of bursting in to confront them or running off in anguish, he masturbates, a yo-yo bouncing up and down from his pumping arm, and then discreetly wanders into the misty night. When he returns to

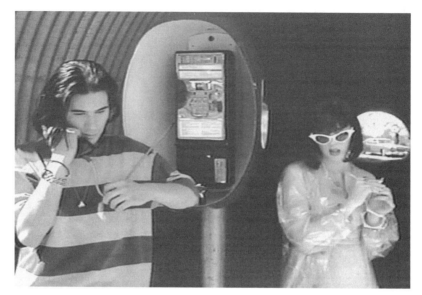

Amy waits while Jordan calls home in *The Doom Generation*. His parents'
answering machine hangs up on him.

their room, Amy's explanation captures inarticulate slacker speech at a
time when pop culture has made lengthy speeches unnecessary: "Just because he and I, it doesn't mean that I'm all that, whatever." This scene has
been played out so often in youth films that her stammered simulation
will suffice. Jordan responds, "I know," and they kiss.

Amy, Jordan, and Xavier represent the empty and amoral end-products
of twentieth-century youth films. Their drug-addled minds, fueled by
frequent fast-food binges, are barely capable of remembering anything
from one moment to the next. Even so, they are not identical; individuality persists despite the deadening conformity of commercialism. Each
one of the three rebels represents an aspect of rebel iconography reconstituted for the slacker nineties: Xavier is brutal; Amy is sarcastic and
insulting; and Jordan is sweet and childlike. Ultimately it is Jordan, who
loses his life, who emerges as the most interesting character, for he represents the persistence of tolerance in an intolerant age. He consistently
forgives Amy and Xavier for their inconsiderate behavior. A conversation
between Amy and Jordan early in the film illuminates the difference between them. Amy has just thrown Xavier out of the car. Jordan says, "I
swear, Amy, you can be so harsh." Amy responds, "He was an anus face."
Jordan tells her, "What were we talking about the other day? About try-

ing to be less judgmental of people?" Amy says, "Fuck that." Jordan is a
Generation X Christ figure, walking through life in a confused but gentle
stupor (for a while nude and wrapped in a scarlet sheet). His "crucifixion"
at the hands of the homophobic neo-Nazi thugs signals the final loss of
innocence in the film's sordid world.

One could accuse the film of cowardice at the end for withholding
sex between Xavier and Jordan, interrupting them with the thugs' attack,
but the interruption is the film's way of signaling its pessimism. To para-
phrase Amy's cliché from early in the film, there just isn't a place for
them in this world. What remains at the end is the disturbing vision of
Amy and Xavier speeding away down the beach, alone with their amoral
brutality, having lost the kindness that Jordan brought to their lives. This
film cautions that the future is likely to be scary. Its religious overtones
are partly ironic and partly a search for something meaningful in a putrid
swamp of human vapidity ruled by phony-baloney authorities and their
mass-produced media clichés.

Media clichés, many from the teen film genre, and intolerance of difference are also themes of *Boys Don't Cry*, a highly successful low-budget
independent film directed by Kimberly Peirce and released in 2000. The
film's plot is loosely based on the actual life of a young Nebraskan transgender teen—Teena Brandon—who, born female, lived as a boy. He
had girlfriends, used a variety of aliases, and was occasionally arrested for
petty crimes. In 1993, on probation for a forgery conviction, he settled
in the small town of Falls City, Nebraska, where he temporarily found
refuge with a new girlfriend and her family and friends, until two of those
friends—ex-cons with a history of violence—discovered his sex. They
viciously beat and raped him, and after he reported the crime to the local
police (who interrogated him about the crime with brutal insensitivity),
they shot and stabbed him to death, also murdering two of his friends.
The murder spree took place on New Year's Eve in 1993; Brandon had
just turned twenty-one. He was a genuine teen rebel who rejected his
culture's most basic dictates. Adapting his life for film presented the challenge of avoiding teen rebel clichés handed down through decades. *Boys
Don't Cry* wisely acknowledges those clichés and gives us a new perspective on them by uncovering their latent gender and sexual ambiguities.

Boys Don't Cry opens as Brandon (Hilary Swank) is leaving Lincoln,
Nebraska. The film fictionalizes some aspects of the events—creating
some characters, eliminating others, using an alias (Brandon Teena) that
Brandon never used (he used a series of other names)—in order to focus
attention on Brandon's transformation and attempt to find a safe place in

the world. Brandon's metamorphosis in the film relies on a well-known stock of mannerisms and clothing choices to signify masculinity, for Brandon puts on masculinity to pass as male. As film scholar Michele Aaron points out, "*Boys Don't Cry* is a tale of passing," but unlike other popular cross-dressing films (such as *Some Like it Hot* [Billy Wilder, 1959] or *Victor/Victoria* [Blake Edwards, 1982]), it refuses to turn cross-dressing into a joke for the amusement of an audience accustomed to expecting that by the film's end they will receive reassurance that the cross-dressing character has resumed a biologically "true" identity.[17] Aaron shows that *Boys Don't Cry*'s unconventional address to the audience divulges "the knowingness or complicity at the heart of spectatorship"[18] as it uses passing not as "a means to an end, as in the comedies, but as the end itself."[19] In *Boys*, it is not only Brandon who has studied twentieth-century American cultural codes of masculinity in order to master them, but all of the characters—male and female—who base their self-presentations on clichéd gender conventions and thus can be seen as engaging in gender performance. One of the film's revelations is that gendered mannerisms and attire are always a masquerade, but that insecurity prevents some people from acknowledging their own participation. Brandon is punished with death for the transgression of challenging two insecure young men unwilling to face the constructedness of their own masculine personae.

By showing Brandon put on masculinity, the film deconstructs the gender codes usually rendered invisible by teen rebel films, in which boys are boys and girls are girls. But Brandon's performance of masculinity has antecedents in the fifties rebel actors' styles. Analyzing Dean, Brando, and Clift, Graham McCann writes:

> through questioning their sexual identity (its "feel," its objects of desire, its modes of appearance), [they] underlined the arbitrariness of all images of "manhood." More lasting than any of their own personifications of masculinity was their critique of the constraining aspects of the conventional, contrived sex roles in modern society. They were eminently prepared for "playing at being masculine"; they had been doing so for many years.[20]

While most teen rebel films have downplayed the gender transgressions of Dean, Brando, and Clift, usually ignoring them entirely and taking gender differences for granted, *Boys Don't Cry* renders them obvious and explicit.

In fact, the transgression of gender conventions is not entirely antithetical to melodrama, the genre that exerted the most influence on fifties teen rebel films. It is featured in more subtle forms in classic melodramas such as Douglas Sirk's *Written on the Wind* (1956) and Michael Curtiz' *Mildred Pierce* (1945). And even though *Rebel Without a Cause* ends by validating conventional gender roles, it does so at the expense of Plato, who poses the greatest threat to convention, and whose death, like Brandon's in *Boys Don't Cry*, exposes the hypocrisy of the status quo. Plato is the soft, needy side of Jim Stark, the part that is destroyed so that Jim can be returned to the family fold. Brandon combines aspects of Plato and Jim, and we watch in awe as he crafts his composite persona and tries to master his intricate performance of masculinity smack in the middle of the American heartland.

The masculine style aspired to by Brandon is the type represented by the Midwestern James Dean: the Hoosier farm boy in jeans, boots, cowboy hat, dangling cigarette, and slow swagger. It is the persona Dean drew on for his performance of Jett Rink in *Giant,* and the attire and attitude parodied in *The Doom Generation* when Xavier clothes himself in cowboy regalia and shows off his titillating bucking bronco belt buckle. Brandon in *Boys Don't Cry* dons a ten-gallon hat before entering a roller-skating rink to pick up girls, but his cousin Lonny, who discourages Brandon's cross-dressing for fear that it will incite violence if discovered, plucks it off his head and says, "You look like a fuckin' idiot in that hat." Brandon, though, is happy to look like a fuckin' idiot as long as it's a male fuckin' idiot. His suiting up in front of mirrors is a motif in the film. Early on, after he gets his hair cut short like a boy, Brandon admires himself in a mirror, smoothing down his hair with spit and then reaching for the requisite cowboy hat and cigarette to complete the look. Later, in Falls City, he goes through a more elaborate process of dressing in front of a mirror, binding his breasts, packing his jeans, and then gazing admiringly in the mirror with his hands cocked like pistols, marveling gleefully, "I'm an asshole."

The young women in the film like what they see; Brandon is a charmer who possesses a magnetic attraction. A girl in the roller-skating rink says to him, "You don't seem like you're from around here." Brandon asks, "Where do I seem like I'm from?" "Someplace beautiful," she responds. The film extends the premise that Brandon brings beauty to a desolate landscape in its depiction of rural Nebraska, which in shot after shot appears hopelessly flat and deserted in what film scholar Julianne Pidduck calls "a stylized hyperrealism."[21] Brandon represents the possibility of escape to "someplace beautiful," especially for his Falls City girlfriend Lana (Chloe Sevigny), who quits her factory job and dreams of traveling to Memphis, or anyplace, with him. She is repulsed by her life in Falls City, by her tedious dead-end existence, and people with pinched, inflexible minds. She and her friends escape into booze and drugs, and when nothing else is available, get high on aerosol cans while spinning in trapped little circles on a playground merry-go-round.

Lana's true escape from entrapment, the film suggests, is through her relationship with Brandon. He provides an alternative space, not unlike *Rebel*'s Jim Stark, who offered escape from suburban hell for Judy and Plato when they set up a temporary refuge in a secluded and abandoned house. But in the flat expanse of Nebraska, filmed in a way that emphasizes its endless desolation, Brandon and Lana are too exposed, unable to find a safe haven. The film nonetheless suggests an alternate universe for the pair. Michele Aaron observes that *Boys* uses a science fiction aesthetic to create a transcendent space, "a community of aliens and dreamers," for Brandon and Lana, "from the cinematographic distortion of light, and time—periods of day and night are shown passing at warp speed—to the film's images of factories with the smoke and metallic splendour of space-stations, and of parked cars with the luminosity of flying saucers."[22] The closest that *Boys* can get to identifying an actual refuge for the lovers is in a broken-down rural shed where they make love shortly before Brandon is killed, and this time, unlike earlier, Lana is fully aware that Brandon is biologically female. Like the abandoned mansion in *Rebel*, only on a much smaller scale, this shed offers, at least for a short time, a space in which to pretend that everything might still work out.

Ironically, even though Brandon offers an escape route for Lana, he does not share her desperate urge to flee Falls City for a different life. Quite the contrary, Brandon reveals excitedly to Lana that what he wants more than anything is for the two of them to settle down in Falls City in an Airstream trailer. She stares at him in dumbfounded amazement, unable to assimilate the fact that he actually wants to stay in a place she perceives as a total hellhole. Analyzing the actual Brandon's desire to remain in Falls City, journalist and novelist Stacey D'Erasmo writes in *Out* magazine, "If you were having a hard time managing women and checks and things in Lincoln, Falls City might feel like a more manageable place to be. Smaller. Safer."[23] Brandon is a dreamer who imagines—naively, as it turns out—that this smaller place will be safer and will let him live his chosen life. What Lana does not understand is that Brandon likes the clichéd accoutrements of masculinity that are plentiful in Falls City; they allow him to forge the "asshole" identity he associates with being male. His new friends, John Lotter (Peter Sarsgaard) and Tom Nissen (Brendan Sexton III), accept him (as long as they think he is a boy), and he admires their brash machismo. Hilary Swank, who played the role of Brandon, comments on the actual Brandon's relationship with the young men who later would murder him: "When he hung out with those guys in Falls City, who, yes, were trouble, he did it because he didn't have a role model . . . They became his role model of what guys look like, what guys act like. All of a sudden he was accepted as this boy—his family never accepted him for who he wanted to be. So once he was accepted, he was staying." [24]

Brandon hones his male masquerade; he frequents bars where he befriends lonely girls moving to the languid rhythm of country ballads while bathed in neon lights and a smoky haze. He is the gallant suitor who defends his girl against the crude advances of a redneck twice his size ("Why don't you leave the lady alone; I don't want any trouble here"), and beams with exhilaration when he suffers a black eye in the ensuing barroom brawl. Brandon is a thoughtful young man who inspires girls to confide in him. In a tense conversation between Lana and her former boyfriend, John (who with his friend Tom will rape and kill Brandon), after John has learned that Lana is involved with Brandon (whom he still thinks is a boy), the subject of Brandon's style of masculinity comes up:

John: What do you see in him? I know he's like nice and everything, but he's kind of a wuss.

Lana: I know he's no big he-man like you. But there's just something about him.

John: (in a mocking tone) There's just something about him.

Lana: Stop making fun of me.

Brandon is "no big he-man," but he likes to take risks: drag racing and bumper skiing are *Boys Don't Cry*'s version of *Rebel*'s chicken run. But while Jim Stark knows when to jump out of his car before it goes over the cliff, abandoning a high-risk version of masculinity in order to save his life, Brandon pushes himself further into the danger zone. His performance of masculinity is more intense than that of the "real boys." His is a hyper-masculinity adopted to avoid being unmasked, and he values accoutrements conventionally associated with masculinity, including fast cars. *Boys Don't Cry* opens with a car driven by Brandon racing down a dark country road at night pursued by a police car. A shot of Brandon's eyes in the rearview mirror reveals apprehension mixed with exhilaration. Fast cars are a rebel accoutrement he appreciates. In an analysis of James Dean's love of cars, Graham McCann writes that

> the car enabled Dean to feel self-accountable, an extension of Emerson's cowboy self-reliance which remains so central to the American male. Driving fast involved control, and the real possibility of losing it, with facing (even relishing) fear, injury and death. The excitement of the activity involved weighing the odds between danger and safety, suspense and relief.[25]

Brandon weighs the odds too, not only when he's squeezing the accelerator to escape a cop, but also when he walks into a room with a cocky, confident swagger, knowing he could lose everything if his performance is uncovered. For the spectator, Brandon's performance is known from the film's beginning, prompting the realization that "passing *is* failing," and that "passing is tinged with the threat of punishment" in an intolerant locale.[26] Brandon has a lot more on the line than does Jim Stark in *Rebel*. While Jim's defiance is directed against his annoying parents and insipid authority figures, Brandon's is aimed at an entire culture's sacrosanct belief in the equivalence of sex and gender and the unwavering fixity of gender roles. Brandon in fact is generally polite to adults—he even calls his girlfriend Lana's mother "Mom"—and takes their annoying habits in stride. His rebellion is more abstract and more radical, and the risks he takes are much more serious.

Boys Don't Cry joins other teen rebel films in locating its risk-seeking youths in a derelict setting, where meaning and purpose are obliterated in a dispiriting bleakness, a "blank expanse" that connects the film with "a widespread cultural articulation of small-town middle America with 'trailer trash' anomie, intolerance and murder."[27] On the phone to his cousin in Lincoln after finding himself in rural Falls City one morning, Brandon says, "I don't know where the fuck I am. [He glances at a newspaper.] Falls City." His cousin exclaims, "What are you doing down there? I mean, it's not even on the map!" Rebel films' wastelands are not always rural; *Rebel Without a Cause* indicts suburban America as a vapid land of loneliness and isolation, and *The Doom Generation* takes up the indictment by showing its trio roam through an endless and despoiled suburban California. The emblem for contemporary meaningless vapidity in both *The Doom Generation* and *Boys Don't Cry* is the convenience store. *The Doom*

Generation has its Quickie Mart, while *Boys Don't Cry* has its gas station mini-mart. As a metaphor, the convenience store represents an emptiness at the core of contemporary American existence hidden by the illusion of plenitude: the shelves are fully stocked with soft drinks and Doritos under bright fluorescent lights, but it is all disposable junk; there is no real sustenance or substance to be found.

Meaninglessness is a long-standing theme of teen rebel films. In *Boys Don't Cry*, Lana and her listless, self-destructive friends manifest the rebel film's typical emphasis on alienation from parents, jobs, and authority figures, but Brandon's alienation is more subtle and complex. Although he steals and flees from cops and judges, who have locked him up before, Brandon wants to belong, to take his place among the good old boys around town. Unlike the bored and cynical local youths he befriends, he perceives beauty in trailer parks and seedy honky-tonks. But although Brandon embraces the mundane, his very existence is a challenge to the culture's gender norms. Film scholar Rachel Swan describes the film as "an apt allegory for a society coming to terms with 'alternative sexualities' and their destruction of a sacred order in the universe."[28] Brandon is profoundly alienated from, and a direct threat to, that sacred order.

Brandon, however, is not alone in engaging in masquerade; it is just that his masquerade short-circuits the norm. *Boys Don't Cry* suggests that masculinity and femininity are always performances. Its young men and women have studied the poses and mannerisms deemed suitable for their sex, and they dutifully perform their parts. The film's metaphor for performance is karaoke. In a dingy bar, sitting at a table with his new friends John and Tom, Brandon sees Lana for the first time as she awkwardly walks onto a small stage with two friends and sings karaoke to the song "Bluest Eyes in Texas." The moment is composed and shot to exhibit the hallmark conventions of performance in contemporary American culture. Lana and her two friends are in their usual listless daze as they go through the perfunctory motions of women performers. They are on display, and Peirce shoots the scene to emphasize that the cultural conventions of performance they have grown up with are suffused with gender clichés. As Rachel Swan writes in describing this scene:

> Brandon watches with John and Tom. Again, gesture becomes an important vehicle of communication in this scene. As she sings, Lana slumps, self-consciously aware of the male gaze upon her. Brandon, Tom, and John sit with their legs spread and their heads cocked unabashedly, each pinching a cigarette between his thumb and index finger. The three male

John Lotter (left), Brandon Teena (right), and Tom Nissen (offscreen right) watch Lana and her friends sing karaoke in *Boys Don't Cry*.

characters' gestural symmetry suggests that watching women is for them a fraternal activity, a way in which to assert their shared masculinity.[29]

For John and Tom, masculinity means power and control, but Brandon gazes more respectfully at the singers, and he singles out Lana with love-struck awe. Lana appears to be self-consciously aware of being an object of desire. She responds with her usual lethargy, but it is combined with awareness of her power to attract male admiration. Later in the film, she seizes on the idea of karaoke as her ticket out of Falls City. She announces excitedly to Brandon that they could move to Memphis, where she could earn money as a karaoke singer. As naive as Brandon, she imagines getting paid to sing karaoke, earning a living at a form of entertainment that does not in fact pay its performers but instead requires them to pay. In her fantasy Lana can only imagine a future in which she sings a part already sung by someone else, and her performance of gender is likewise based on "feminine" mannerisms already established by others. She sees no room for individual assertion of uniqueness.

Lana and Brandon both perform their genders, and the film uses mirrors to reveal the parallels. Rachel Swan describes the film's juxtaposition of two mirror scenes:

Lana performs femininity while singing karaoke in *Boys Don't Cry*.

Lana stands before a full-length mirror and scrutinizes her female body. She slumps her shoulders and clasps both hands over her belly, sucking it in self-consciously, as though to express the desire for an aesthetically appealing female form, the ideal object for a male spectator. The camera cuts to a parallel shot of Brandon in men's briefs, his breasts bound tightly to his chest with elastic gauze. In this shot Brandon is positioned in the same way as Lana was, standing before a full-length mirror with his hands clasped over his flat belly.[30]

Lana poses in front of a mirror to practice femininity, just as Brandon poses in front of a mirror to practice masculinity. Mirrors are a primary motif in the film, reminding the spectator that the characters feel compelled to stop and compare themselves to a gender ideal. A psychoanalytic reading would suggest that the mirror motif continually places the characters in the stage of infant development referred to by Jacques Lacan as "the mirror stage," when the infant initially starts to recognize its autonomous existence at the same time that it still yearns for the comfort of complete union with its mother. Lacan argues that the mirror stage signals the subject's initiation into the symbolic realm of culture and language.[31] In *Boys Don't Cry*, the symbolic realm inculcates gender; it instructs boys how to be boys and girls how to be girls, and the mirror signifies their periodic return to the moment before their roles have been learned in order to inspect the effectiveness of their performance. What results is a culture-wide and all-inclusive game of impersonation, one in which the film's audience is also implicated, for watching the film, with its inducement to identify with characters onscreen, is comparable to gazing into a mirror.

Boys Don't Cry demonstrates what can happen when male cultural insiders refuse to acknowledge that they too have learned to be masculine, have been acculturated in the proper gestures, language, and garb to be perceived as men in their particular cultural context. John and Tom are also impersonating masculinity, and the film indicates that even for them, the impersonation is difficult and has taken its toll. John is filled with rage and his friends have learned that he can erupt in extreme violence. His explosions are irrational and scary. Tom is likewise destructive, but he directs his violence inward by cutting himself with knives. Brandon gazes with horrified fascination when Tom reveals the ragged scars across his body where he has carved his own flesh. Tom challenges Brandon to cut himself too, to prove his masculinity, to prove that he's tough. Brandon's face is tense as he ponders a way out and finally finds it, saying, "I guess I'm a pussy compared to you." Brandon has defused the tension by deferring to Tom's greater "manliness." But although John and Tom present a "manly" exterior to the world, their own identities are layered and complex, and not only because of the latent violence they contain. John, for one, surreptitiously gazes at Brandon, whom he thinks is a boy, with unmistakable desire. John is portrayed as secretly bisexual, and his rages can be interpreted as erupting from his own self-loathing, a result of having internalized his culture's homophobia. His heterosexual masculine masquerade is especially aggressive because it functions to hide his true desires. By equating masculine performance with Tom's self-destruction and John's crazed fits of violence, the film suggests that the cultural expectation that men be tough can cause irreparable psychological damage, not to mention irreplaceable loss, when people who don't conform to cultural norms are destroyed.

Brandon's death was of course not isolated, as Stacey D'Erasmo points out:

> Violence destroys context, destroys history, makes memory go blank. It enforces solitude. Violence against transgender people is by no means rare; Gwendolyn Ann Smith's "Remembering Our Dead" website lists more than 120 recently murdered transgender people.[32]

The enormous success of *Boys Don't Cry* suggests that it helped to heighten awareness of violence against, and to foster acceptance of, transgender people. The degree of success attained by the film can be measured by its wide release on multiplex screens (after first circulating in small art film theatres, where low-budget independent films typically remain), the journalistic coverage it elicited, and the prestigious awards it won, including the Academy Award for best actress for Hilary Swank, the Best Supporting Actress Award from the Los Angeles Film Critics Association and the Boston Society of Film Critics for Chloe Sevigny, and the Debut Director Award from the National Board of Review and the Best New Director Award from the Boston Society of Film Critics for Kimberly Peirce. Newspapers ran large-print ads that trumpeted the film's awards and quoted critics' praise. (Scott Heller from the *Boston Phoenix* is quoted as saying, "A tremendous performance by Hilary Swank depicts Brandon as Thelma, Louise and James Dean rolled into one.")[33]

Despite the film's success and hopes that it might have had a positive effect on the acceptance of transgender individuals, there were disturbing signs that the machinery upholding the status quo was hard at work to defuse its challenge. Most obviously, there was a concerted media campaign to feminize Hilary Swank. At the Oscar ceremony, Swank wore a clinging gold gown with plunging neckline. Media coverage of the event emphasized her femininity (and implicitly her heterosexuality), and there was a great deal of press devoted to her designer gown as well as her failure to thank her husband. The campaign to distance her from Brandon Teena's transgressions continued, and can be seen clearly in the contrast between two magazine cover stories about her, one in *Out* in October of 1999 and the other in *InStyle* in August of 2001. *Out*'s cover shows Swank in close-up in three-quarter profile with short hair, minimal makeup, not smiling, and wearing a black turtle-neck sweater.[34] *InStyle*'s cover shows Swank facing the viewer head-on, smiling seductively, with chin-length carefully styled hair, glamourous makeup, and wearing a skin-tight fire-engine-red halter gown with a deeply plunging neckline. A jeweled necklace dangles suggestively between her breasts.[35]

InStyle's Swank is the anti–Brandon Teena being sold by the star makers who manage her career. While the article in *Out* documents a somber visit to Falls City by Swank and the author Stacey D'Erasmo, the *InStyle* article ("A Woman in Full") is about Swank's playfulness, her husband, and her many pets, and is accompanied by full-page photographs of her in stiletto heels and extravagantly frilly and transparent designer dresses. She is quoted as saying: "When I finished *Boy's Don't Cry* I felt like I'd lost a piece of me . . . I think I had been hiding my femininity for so long that I felt I wasn't gonna get it back." (She has apparently forgotten that she actually acquired a piece in *Boys Don't Cry*.) This is followed by "Here she proves otherwise in a gown by Yves Saint Laurent."[36] On another page: "'I'm comfortable in myself. I like putting on a pretty dress,' says Swank in a Givenchy dress and heels by Manolo Blahnik. 'If that means showing my cleavage, I'm comfortable with that. But that's not me all the time.'"[37] There is something desperate about the extent to which the article and photos attempt to disavow any similarities between Hilary Swank and Brandon Teena, and while it is obvious that actors are not identical to the roles they play, the loser is nonetheless Brandon Teena, whose brave challenge to cultural inflexibility is treated like a smelly sock that needs to be shoved aside and hidden far, far away.

Films do not have a monopoly on teen rebel narratives; literary fiction has also made crucial contributions, most importantly J. D. Salinger's *The Catcher in the Rye* from 1951. Just as in the film world, rebel books have ranged across the spectrum from clichéd sensationalism to innovative creativity. Of the many recent rebel texts in circulation around the globe, one of the most brilliant and original is *Wild Child*, a novel by Taiwanese author Chang Ta-chun.[38] Originally published in Taiwan in 1996, it was translated into English by Michael Berry and published in 2000 together with the novel *My Kid Sister*, by the same author. The two novels are the second and third parts of a trilogy that begins with the novel *The Weekly Journal of Young Big Head Spring*. Of the three parts of the trilogy, *Wild Child* is most explicitly about the punctured dreams of lost youth. Like the films *The Doom Generation* and *Boys Don't Cry*, *Wild Child* depicts young people trapped in a wasteland of adult indifference where their most meaningful touchstones are provided by pop culture artifacts. But instead of the United States, these young people are adrift in Taiwan, a nation with a troubled history of foreign occupation and the site of a contemporary struggle over influence among the superpowers.

Taiwan has long been the object of forced takeovers as well as rhetorical disputes about its identity. The island was originally populated by various aboriginal groups, most of whom are thought to be descended from Malayo-Polynesian peoples, and there were occasional encounters with both Japanese and Chinese fishermen and pirates as early as the sixteenth century. Portuguese explorers landed on Taiwan in 1544, but it was the Dutch who colonized the island from 1624 to 1663 as an outpost where the Dutch East India Company could establish plantations and mines, using imported Chinese laborers. The Dutch were defeated in 1662 by

Cheng Ch'eng-kung, the son of a Japanese woman and a Chinese pirate, and the island was a self-contained kingdom until 1683, when it was conquered by the Manchu dynasty, then ruling China. Taiwan remained a Chinese province until 1895, when the Treaty of Shimonoseki granted it to Japan after the Japanese defeated the Chinese Ch'ing dynasty. Remaining a Japanese colony until the end of World War II, Taiwan was handed over to China in 1945 as one of the terms of the Japanese surrender. The Chinese Kuomintang government under Chiang Kai-shek was at the time involved in fierce fighting with Mao Zedong's Chinese Communist Party, and after the Communist victory in 1949, Chiang Kai-shek fled to Taiwan along with between 1 and 2 million loyalists and set up an autocratic government in exile, vowing to someday regain mainland China. He ruled with martial law and tolerated no opposition, dealing harshly with dissidents.[39] Martial law was finally lifted in 1987, and Taiwan's first direct presidential election was held in 1996.

Between 1979 and 1989, Taiwan was transformed into a highly sophisticated technological society in an "economic miracle," while its citizens were involved in a struggle against the repressive dictatorship. At the same time, the People's Republic of China pursued its interest in assuming control of the island, and many in the West consequently think of Taiwan as nothing more than "a piece of the international affairs puzzle."[40] Those living in Taiwan have seen their country repeatedly used as a pawn in other nations' political maneuverings, and their society has long been divided over questions of national identity, with intense hostilities existing between all of the different indigenous people and immigrant groups who have settled the island over the centuries. The Taiwanese language distinguishes between Chinese settlers from different time periods, and there is a lingering feeling that recent immigrants are not really Taiwanese. The question of who really is Taiwanese is deeply divisive and is compounded by the question of which is the "real" China—Taiwan or the mainland. This "absence of consensus regarding national identity"[41] joins with uncertainty about the nation's future to create a sense of instability among the island's inhabitants.

The author of *Wild Child*, Chang Ta-chun, has frequently made politics a component of his distinctive experimental style. His literary response to Taiwanese political and social life is consistently irreverent, concentrating frequently on the underside of Taiwan's "economic miracle," which brought great affluence to a small percentage of the population while neglecting many others, including adolescents, who fell through the cracks, not unlike the situation in the U.S. following World War II. The rapid technological growth of Taiwan's "miracle" was accompanied by deep corruption and produced profound social changes, including family fragmentation. Taiwanese literature professor Chu Yen writes that "the generation gap, something rather alien to traditional Chinese culture, has become a thorny social problem" and reports that juvenile delinquency has become widespread.[42] "Young lives in a world dehumanized by materialization, barbarization, and promiscuity are miserable beyond description," he writes, for they are "weltering wretchedly in a lurid confusion of glittering economic prosperity" and "suffer silently or rebel without a cause."[43] Chu Yen's words evokes the 1950s American experience of juvenile delinquency, which accompanied its own moment of economic affluence.

Chang Ta-chun sees little reason for optimism, and his fragmented style, with its bricolage strategy, captures the splintered nature of Taiwanese society. *Wild Child* follows the adventures of middle school student Hou Shichun, known as Big Head Spring, and depicts the experiences of adolescent social castaways who from their position on the margins—they literally live in a junkyard—can perceive the flimsy façade of lies erected by the affluent and respected members of Taiwanese society. Chang draws on the teen rebel tradition of disaffected and confused adolescents for his protagonist Hou Shichun's disarming innocence, an innocence that prevents him from understanding much of what happens around him. His rejection of the status quo from a position of youthful innocence links him to Jordan in *The Doom Generation*, Brandon Teena in *Boys Don't Cry*, and the Ur-adolescent, Jim Stark in *Rebel Without a Cause*. In keeping with *Rebel*, *Wild Child*'s young protagonist rebels against authority figures, his family, and school, but he finds himself contending with more than annoying parents and schoolyard bullies; he lands in the middle of the criminal underworld, where he learns what it means to live on the edge.

Fourteen-year-old Hou takes flight from home after he has rammed his head into the stomach of an abusive teacher who falsely accused him of setting fire to a stack of geography exams. While hanging out in a video arcade, Hou is mistaken for someone else by a gang member, and he finds himself taken in by a gang led by the enigmatic Uncle Xu, who runs a parking lot but whose goal in life is to own a harbor port, to be a man of great influence. Uncle Xu's gang consists of a motley crew of young men and women who live in a junkyard and typically bungle their crimes and their deadly encounters with a rival gang. For Hou, the gang's activities are mystifying, but despite his confusion, his discomfort, and the dangers of life in the street, he finds gang life more agreeable—more comforting, even—than family life. When circumstances force him to remain with the gang, he does not mind, having chosen the perilous existence of gang life over mainstream society's sanctimonious hypocrisy. Ironically, Hou fulfills his vituperative teacher's prophecy that "a piece of work like you, even if you wiggled your way into some gang, you'd still be nothing but a petty thief!" (137).

For fourteen-year-old Hou, the adult world is utterly bankrupt, and the novel's short chapters, each a vignette from his life on the run, chronicle his disillusionment. Hou represents Taiwanese young people who cannot find a footing in their society and end up discarded. As Chang Ta-chun stated in an interview, Big Head was wasted even before he ran away from home, just as Annie, a prostitute in the gang, says, "all the cars in the junkyard were wasted before they were even delivered there" (xi). In school, Hou's abusive teacher, when not clobbering and deriding Hou, makes a fool of himself in front of the students. Hou has no respect for the school, and even his friendliness toward several classmates fades after he has been in the streets for a while. After an unsatisfying telephone conversation with a classmate, Hou knows that he'll never again be as childish as his friends from school.

His home offers little more peace than his school. Hou's parents smolder with resentment and anger, with both his mother and father keeping secrets from each other until they divorce and his father takes flight. After Hou leaves home, he retains one fond memory of a facial expression his mother makes while she parks her car, but his warmth for her evaporates after she launches a slick campaign to find him. His mother, it turns out, is Jade Aroma Chen, known as the "Commercial Queen," a television celebrity whose public efforts to locate her son ring insincere. As in *Rebel Without a Cause* and *The Doom Generation*, there is an enormous gap between the official rhetoric of concern for adolescents and actual adolescent experience. A newspaper article oozes with phoniness, stating,

> As ill fortune has already befallen Mrs. Chen, she has resolved to draw a lesson from her painful experience. Paying no heed to the social convention of "not washing one's dirty laundry in public," Mrs. Chen has bravely stood up. She has taken her own bitter experience as the inspiration and theme in designing a fund-raising activity poster for the New Era Cultural and Educational Foundation, which has long been concerned with problems facing today's adolescents. In the text of the poster, Jade Aroma Chen uses her own experience as a point of departure.

Written in the first person, Mrs. Chen's sincere and highly personal message confesses her own heartfelt emotions. She writes: "My child! Your mother is here, your family is here. The road back is in your heart; give your mother a chance; let us grow together!" The Foundation will assume the responsibility of printing the posters and distributing them to supermarkets, convenience stores, karaoke clubs, and other places frequented by adolescents. (212)

Hou contemplates the text and concludes that it was "unlike anything that my mother would normally say," thinking to himself, "Why don't you just go on eternally searching for me!" (213). Another newspaper article states that the Department of Education and the Police Department have contacted Hou's mother, and that "both departments have expressed that the increasingly critical nature of adolescent problems requires a concerted effort of cooperation between the family, schools, and related governmental departments in order to reach a resolution" (212). This pretentious rhetoric is deflated by the gang leader's unembellished response: "It's not so bad," says Uncle Xu. "So far they don't have shit" (212).

A desire to keep up appearances animates the efforts of the authorities and Hou's mother. As long as it looks as though the police and the school department care about adolescents, and as long as it looks as though Jade Aroma Chen is doing all she can to be reunited with her son, satisfaction prevails. The bureaucracy and the media keep grinding along, perpetuating the illusion of Taiwanese society as a smoothly functioning modern success story. Hou learns that well-to-do members of society maintain their distance from the poor and justify their own prosperity by referring disdainfully to poor people as "good-for-nothings" and "losers," and he wonders about the meaning of these dismissive terms; only after living in the streets for a considerable length of time does he have a revelation. "Good-for-nothing," he realizes, is "something that 'is already of no use, yet continues to be used and taken advantage of by other people'" (170). From his new vantage point among so-called losers, he perceives an exploitive economic system that relegates some people to the bottom of the hierarchy, where they are continually victimized for the benefit of those who are better off.

Hou's disillusionment extends not only to his parents and other authority figures but eventually even to the gang members he initially idealized. He is frequently struck by the gap between his expectations and the reality of gang life, much of it spent doing nothing at all. His greatest disappointment comes when he observes a high-level meeting between

Uncle Xu and a more powerful rival, Horsefly, in the lobby of a Sheraton hotel; from the moment Horsefly and his men arrive, it looks all wrong to Hou:

> Horsefly and his two men walked in a row as they entered the Lai Lai Sheraton, but they didn't walk up the steps in slow motion as I had imagined. Actually, they walked quite briskly, as if they were in a rush; Horsefly even almost slipped—the floor was probably too slick. What's more, they didn't look like they were about to go on any killing spree. In fact, after carefully observing the area from their waists to their torsos, I saw that not only weren't they packing any heat but they weren't even carrying Rambo knives or ice picks! (246)

Hou later listens to a recording of the gang leaders' negotiations at the hotel bar, and he is utterly perplexed by the mundane nature of their conversation, which falls far short of the movie version in his head, just as the arrival of Horsefly and his men pales compared to the conventional cinematic rendering of backstreet gang intrigue. Hou often mentally reconstructs events, explaining, "I take all the things I have experienced and recompose them in the same manner that a Transformer goes from robot warrior to car" (154). He transforms his life into pop culture clichés, most strikingly as he tries to fall asleep the night after his first day on the streets and he imagines himself and his new gang associates fleeing from the cops, "ducking here, dodging there, escaping only by the skin of our teeth" in a stolen police car (154). His favorite "scene" from the story, the one he really loves, is "when Uncle Xu, Ahzhi, Old Bull, and I stepped out of the police car. The four of us, lined up side by side stretching across the entire alley, strutted forward in slow motion. In the heart of the night, we walked with style" (154). Hou aspires to a cool attitude he has seen countless times in widescreen and slow motion.

Hou, a young runaway lost in the big city, pummeled by a gang member, unsure of what the next day will bring, has good reason to stifle his emotions by affecting a cool demeanor. Contemporary cool, argue Dick Pountain and David Robins, is more than just a matter of fashion; it is "not simply emotional shallowness, lack of passion or enthusiasm, as it is sometimes parodied. Cool's real work is done inside."[44] When a person has attained a cool appearance, scary emotions can be controlled: "A carefully cultivated Cool pose can keep the lid on the most intense feelings and violent emotions."[45] When Hou conjures up a slow-motion swagger down the alley in his mind, he keeps the lid on panic, but the effect is temporary, for he wakes up the next morning in extreme physical pain, a result of a beating he sustained. But physical pain fades, and emotional pain can always be suppressed, with pop culture providing a carapace of cool.

Hou's own identity in the gang owes its existence to global pop culture; the gang calls him "Bull-man," "that little Bull-boy," "Bull," "Bull-tail," (140) and other related names, all because they find him wearing a Chicago Bulls T-shirt with Michael Jordan's famous number 23 on it. As "Bull-boy," Hou is fortified against distressing information. He listens to Annie's devastating story of having been abducted by a brutal gang leader when she was a teenager and kept in a big iron cage on a rooftop, where she was raped and forced to take care of the thug's disfigured mother until the elderly woman died a year and a half later. Annie never saw her family again. Hou shields himself from the pain of Annie's life by exclaiming to her, "Your story is super cool, you could make it into a movie!" (194). He then proceeds to tell her, "If the part about the gang leader was a little more developed, it would be even more interesting" (195), and he takes issue with the end of her story, for the gang leader's brothers failed to avenge his death; her ending, he insists, "is not what you'd expect from a true gang brother" (195). For Hou, a true gang brother is the fictional one he has seen in films. The world of simulation is preferable to reality for him, and the slick clichés he has absorbed from pop culture help him compartmentalize the ugliness around him.

Chang Ta-chun, however, is too smart to suggest that reality and fiction are opposites. Quite the contrary, in *Wild Child*, storytelling permeates everything, making the point that raw reality is only accessible to us via stories, and the story told depends on the teller. Everyone tells stories, family members and gang members alike. Some stories are easy for Hou to reject, and others, such as those of a classmate with a wild imagination, are compelling. Not only is Hou a discerning listener; he also tells stories, and he appreciates those who listen: "If I were to think back to how I fell in love with Annie, I would tell you it started the night she listened to me telling stories" (185). The novel ends with Hou remembering a storytelling game he played with Annie, in which one question prompts another. His last comment to her is, "I don't want to know what you forgot . . . I want to know how you forgot" (256). Stories are as much about forgetting as remembering, a notion that has particular resonance in Taiwan, with its battleground of conflicting stories about the country's history and contemporary identity. What Hou wants to know from Annie is how to forget, how to resist sinking into despondency and a ghost-like existence, how to keep on living despite the pain of accumulated memories. The novel ends before Annie answers.

Earlier in the novel, Hou has indicated that life in the streets has left him thoroughly disillusioned. In a short, two-sentence chapter titled "Junk-yard Notice," he declares, "All that is left in this world are gang leaders, good-for-nothings, and dead people. Teenagers are already a thing of the past" (133). Teenagers as constructed by romanticized Hollywood films are definitely a thing of the past, if they ever existed at all. Actual young people face obstacles far more serious than the minor annoyances concocted by mainstream films. By 2004, adolescents in the U.S. were hard-pressed to find even low-paying summer employment, for the dead-end service jobs previously available were being monopolized by adults in a decrepit economy. Unemployed American young people with limited prospects became vulnerable to military recruiters who sought them out to fill the ranks of troops sent to the war in Iraq, with its steadily mounting death and wounded rates. Hou, commenting in *Wild Child* from the turbulence of Taiwanese gang violence, has reached the conclusion that there are no easy Hollywood-style resolutions, no ways to prettify the vapid and dangerous lives faced by young people set adrift in the contemporary world.

Reaching the same conclusion is the 2003 Swedish teen rebel film *Lilya 4-Ever*, directed by Lukas Moodysson and set in a bleak poverty-stricken city in the former Soviet Union, where sixteen-year-old Lilya (Oksana Akinshina) endures the grinding monotony of life in a barracks-like apartment complex surrounded by trash, gray skies, unemployment, cold, and hopelessness. Stylistically indebted to the French New Wave, the film's fractured editing and swirling camera movements, combined with the sound track's harsh and guttural punk music, convey a chaotic world where everything is too quick and irrational to understand. Lilya's cultural touchstones are from American pop culture, and she takes great pride in sharing her birthday with Britney Spears. Lilya is overjoyed when her mother announces that they are moving to the U.S., but her mother departs without her, giving in to a boyfriend who resents the encumbrance of a child. Lilya's despair at her abandonment is compounded by an aunt who appropriates her apartment and leaves her penniless to fend for herself in a filthy rat hole of a flat. As Stephen Holden writes in his review, "One ugly message the film keeps hammering home is that poverty and hopelessness have stripped the adults of their humanity along with their hope, and their children must make their way in a Dickensian nightmare of indifference and abuse."[46]

Adult inhumanity is starkly displayed when a bureaucrat informs Lilya that her mother, in her first communication from the U.S., relinquishes all parental responsibility for her and asserts that Lilya has always been an unwanted child. Lilya is left entirely without adult supervision, prey to classmates who rape her, with only one friend, a younger boy, Volodya (Artiom Bogucharskij), who is victimized by his brutal father and haunts the streets and an abandoned factory until Lilya rescues him. Volodya, a sweet boy who idolizes Michael Jordan and shoots hoops with a tin can, is devastated when Lilya abandons him after she is lured to Sweden with false promises of romance and decent employment.

Sweden turns out to be as gray and harsh as Lilya's Eastern European home, and she is immediately locked into a high-rise apartment, the prisoner of a pimp who rapes her and sells her to a series of men, depicted from Lilya's point of view, grunting and thrusting themselves into her. Visions of Volodya sporting angel wings—he swallowed a massive overdose of pills after her departure—guide her; he comforts her from beyond and gently urges her not to give up. She does give up, however, choosing to leap from a highway overpass after a brutal beating from the pimp. With nowhere to turn, and no experience of adult sincerity, she chooses suicide and is last seen on a rooftop with Volodya, both possessing angel wings, happily dribbling and passing a basketball, experiencing the joys of childhood only after death. The film's fragmented style, with its rapid editing between extreme angles and restlessly moving camera, implies that Lilya's life leads inevitably to her tragic death. Events occur too quickly and ruthlessly for her to find an alternative to suicide.

Lilya 4-Ever is an antidote to the characterization of teens as superpredators: Lilya sniffs glue, gets drunk, swears at adults, and resorts to prostitution to buy food and a basketball for Volodya's birthday, but adult crimes against her are infinitely more cruel. Like Annie in *Wild Child* and like all the young people, many of them still children, exploited by sex traffickers, she is held captive in a nightmare created by predatory adults. The fall of the Soviet Union in the early 1990s created enormous poverty, and young women there have fallen prey in record numbers to sexual exploitation at the hands of organized criminals. Sexual exploitation is a problem worldwide, but in Russia and Ukraine, human trafficking has reached epidemic proportions. "In Ukraine alone, sex traffickers moved some 500,000 women west between 1991 and 1998."[47] *Lilya 4-Ever* humanizes those nameless victims while also acknowledging its debt to earlier films with stories of abandoned children, among them Vittorio De Sica's *Shoeshine* (1946), François Truffaut's *The 400 Blows* (1959), Hector

Babenco's *Pixote* (1981),[48] and Martin Bell's *Streetwise* (1984). *Lilya 4-Ever* adds a contemporary perspective to show that adolescent outsiders may dream of celluloid-inspired romantic alienation, but their lives are actually filled with perils of a much uglier and more deadly sort.

Lilya's abandonment brings us full circle to James Dean, abandoned as a child by his father after his mother's death. Dean translated this early rejection into a metaphysical sense of abandonment in his stage and screen performances and, to a large degree, in his life, exuding an aura of incurable loneliness. Even now, over fifty years after Dean's death, abandonment is still a powerful metaphor for the teen rebel's predicament, and it has become more accurate than ever in describing young people in a globalized world who are discarded by older generations unable to provide employment or an effective education, much less a compelling vision of the future. Young people are inheriting a ravaged environment and a stratified, war-torn world of immensely rich and desperately poor people. The irony of the teen rebel figure is that despite its conventional association with an ennobling outsider stance, its more accurate meaning currently is someone cast aside and scorned. Rather than admit culpability in the neglect of young people, the advertising and entertainment industries continue to romanticize youthful outsiders and mask the true deprivations of adolescent existence.

CHAPTER 5

The Postcolonial Rebel

In the years since the birth of rebel iconography, its arc of influence has reached far and wide. Hollywood's domination of worldwide film distribution, maintained with the assistance of the U.S. State Department, has guaranteed that its products receive the widest possible exposure. American films join American fast food, American television, and American pop music in their relentless international dispersion. Although there are good reasons to condemn American pop culture's assault on the world, the situation is complex and rife with contradictions. For many young people internationally, pop culture from the United States, no matter how tainted by commercial interests, can be experienced as meaningful. Rather than function as passive consumers of hegemonic American culture, global youths often integrate American cultural products into their own traditions and practices to create new hybrid forms,[1] and these composite texts frequently make their way back around the globe, influencing production in the cultural capitals. Considering this international exchange of commodities, scholar of African American studies and philosophy Kwame Anthony Appiah writes that "if there is a lesson in the broad shape of this circulation of cultures, it is surely that we are all already contaminated by each other."[2] While the rebel figure's presence internationally is on the one hand evidence of American cultural hegemony, on the other hand there are endless possibilities for appropriation. Rebel iconography can be turned back against the American interests that produced it, and, as with any ambiguous icon, its meaning is up for grabs.

At the time of the rebel icon's appearance in the fifties, colonial subjects around the world were energized by dreams of independence and the desire to create nations based on nonexploitive principles. Those dreams and desires carried them through the arduous years of wars for independence. When it came, independence was celebrated, but subsequent years brought disillusionment when some of the early leaders who were beacons of hope, such as Patrice Lumumba in the Congo, were assassinated by political opponents, and subsequent leaders were characterized by corruption and profiteering. Countries with great potential have been consigned to poverty by their rulers and by trade policies that favor the U.S. and Europe. Many Third World countries have been transformed into sweatshop factories for the production of the First World's consumables, with workers earning pennies per hour and often laboring in unsafe conditions under armed guard.[3] These postcolonial realities have replaced the obvious colonial enemy of the past with much more diffuse and anonymous enemies against whom resistance can feel futile.

Two films that explore the postcolonial dilemmas of disillusioned adolescents are *Touki-Bouki*, a 1973 Senegalese film directed by Djibril Diop Mambety, and *La Haine* (*Hate*), a 1995 French film directed by Mathieu Kassovitz. Both films depict young people dissatisfied with their stifling environments and limited prospects. The postcolonial world they have been born into relegates them to the margins and regards them with racist distrust. They are estranged from their parents' generation and from the opportunities that independence was supposed to bring. Their struggle is complicated by their inability to find an authentic means of expression for their dissatisfaction, since the American and European pop culture that dominates their lives has already appropriated and packaged the concept of rebellion. The western-style rebel icon is a readily available but woefully inadequate role model that cannot overcome these young people's powerlessness in the face of entrenched institutional authority. Like their teen rebel precursors on screen, they also feel deprived, but the causes are rooted in colonial erasure of their cultures' histories and in postcolonial perpetuation of Eurocentric ideology. *Touki-Bouki* and *La Haine* reveal the futility of mimicking the rebel icon, which offers a seductive pose but fails to produce actual change.

Touki-Bouki was made by director Djibril Diop Mambety (1945–1998), who was twenty-eight years old when the film was released in 1973. Mambety grew up in the small town of Colobane near the Senegalese capital of Dakar, the son of a Muslim cleric, and studied theatre in Dakar before turning to film. He was reportedly expelled from acting school because of his rebellious lack of discipline.[4] *Touki-Bouki* was highly acclaimed, winning the Special Jury Award at the Moscow Film Festival and the International Critics Award at Cannes. It is a stunningly powerful film about alienated Senegalese youth in which Mambety's piercing gaze "destroys the possibility of illusion."[5]

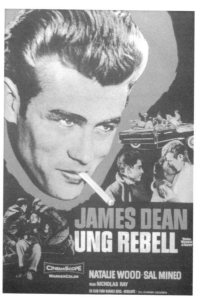

Posters for James Dean's films from around the world. (The David Loehr Collection)

Like many African films, *Touki-Bouki* is concerned with postcolonial tensions between African traditions and western influences. It takes place in the early 1970s in the West African nation of Senegal, which achieved independence from France in 1960. Its interest in the destructive legacies of colonialism links it to the extremely influential book *The Wretched of the Earth*, written by the psychologist Frantz Fanon in 1961, based on his experience working in an Algerian hospital during the French-Algerian war, in which he describes the process of African decolonization and the dangers facing newly independent African nations suffering from the af-

termath of colonial devastation. Fanon's analysis of neocolonial identification with the former colonial power is especially relevant to *Touki-Bouki*. Fanon writes:

> During the period of unrest that precedes independence, certain native elements, intellectuals, and traders, who live in the midst of that imported bourgeoisie, try to identify themselves with it. A permanent wish for identification with the bourgeois representatives of the mother country is to be found among the native intellectuals and merchants. This native bourgeoisie, which has adopted unreservedly and with enthusiasm the ways of thinking characteristic of the mother country, which has become wonderfully detached from its own thought and has based its consciousness upon foundations which are typically foreign,

will realize, with its mouth watering, that it lacks something essential to a bourgeoisie: money.[6]

In *Touki-Bouki*, postcolonial tensions crystalize in Mory (Magaye Niang), a young man torn between conflicting desires for an African identity and western trappings of wealth and power. Mory is neither an intellectual nor a merchant, but he desperately wants to distinguish himself from his fellow Senegalese. Fanon refers to the national bourgeoisie's "contemptuous attitude toward the mass of the people,"[7] and Mory illustrates the attitude perfectly with his venomous words, "You street-sweeping niggers, you city nigger. I'm not one of you." Mory is guided by a Eurocentric belief that freedom and happiness lie outside of Africa, in Europe, where fame and fortune await his arrival.

Mory is a former shepherd who lives in rural Senegal on the outskirts of Dakar but emulates the lifestyle of an American motorcycle rebel; he dreams of escaping Senegal for Paris. His youthful anger, directed at authority figures and the monotony of village life, is expressed in a culturally hybrid style; he roars through the countryside on a western motorcycle, but it is decorated with African ornaments—steer horns mounted on the handlebars and a Dogon cross, a Malian fertility symbol, on the back.[8] The film follows the misadventures of Mory and his university-student girlfriend, Anta (Mareme Niang), as they tear through the countryside on Mory's motorcycle, trying through various bungled schemes to steal enough money to book passage to Paris on an ocean liner. In Dakar, the two finally commit robbery successfully and, dressed in expensive stolen western clothes, start to board a ship bound for Paris. Mory, however, hesitates on the boarding ramp, and, after exchanging a long and silent gaze with Anta, runs back into the city. Anta embarks by herself on the journey to France.

Though they take different paths at this juncture, both Mory and Anta choose to be "hyenas" by adopting a rebel stance in defiance of their elders and traditional village life. *Touki-Bouki* means "the hyenas' journey" in Wolof. Scholar of African films Nwachukwu Frank Ukadike writes that "in West African oral tradition, this animal (symbolic of 'trickery and social marginality'), [is] notoriously known for its greed and mischievousness, and for its repulsive, nasty smell."[9] Scholar of African films Françoise Pfaff asserts that "the animal is used by Mambety [the director] in his story, which again opposes nonconventional individuals to the established mores and laws of society."[10] As hyenas, Mory and Anta live on the perimeter of their culture, disdainful of the tiresome routines of village life and adults' expectations of them. As a result, adults assail them with criticism. Anta's mother and another woman shout at her that she doesn't respect tradition, to which she responds, "To hell with the traditions!" As she dashes off, her irate mother calls after her, "You'll wind up emptying chamber pots. And your university won't change that . . . I'm ashamed for you. You and that Mory. What's he riding today? A motorbike or an ox? And that university where you lose all respect. God will punish you someday." Mory, too, is denounced by a woman known as the sorceress, who brandishes a bloody knife she has been using to skin a slaughtered goat and shouts at Anta that Mory is a "bum, parasite, and good-for-nothing." Mory and Anta are rebel malcontents who reject the older villagers' conformity and limited perspectives.

The film's director, Djibril Diop Mambety, discussed his interest in marginalized people in an interview:

> I believe that they do more for the evolution of a community than the conformists. Marginalized people bring a community into contact with a wider world. The characters of *Touki-Bouki* are interesting to me because their dreams are not those of ordinary people. Anta and Mory do not dream of building castles in Africa; they dream of finding some sort of Atlantis overseas. Following their dream permitted me to follow my own dreams, and my way of escaping those dreams was to laugh at them. Mory and Anta's dreams made them feel like foreigners in their own country. So they were marginalized people, in that respect.[11]

Mambety values marginalized people for contributing unconventional dreams of alternative lives, but in *Touki-Bouki* Mory's and Anta's dream of fulfillment in France is unproductive, based on a Eurocentric disdain for all things African and a belief in European superiority. Their desire for wealth and power exists in a postcolonial context that deprives them of self-esteem and pride in their cultural heritage.

Touki-Bouki is Mambety's indictment of Senegal's postcolonial dependence on France. In the film, the French presence is everywhere in Senegal, in the economic infrastructure as well as in the dreams of Senegalese youths. Mory builds an elaborate fantasy about striking it rich in France, telling Anta, "It's an easy hustle. All we need is a bit of ready cash, throw it around, tip the right guys, play it like we're loaded, hang out where the money is. France, here we come. Paris, the gateway to paradise, and when we come back, they'll call me Mr. Mory." Mory mimics and identifies with French power, disavowing his Africanness and not seeing that French power rests on Africa's—and consequently his own—subordination, even in the postcolonial era. Mory's dreams are forged by the complex hybrid subjectivity produced by colonialism.[12] *Touki-Bouki* comments on Mory's desires with Josephine Baker singing "Paris, Paris, Paris; it's paradise on Earth" nondiegetically in French as Mory speeds along on his motorcycle. The use of Baker's voice contains a level of irony; her fame in Paris was not based solely on her considerable dancing and singing talents, but was inextricably caught up with her presentation as a "savage" black woman who had to dress in "jungle" attire onstage despite having grown up in St. Louis, Missouri. Baker's praise for Paris as the gateway to paradise in the song may be fueling Mory's fantasy of French glory, but it should also function to warn him about the reality of French racism.

Instead, Mory's neocolonial dream takes over the diegesis. In an extended fantasy sequence, he and Anta are driven through Dakar in a motorcade, coyly waving at the huge cheering crowds lining the streets, celebrating their triumphant return from France. The fantasy sequence occurs after Mory and Anta have stolen money and clothes, and Mory has stripped naked in the backseat of a stolen chauffeur-driven convertible. The stolen car is an American flag on wheels; it is painted with the red, white, and blue stars and stripes, evoking the American Dream of individual wealth and power that has invaded Mory's consciousness. In his fantasy, Mory stands nude, arms outstretched, driven through the dusty countryside, crosscut with shots of cheering crowds and then, heightening the fantasy, he imagines that he and Anta are dressed in fashionable western clothes, receiving the adulation of their wildly enthusiastic fans in Dakar and their village, where villagers dance and sing their praise. The sorceress who earlier cursed Mory for owing her money now leads the celebratory singing and dancing. Mory smugly hands her a large wad of cash.

Mory is destined for disillusionment, and the film foreshadows his disenchantment with a recurring analogy between him and cattle being led to their deaths in a slaughterhouse. The film's opening credit sequence makes the analogy between his shattered dreams and slaughtered cattle with a shepherd boy riding a steer and leading a herd of cattle across the arid land to their slaughterhouse deaths. After the cattle arrive at the slaughterhouse and we see one of them killed in an unflinching long take, the shepherd (who might be Mory as a child) returns alone, slowly and methodically riding his steer, accompanied by the nondiegetic sound of a traditional African flute. The loud roaring sound of a motorcycle intrudes on the shot, jarringly clashing with the flute. A shock cut suddenly places the viewer with Mory speeding through a village on the motor-cycle adorned with cattle horns, while shouting and cheering children run alongside him. The camera tracks quickly, capturing the motorcycle's exhilarating speed while its raucous engine fills the sound track.

Like the cattle, Mory sets a course across the countryside without understanding that he is drawing closer to his destruction, although what awaits Mory is not literal death but rather the death of his dream. When he finally reaches the Dakar harbor and the ship bound for Paris, seem-ingly fulfilling the first step in his dream, he is confronted by the disdain of white racist Europeans for Africans. A sequence of shots onboard a lux-ury yacht presents fashionably dressed, rich white Europeans, young and old, lounging about, loudly condemning Senegal as intellectually barren. A white man opines that "African art is a joke made up by journalists in need of copy," and the Senegalese are put down as "big children" who "have no heart." Meanwhile black men carry heavy baggage onto the ship, doubled over from the weight of their cargo and the insults they endure. When Mory encounters French racism at the harbor, he confronts the exclusion at the heart of the colonial—and postcolonial—experience.

Mory's neocolonial fantasy thus crashes against the reality of racism when he reaches the ship, the symbol of transit between Senegal and France. His decision to flee back into Dakar is rendered nonverbally; it is depicted by way of a complex juxtaposition of sounds and images. Shots of Mory running from the ship are crosscut with the barren white ship's deck, where Anta looks lost and alone, decentered in the static shots, over-whelmed by the cold impersonal ship, which represents white European power. The confident physicality she has exhibited up until that point has been replaced by small hesitant gestures, and she nervously clutches her suitcase like a lifeline. The shots of Mory are in sharp contrast; the camera tracks rapidly as he runs headlong through the streets, his body seemingly flinging itself back into his familiar surroundings, away from the ship's threatened oblivion. Loud, jarring dissonant music and shouts fill the sound track, while the shots of Mory and Anta are crosscut with cattle being put to death in the slaughterhouse. Mory's flight from the ship is a figurative rejection of servitude to France. Although the film's open ending does not provide Mory with a solution to his conflicting desires, he has at least escaped Anta's shipboard confinement and its im-plications for a loss of self.

Postcolonial divisiveness permeates the film. In one powerful sequence, Mory and Anta have stopped in an outdoor stadium where a wrestling match is about to take place. An announcer informs the gathering crowd that this athletic event is part of a long partnership between France and Senegal, and that the proceeds will be used to purchase a memorial honoring General de Gaulle. Mory and Anta, motivated by the dream of obtaining French wealth, steal a large wooden box outside the stadium, hoping that it contains the match's proceeds. Their theft on the one hand signifies a return of misappropriated African wealth to two Africans—Mory and Anta—but, on the other hand, they intend to spend it on their own pursuit of French luxuries. As it turns out, Mory has chosen the wrong box, one containing a skull and amulet, the fetishes belonging to one of the wrestling contestants. The two boxes represent two related concepts: one contains a huge cache of money destined to commemorate Senegalese subservience to France; the other represents Senegalese culture, but it contains a skull, a literal signifier of Senegalese death as a result of the destructive legacy of French colonial power.

In another scene, Anta berates a woman who promises to pay later for vegetables she has taken from Anta's mother's stand in the vast shantytown on the outskirts of Dakar. Anta grabs the produce from the woman and says, "My ass! You pay now. We want a TV too." Anta's mother and the customer shout at Anta that she doesn't respect tradition and she exclaims, "To hell with the traditions!" The scene concisely illustrates the clash of traditional communal values with new western-inspired individualism. For Anta's mother, empathy for her customer outweighs the economic imperative, and their shared understanding is part of the flexible give-and-take of village life. Instead of trying to understand her mother's perspective, Anta flees with Mory, but at the end it appears that her energetic spirit is about to be broken by the crushing weight of French racism.

Touki-Bouki represents Mory and Anta's restlessness stylistically as well as narratively. The film eschews a realist aesthetic in favor of elliptical editing and a disruptive visual style that some critics have labeled avant-garde. In both its characterizations and its stylistic discontinuities, *Touki-Bouki* resembles Jean-Luc Godard's film *Breathless* (1959): Mory is a drifter and petty thief who is full of dreams but is consistently ineffectual, not unlike Michel in *Breathless,* and both young men team up with women students drawn to their nonconformity. Godard's Michel (Jean-Paul Belmondo), a generic hybrid, owes some of his traits to his rebel precursor James Dean. The route from Dean to Michel to Mory follows rebel iconography's trajectory from Hollywood to France to Senegal, each culture inflecting it with its own particular context. While *Rebel Without a Cause* served as an inspiration for films about disaffected young people, it did not inspire stylistic imitation by Godard or Mambety. By 1959, when Godard made

Breathless, Nicholas Ray's overwrought melodramatic Hollywood aesthetic was ill-suited to conveying a young rebel's unsettled edginess, and the same was true for Mambety in 1973.

There is disagreement among critics about whether *Touki-Bouki*'s experimental style derives from western modernism or reflects an African sensibility that captures the fractured inconsistency of postcolonial African life. Nwachukwu Frank Ukadike characterizes the two opposing views: "While non-African critics have read the film as an avant-gardist manipulation of reality, an Africanist analysis would attempt a reconfigurative reading that synthesizes the narrative components and reads the images as representing an indictment of contemporary African life-styles and sociopolitical situations in disarray."[13] Film scholars Ella Shohat and Robert Stam point out that techniques westerners typically perceive as their own avant-garde tradition often have antecedents in the artistic practices of the Third World: "One cannot assume . . . that 'avant-garde' always means 'White' and 'European,' or that Third World art, as Jameson sometimes seems to imply, is always realist or premodernist."[14] Ghanaian-British director John Akomfrah states that *Touki-Bouki* is

> not technically an avant-garde film, if by avant-garde people mean that it's trying to do something weird. It is more a portrait of African urban reality which is profoundly suffused with the tempering of that reality. Everybody knows about the restlessness that you see in towns and cities, in Accra and Lagos. This is one of the few films which actually captures that to-ing and fro-ing—not only through storytelling but also through a narrative parody of that movement. It's very graceful.[15]

Cultural dislocation governs every aspect of the film, from its plot to its style to its critical reception; Mambety made cultural hybridity the inescapable center of his film. When asked where *Touki-Bouki*'s jarring and discontinuous style comes from, Mambety responded that "it's the way I dream" and that "cinema must be reinvented, reinvented each time, and whoever ventures into cinema also has a share in its reinvention."[16] For Mambety, *Touki-Bouki* is a personal film that expresses his particular vision in a manner that he felt was necessary to tell the story of Mory's and Anta's fractured lives.

The motorcycle's exhilarating speed and the rebel stance are powerfully seductive for Mory and Anta, and also for another rebel who turns their quest upside down, replacing their fantasy of opulence with its opposite. He is a young white man who lives in a large baobab tree, wearing

animal skins and long hair and carrying a Stone Age–style ax. He steals
Mory's motorcycle from Anta, who runs in terror from this crazed wild
man who has presumably fled European values in pursuit of a back-to-
nature fantasy. The motorcycle acts as a shared symbol of rebellion for
these very different rebels, but the rebel stance it confers fails as effective
political action. Mambety indicates as much early in the film when he por-
trays the allure of the motorcycle as essentially sexual. When Anta makes
love to Mory alongside his motorcycle, we don't see Mory; instead, we
see close-ups of Anta's hand clutching the Dogon cross on the back of the
motorcycle. By excluding Mory from the shots of lovemaking, Mambety
makes the motorcycle Anta's lover, and, like Kenneth Anger in his film
Scorpio Rising, reveals the sexual energy invested in the rebel's motorcycle
by its love-struck enthusiasts. At the end of the film, the motorcycle has
been destroyed by the white wild man in an accident that has left him
badly injured, with one bystander commenting, "From the baobab tree
to a motorcycle. Now there's a jump that can kill you." Anta has set sail
for France, and Mory is alone.

What undermines Mory and Anta's quest is that they choose to express their marginalization by rejecting Africa and dreaming of luxuries
associated with France. They have chosen to distance themselves from
traditional villagers but have not found a viable alternative. Political activism is ruled out when they are excluded by students involved in political organizing whose disdain for the working-class Mory and misogynistic dismissal of Anta mark them as retrograde elitists and render their
progressive political efforts futile. Mory and Anta, like hyenas, and like
Michel in *Breathless*, respond to their situation by preying on people. Mory
descends on Charlie (Ousseymou Diop), a rich gay Senegalese man who
fancies him. While the stereotypically effeminate and simpering Charlie
waits for Mory in the bath, Mory steals all of his clothing and flees. In the
meantime, Anta has lifted another guest's wallet. They steal Charlie's car
(the one painted like an American flag) and chauffeur and light out for the
travel agency to book passage to France. The film falls back on a buffoon-
ish gay caricature, but includes a self-reflexive joke. Charlie phones the
police department to report the theft; he speaks to an officer, reminding
him of their previous sexual tryst. The officer's name is Mambety.

Mory and Anta are momentarily elated by the robbery, but their dream
cannot sustain them and they are left with less than they had before. Each
is alone at the end of the film: Anta decentered and displaced onboard
the sterile white ship, and Mory running away in panic, without a goal.
Mambety leaves us with two lost souls and an open ending; their future

is uncertain. A flashback to Mory and Anta after they have made love, stretched out beside the motorcycle on a cliff overlooking the sparkling sea, is a brief reminder of a moment of harmony, one that emphasizes the beauty of Africa without fantasies of fame and fortune overseas.

Interestingly, Mambety himself remained curious about his protagonists' fates, especially Anta's, and revisited them nineteen years later when he made his second feature film, *Hyenas* (1992). According to Mambety, "I began to make *Hyenas* when I realized I absolutely had to find one of the characters in *Touki-Bouki*."[17] He explains, "In *Hyenas* the two characters from *Touki-Bouki* reappear: the girl who leaves to cross the Atlantic and the boy who stays on the continent as if he has betrayed her."[18] In *Hyenas*, Mambety's vision has become more lyrical but also more pessimistic, adapting Friedrich Dürrenmatt's play *The Visit* to portray the corrupting influence of greed and indict the ruthless policies of the International Monetary Fund and the World Bank for their elevation of financial profit over human life. *Hyenas* was Mambety's last feature-length film. He died of lung cancer in 1998 at the age of fifty-three.

The 1995 French film *La Haine*, directed by Mathieu Kassovitz, can be seen as an alternative vision of what might have happened to Mory and Anta (or, more accurately, to their children if they had had any), had they sailed to Paris together. Mory dreamt of French riches and of the glamour promised by Josephine Baker's lyrics, but in *La Haine* the lives of dispersed postcolonial subjects in France are anything but glamourous. As the title suggests, *La Haine*, which won the award for Best Director at the 1995 Cannes Film Festival, is shot through with rage at the continued existence of French racism and institutionalized injustice.

La Haine concerns three young men who live in an HLM (*habitation à loyer modéré*), a low-income housing project in a working-class *banlieue* outside Paris. Each of the three friends represents an immigrant group: Sayid (Saïd Taghmaoui) is of Arab descent, Vinz (Vincent Cassel) is Jewish, and Hubert (Hubert Koundé) is of African descent. *La Haine* revolves around the violence and frustration of everyday life in the *banlieues*, where residents encounter constant hardships that include their vilification by the police, the media, and the French political right wing. As professor of French studies Kevin Elstob writes in a review, "*Hate* covers much terrain. It interweaves root causes of social and political unrest in France today: immigration, racism, exclusion, poverty, crime, and violence."[19]

What Mory and Anta in *Touki-Bouki* did not realize is that one of the legacies of French colonialism is a strong French right-wing hatred of immigrants from the former colonies. The issue of immigration has generated enormous tension in France and has revealed the depths of right-wing racism in the xenophobic rejection of immigrants and their descendents. The official French policy of transforming colonial subjects into French citizens through education never resulted in widespread acceptance of those new French citizens in France. According to Alec G. Hargreaves and Mark McKinney,

> Tensions are nowhere more acute than in relation to minorities originating in ex-colonies who have now settled in France. French-speaking to a very large extent, yet culturally distinct in other ways and still marked by exclusionary memories of the colonial period, these minorities defy the political logic of francophonie by being residents and in many cases citizens of France while appearing to many among the majority population to belong elsewhere.[20]

Hostility is directed not only at the immigrants themselves, but also at their descendents. As Hargreaves and McKinney write, "These aspects of the neo-colonial gaze affect second- and third-generation Maghrebis [North Africans] as much as their immigrant forebears."[21] There have of course been a few immigrants who have been treated as dignitaries in France, including Leopold Senghor, the first president of Senegal after it gained its independence from France in 1960, who held office until 1980, retired from politics to Normandy with his French wife, was elected to the Academie Française, and on his ninetieth birthday was honored by French president Jacques Chirac.[22] Hargreaves and McKinney observe, however, that

> the majority of France's post-colonial minorities are to be found in more humble milieux, foremost among which are the *banlieues* (literally, "suburbs"), which in the 1990s have become a byword for socially disadvantaged peripheral areas of French cities containing relatively dense concentrations of minority ethnic groups.[23]

Mory and Anta, unlike their countryman Leopold Senghor, might easily have ended up in a *banlieue*, and if they had had children, those children might have grown up in the milieu depicted by Mathieu Kassovitz in *La Haine*.

Vinz, Hubert, and Sayid are angry, disaffected rebels stuck in a low-income concrete *banlieue* and contemptuous of conformist drones. They wear tight jeans and leather jackets and swagger like the juvenile delinquents who caused a nationwide panic in the U.S. in the 1950s. The rebel swagger fortifies the three French friends against a consistent pattern of police brutality directed against minority racial and ethnic groups relegated to the desolate margins of the city. The three friends are fully aware of their outsider status, and it is their shared sense of entrapment in a rigid class system that allows their friendship to transcend the conflicts that divide their ethnic and racial groups. When they get annoyed with each other, they often hurl racial and ethnic epithets, but the insults are used loosely and metaphorically, so that even the Jewish Vinz asserts that he doesn't want to be "the next Arab iced by the pigs." These are rebel outsiders whose lives are in jeopardy every day. The film centers on two themes: the first is the nature of the police force and its relationship to discontented young people, and the second is the problem of where alienated youths can turn for meaningful guidance. Unlike the protagonists of fifties teen rebel films, the three young men in *La Haine* do not expect much from their families. Instead, like the young castaways in *The Doom Generation*, *Boys Don't Cry*, *Wild Child*, and *Lilya 4-Ever*, they turn to pop culture and the media for their life lessons.

The three young men's bleak lives are conveyed in *La Haine*'s stark black-and-white cinematography and in their aimless drift through about twenty hours, which is given structure by means of intertitles announcing the time of day. The narrative begins at 10:38 one morning and ends at 06:01 the following morning. This structural precision contrasts sharply with the unstructured quality of the young men's lives, which are at once chaotic and static. At several moments in the film, an intertitle announcing a change in time interrupts a scene, only to return to the same scene and virtually the same shot: nothing has changed. The stasis implied by the film's repetitive shots captures the young men's sense of entrapment. But *La Haine* is not only a film about bored, restless kids without purpose in their lives, for these young men are caught up in fierce social conflicts and political battles. The dilemma they face is how to respond effectively, how to be authentic rebels when the rebel stance packaged by the media is hopelessly incapable of providing clarity or producing results.

The film's main theme is the question of how to respond to violence. It is introduced in the prologue when, accompanied by a black screen, a voice-over asks, "Heard about the guy who fell off a skyscraper? On his way down past each floor he kept saying to reassure himself: 'So far so good.'" The black screen dissolves to a long shot in color of the Earth in space, and the voice continues: "How you fall doesn't matter. It's how you land." At this point, a Molotov cocktail falls to Earth from space, and the planet explodes, followed by a black-and-white shot of an exploding car and the unfolding confrontation between protesting young people and riot police. A television newscast reports that the riots, in which young people attacked a police station in the Muguet projects, began two days ago in response to alleged police brutality. A local teenager was severely beaten under questioning and the police officer responsible was suspended. The victim, Abdel Ichaha, is hospitalized in critical condition.

The planet Earth, destroyed in the prologue by the Molotov cocktail, is a motif in the film, appearing on billboard advertisements accompanied by the words, "The world is yours" (*Le Monde est à vous*). This phrase refers to the 1932 gangster film *Scarface* (Howard Hawks), in which the rise and fall of kingpin Tony "Scarface" Camonte (Paul Muni) is underscored by a sign emblazoned with this phrase. When Tony is at the height of his power, surrounded by wealth and luxury, the world is indeed his, but at the end of the film, the same phrase is cruelly ironic; Tony's world has crashed around him and he is killed by the police. In *La Haine*, the phrase is never anything but ironic, since the three young men never experience a rise to success. To them, the phrase is a cruel taunt, causing one, Hubert, to squeeze his eyes shut in an agonized grimace when he reads it, and another, Sayid, to spray paint the word *vous* to read *nous*, meaning "The World is ours." By the end, it is clear that the world is anything but theirs.

The idle young men in the *banlieue* have been left behind by the system; they have no hope of employment or escape from poverty. Gangsta rap music surrounds them, giving at least some vent to their frustration and providing them with a contemporary version of classic gangster tales like *Scarface*. *La Haine* illustrates three different styles of resistance to the system: Sayid is an opportunist and hustler who tries to turn situations to his advantage; Vinz tries to turn the violence of the system against it, becoming brutal in response to brutality; and Hubert desperately wants to escape and seeks a conciliatory stance that will end the self-perpetuating cycle of death. Sadly, the social forces they oppose prove too powerful for any of their strategies, and two of them are destroyed at the end of the film. Sayid, the opportunist, survives, but only through happenstance; clearly, he could be the next victim.

The teasing, bantering name-calling indulged in by the three friends contrasts with the virulent racism they encounter elsewhere. Most horrifically, Hubert and Sayid are tortured by a cop who has tied them to chairs in an interrogation room and beats and insults them. Before bringing them in, he proves himself no different from the criminals he is supposed to stop; he finds cocaine on Sayid and says "Good stuff, I'm keeping it" and

Hubert (left), Sayid (middle), and Vinz (right) get their bearings in downtown Paris in *La Haine*.

launches into a monologue on the merits of various kinds of cocaine. At the police station, he tells Hubert, whose arms and legs are bound, to pick something up with his feet "like your people do back home." The torturer tells another cop, "They're great with their feet." Sayid is called an "Arab sonofabitch" by the same cop. The cop's viciousness is a far cry from Jim Stark's gentle treatment in the police station in *Rebel Without a Cause*. Jim has a heart-to-heart talk with Ray (Edward Platt), an avuncular police officer who encourages him to punch a desk to let off steam and invites him to come back anytime. Hubert and Sayid are tortured. The cop in *La Haine* is a racist and psychopathic sadist, and the question posed by the film is whether he is an anomaly who has found an officially sanctioned niche to practice his violence or whether his brutal racism is instead a manifestation of the French power structure it is his job to protect and maintain.

There is ambiguity early in the film about whether the police are all corrupt thugs. A police lieutenant intervenes after the three friends get in a scuffle with police guarding the hospital room of their comatose friend, Abdel, the victim of police brutality. They are not allowed to see Abdel, and Sayid is arrested for his persistence. When the lieutenant tells Hubert and Vinz that the police are protecting Abdel, Hubert asks, "Who protects us from you?" Even after the lieutenant arranges for Sayid's immediate release, the three friends remain suspicious, and Vinz responds with disgusted rage when Hubert and Sayid agree to shake the lieutenant's hand. This cop appears to be concerned about their welfare, but Vinz rejects his goodwill. The film scorns the rhetoric of institutional benevolence. Even Hubert's moderate stance—his rejection of acts of violent retribution against the police—is only an acknowledgment of the overwhelming power of the police force, not a belief in the possibility of police altruism.

In a pivotal scene in a public restroom, Hubert and Vinz argue about the appropriate response to police brutality. Vinz has possession of a policeman's gun and has declared that he will shoot a cop if their friend Abdel dies. Their conversation begins as Hubert and Vinz relieve themselves, and Hubert says that "wanting to kill a cop is jackshit." Vinz responds that he didn't say that, only that if Abdel dies, he'll kill a cop, adding that without his gun back there (they just escaped from a pursuing cop when Vinz drew his gun and prepared to shoot, but Hubert, a boxer, punched the cop to prevent the shooting and allow them to flee), they would've been history, "or my name's not Rodney King." Hubert answers, "It's not the same thing." Vinz then accuses Hubert and Sayid of doing nothing to change things even though "we live in rat holes." He repeats that if Abdel dies, he'll kill a cop "so they know we don't turn the other cheek now!" Sayid interjects: "Wow! What a speech. Half Moses, half Mickey Mouse." Hubert points out that if Abdel dies, they lose a friend; but if Vinz kills a cop, cops don't all go away, adding, "You're just one guy. You can't blow them all away." Vinz asks, "Who made you a preacher? You know what's right and wrong?" Hubert responds that "in school we learned that hate breeds hate." Vinz answers, "I didn't go to school; I'm from the street. Know what it taught me? Turn the other cheek, you're dead, mothafucka!"

The film's tragic irony is that after a series of events propel Vinz to reject his vengeful stance, a new situation suddenly invalidates both of their positions and destroys them. First, a television news report announces that Abdel has died from his injuries. Sayid and Hubert abandon Vinz; Sayid says, "You want to kill a pig, go ahead. But you're on your own. We're outta here." Shortly after, a group of racist skinheads attacks Sayid and Hubert, but Vinz appears with his gun. All the skinheads but one scatter, and Vinz holds the remaining one at gunpoint, shouting to Hubert, "You think I'm all talk? Watch! Try and stop me!" Sayid does try to stop him, but Hubert takes the opposite approach, sarcastically urging Vinz on: "Go ahead and do it. Do your good deed! The only good skinhead is a dead skinhead: shoot him! . . . Do it for Abdel." After an agonizingly long pause, Vinz is unable to shoot the trembling skinhead. The prospect of shooting an unprotected human being at close range leaves Vinz shaking and gagging.

After Vinz' change of heart, events quickly come to a crashing end. The three friends catch the first morning train out of Paris to their housing project. Back home in bright daylight, they part in the courtyard, yawning after their night in the streets. Before he leaves, though, Vinz gives his gun to Hubert, signaling that cop killing is no longer his goal. Vinz and Sayid walk away, only to have a police car careen to a stop beside them and two policemen jump out and grab them. The cops hurl insults at them, and one cop points his gun directly at Vinz' head, taunting him and pretending to shoot. The gun suddenly fires, and the cop stares in surprise as Vinz slumps, dead, to the ground, killed as a result of a cop's cruel, careless bravado. Hubert has meanwhile run over to join his friends, and when Vinz is shot, pulls the gun Vinz had just relinquished to him and points it at the cop who fired the shot. The cop simultaneously trains his gun on Hubert. The cop and Hubert hold guns at each other's heads in an anguished stand-off that symbolizes the destructive futility of the larger confrontation between the police and angry youths. The voice-over from the opening of the film returns with the lines, "It's about a society falling. On the way down, it keeps telling itself, 'so far so good, so far so good, so far so good.' How you fall doesn't matter." The camera zooms into a close-up of Sayid's horrified face. As he shuts his eyes in a helpless grimace, there is an offscreen gunshot. The screen goes black as the narrator finishes, "It's how you land."

The film does not reveal who was shot, Hubert or the cop, but, clearly, Hubert is doomed either way. In a split-second decision, Hubert has sacrificed his life out of unspeakable outrage at the brutal murder of his friend Vinz. The film thus ends with an ironic and tragic twist that renders futile Hubert's avoidance of violent confrontation, because state-sanctioned police violence seeks out young minority men condemned as troublemakers. Up until the end, the film could be read as endorsing Hubert's pacifist stance, but that is no longer possible—or at the very least it is problematic—after the cop blows away Vinz.

Hubert, Sayid, and Vinz cast about for an effective response to state-sponsored violence, but their reference points are banal and trap them in incomprehension and paralysis. The "truths" to which the three friends turn time and time again all derive from pop culture and are incapable of providing adequate role models or solutions—or even posing the right questions. The references in the film are mostly, but not exclusively, from American films and TV programs. As Kevin Elstob writes,

Today's suburban Parisian youth thrive on Anglo-American rap, reggae, and rock music, incorporate American and African fashion into their dress code, and spray-paint New-York style graffiti on walls and bridges. At the same time, the immigrants among them are expected to assimilate in a country where 15 percent of voters back the National Front, the extreme right-wing political party whose xenophobic, reactionary platform advocates, among other things, repatriating all immigrants.[24]

The three friends in *La Haine* turn to the media to fashion their rebel personae, gazing into mirrors to practice the style they have chosen, much as Brandon Teena depends on mirrors to craft his good-old-boy persona in *Boys Don't Cry*. In his mirror, Vinz practices drawing a gun and mimics the notorious lines of Robert De Niro's character Travis Bickle in *Taxi Driver* (Martin Scorsese, 1976): "You talkin' to me?! You talkin' to me?!" Like Travis Bickle, Vinz has shaved head and bare chest. He chooses vigilante violence more because his idol Bickle resorts to violence than because he understands the ramifications of his choice.

Pop culture figures are the models for Vinz and his friends' self-creations. In his mirror, Sayid makes faces and says, "I'm Señor Duck: I fucka you, I fucka her, I fucka him . . ." He then asks Vinz to give him a haircut so he can get lucky with a girl that night. When Vinz butchers his hair, Sayid is furious, and Vinz tries to placate him by saying, "It's the style in New York. The killer cut. So stop whining." New York is their cultural mecca. Later, walking through the Parisian streets at night, they engage in an impassioned debate about the merits of American cartoon characters.

> Vinz: Coyote's a bad motherfucker. Roadrunner's a pussy. Pick between Tweetie and Sylvester.
>
> Sayid: . . . I say Sylvester's the real gangsta.
>
> Vinz: . . . I say Tweetie's the baddest. He always wins.
>
> Hubert: Sylvester fucks Tweetie and you! . . . Anyway, Sylvester's a black brother.

Their experiences are all filtered through entertainment. It envelops their lives, providing touchstones that are sometimes ridiculous (while botching an attempt to hotwire and steal a car, one asks the others, "How'd they do it on TV?" as they try to remember MacGyver's technique) and sometimes poignant, as when Hubert says that he identifies with Sylvester as a black brother.

Mass media imagery and iconography constitute a large part of the young men's shared experience in *La Haine*, but they are left without representational models equal to the complexity of their circumstances. Neither Travis Bickle nor the full roster of American cartoon characters can teach them how to effectively oppose racism, unemployment, poverty, or police brutality. *La Haine* shows that *banlieue* dwellers are not simply passive consumers of pop culture; they appropriate it passionately, but it lets them down. As Hargreaves and McKinney write,

> The markers—graffiti, music, dancing, dress codes, etc.—through which young *banlieusards* (literally, "suburb dwellers") seek to reterritorialize the anonymous public housing projects in which they are corralled are saturated with references to global networks of multiethnic youth culture in which they participate daily through the mass media.[25]

This reterritorialization, however, does little to touch the larger structural factors that keep youth so corralled. Kevin Elstob describes a significant scene in the film when the peacefulness of a quiet afternoon is shattered by music coming from two enormous speakers placed in the window of a fifth- or sixth-story apartment. A young disc jockey there mixes and samples Edith Piaf singing "*Je ne regrette rien*" (I Have No Regrets) and "Police," a powerful anthem by the French rap group Supreme NTM, sung in French with a chorus that includes the English line "Fuck the police."[26] The sampled music succeeds in providing a heightened sense of community among the disaffected young people in the *banlieue*, loudly announcing their rage and sense of alienation, but it cannot provide a solution to the young men's dilemma of how to respond to police brutality.

Ultimately, the film is ambiguous about whether pop culture is entirely a paralyzing trap for the young men or whether it also gives them a symbolic sense of strength. Traps are everywhere in the film's mise-en-scène, with its emphasis on circular courtyards, walls, locked doors, narrow corridors, claustrophobic rooms, and tunnels. Perhaps pop culture is as much a trap as the physical environment that prevents these young men from escaping oppression. However ineffective American pop culture is in the film, *La Haine* acknowledges that it is an undeniable aspect of young French people's lives, and the film does not endorse its control by the French state. A feature of French right-wing ideology is the desire to protect the French language from "corruption" by English phrases, and it was in this spirit that French president Chirac's administration was "fighting a hopeless rearguard action against the ever-widening inroads made by the English language and American popular culture into the everyday cultural practices of the French."[27] Hargreaves and McKinney point out that

> the latest innovation in this unequal struggle consisted of revised quotas, introduced at the beginning of 1996, requiring radio stations to prioritize "French" songs over those in other languages. One of the ironies of these and earlier quotas has been to facilitate the emergence of rap as a major force on the contemporary music scene in France. Short of new songs meeting the official quota criteria, broadcasters have filled their vacant air time with rap recordings by minority ethnic *banlieusards* featuring French-language vocals adapted from black American models.[28]

The French state's efforts to preserve an ideal of French purity are doomed given the hybrid nature of lived experience, certainly in postcolonial times, but even long before. Cross-cultural borrowings have a history that predates even the European "age of exploration." The notion of national purity is a mythic one:

> Few, if any, individuals are entirely mono-cultural. Although they may not always realize it, most people participate—whether as producers, consumers or intermediaries—in a variety of cultural communities. To the extent that a sense of identity is derived from such communities, multiple identities are the norm, rather than exceptional features of personal experience. The proliferation of ever more sophisticated communication networks implies, moreover, a constant challenge to simplistic notions of neat demarcation lines between "national" cultures. To a greater or lesser degree, all cultures are engaged in a constant process of renewal, which is driven in part by borrowings from elsewhere.[29]

One way in which pop culture's rebel stance shapes the young friends in *La Haine* is to validate their machismo. The fifties screen rebel's sexual ambiguity has been abandoned by these young men in favor of swaggering heterosexuality. Women in the film are primarily sex objects, and the young men treat them with a mixture of predatory fascination and disdain.

No matter how persecuted the young men in *La Haine* feel, they gain a sense of power from being men, but always at the expense of women. And while the three friends' bonds are tight, they lack homoerotic overtones.

La Haine broadens its context from the fifties rebel films' nuclear family to encompass vital political issues. The problems faced by Vinz, Hubert, and Sayid are more critical than those faced by Jim Stark in *Rebel Without a Cause*, who only had to contend with a dysfunctional family and high school bullies. *Rebel* leads us to believe that the police shoot Plato out of helpless ignorance, not viciousness, while *La Haine* shows us a consistent pattern of police violence against young residents of *banlieues*. The film refuses to engage in vilifying the young men's families for their problems, and it avoids *Rebel's* armchair psychology. The three friends in *La Haine* would have little to gain from reconciliation with their fathers; their problems are much larger and more profound.

La Haine is intelligently self-conscious about rebel film conventions and enlists them ironically, acknowledging that audiences expect to see certain conventions in films about teenagers but refusing to reduce the young men's circumstances to fit the conventional molds. The film pokes fun at its own status as a rebel film, with characters who shrug in clichéd despair at the state of kids today. In one scene, the three friends have been thrown out of an opening at an upscale Parisian art gallery for causing a disturbance. At the door, Hubert shouts back into the gallery, "Go suck cocks in hell." The gallery director turns to the elegant patrons and shrugs, saying, "Troubled youth!" But Sayid falls back on the same cliché after he berates his younger sister for skipping school and hanging out with her friends in the projects. "Kids these days!" he mutters in an exasperated tone. In yet another twist on the cliché, Vinz is chastised by his grandmother, who thinks he is responsible for burning down the school, and she predicts the trajectory of his bad behavior: "You'll start that way and then you'll skip Temple." Rather than condemn the grandmother for misunderstanding Vinz, the film and Vinz himself treat his grandmother with gentle amusement.

Rebel iconography, launched into the world in the fifties from the Southern California dream factory, is still a model for alienated adolescents, and alienation is an understandable response to the conflicts and tensions of the postcolonial world. In the rebel icon, disaffected postcolonial youths find the archetypal outsider, still exerting a powerful influence after half a century. While acknowledging the appeal of the rebel stance, *Touki-Bouki* and *La Haine* also challenge its ability to provide an effective position from which to oppose injustice. Eurocentrism, racism, poverty, and police brutality are crushing adversaries. Rebel iconography is no match for their devastating exclusivism and violence.

Even though Jim Stark's suburban existence in *Rebel Without a Cause* is far removed from colonial turmoil, James Dean's life was not. When he died in 1955, colonial subjects in Africa, Latin America, and Southeast Asia were organizing resistance to their European colonizers, and their efforts would soon erupt into violent wars of independence. Colonialism was on its way out during James Dean's life, and Dean's road to fame led him for a brief time into its sphere: for two weeks in 1954, he had a part on Broadway in the play *The Immoralist*, playing the role of Bachir, a gay young Arab in North Africa whose interactions with a visiting newly-wed French archaeologist are steeped in the tensions evoked by colonial power relations.

Written by Ruth Goodman Goetz and Augustus Goetz, *The Immoralist*[30] was adapted from André Gide's semi-autobiographical 1901 novel titled *L'Immoraliste*.[31] The plot of *L'Immoraliste* revolves around a French archaeologist, Michel, who arrives in ill health with his bride in French-colonized Algeria and there becomes enchanted by beautiful Algerian boys. Bachir, played by Dean in the stage version, is the young seductive servant who awakens Michel's desire. Upon first meeting Bachir in Gide's novel, Michel declares, "I notice that he is naked under his skimpy white *gamdoura* and patched *burnous*."[32] Smitten by Bachir and a succession of other boys, Michel resolves to regain his health. Gide writes, "This was more than a convalescence—this was an increase, a recrudescence of life, the afflux of a richer, hotter blood which would touch my thoughts one by one, penetrating everywhere, stirring, coloring the most remote, delicate and secret fibers of my being."[33] Michel's interest in Bachir only increases when he observes that Bachir is a thief—he resolves not to tell his wife that the young man has stolen her scissors—and he keeps from her his attraction to Bachir and the other boys he meets. The novel ends after the death of Michel's wife, Marceline, who has wasted away while Michel has recovered and led a double life in the company of the lovely boys he covets. The play ends differently. Rather than dying, Marcelline becomes pregnant. (The Goetz play spells her name with two els.) Michel leaves Biskra to follow his wife to France, where they tentatively agree to stay together and try to make their marriage work.

Rehearsals for *The Immoralist* were fraught with conflict having to do in part with what some of the cast members and other personnel perceived as Dean's rudeness and lack of discipline. Biographer Donald Spoto quotes

James Dean performs his alluring "scissor dance" as Bachir in *The Immoralist*, February 1954. (The David Loehr Collection)

playwright Ruth Goetz as saying, "The little son of a bitch was one of the most unspeakably detestable fellows I ever knew in my life. The little bastard would not learn the words, would not really try to give a performance, would not really rehearse. He drove us up the wall."[34] Louis Jourdan, who played the part of Michel, also found Dean intolerable, as did Daniel Mann, who replaced director Herman Shumlin near the end of the rehearsal period. But Geraldine Page, who had the role of Marcelline, sympathized with Dean and became his friend. He produced a very fine performance, and several reviewers gave him high praise, particularly for his sensuous "scissor dance." Dean, however, resigned, giving his two-weeks' notice just after opening night, and soon after left New York for Los Angeles and the part of Cal Trask in *East of Eden*.

A brilliant 1996 short story by American fiction writer and English professor Robert Ready, titled "Jimmy the Arab," extrapolates from Dean's brief stint as Bachir to explore the convergence of colonialism, sexuality, and stardom.[35] The story is told in the late twentieth century from Bachir's point of view after he has grown old and is under house arrest for his gay sexuality in postindependence Algeria. In Ready's story, Bachir/Dean challenges colonialism, myths of masculinity, and homophobia. The story derives its strength from the unexpected juxtaposition of James Dean with Orientalist ideology. In his highly influential analysis of Orientalism— western discourses about "the Orient"—the late Edward Said argues that "European culture gained in strength and identity by setting itself off against the Orient as a sort of surrogate and even underground self."[36]

> Taking the late eighteenth century as a very roughly defined starting
> point Orientalism can be discussed and analyzed as the corporate institu-
> tion for dealing with the Orient—dealing with it by making statements
> about it, authorizing views of it, describing it, by teaching it, settling it,
> ruling over it: in short, Orientalism as a Western style for dominating,
> restructuring, and having authority over the Orient.[37]

André Gide drew on standard Orientalist stereotypes of the Arab world, characterized here by Said: "The Arab is associated either with lechery or bloodthirsty dishonesty. He appears as an oversexed degenerate, capable, it is true, of cleverly devious intrigues, but essentially sadistic, treacherous, low."[38]

In Ready's story, Bachir has a double consciousness: he is the Orientalist caricature of an Arab, but he is also simultaneously aware of, and amused by, his status as a western stereotype. Ready gives Bachir knowledge of his own Orientalist origins in order to turn Orientalist discourse against itself, writing, "Though Michel couldn't accept himself, I was what Michel expected me to be, nothing more. By telling Michel to be Michel in the orchards, I was his image in the dark mirror, his way into himself at last. How convenient for him to find clarity for his European soul in the native Arab houseboy!" (65).[39] Bachir is sarcastic and mocking because he understands his origin in western myth, and he applies this knowledge to understanding the phenomenon of James Dean, who was also the object of projected fantasies, particularly sexual fantasies, and who was posthumously transformed into myth. Dean and Bachir both function as the "hypersexualized Other," a product of overheated colonialist ideology.[40] Ready's story disrupts Orientalist discourse and also disrupts mainstream James Dean iconography by asserting that Dean was the equivalent of an Orientalist "Arab" in fifties America. Ready's story states, "Jimmy and Bachir were once the same, just before James Dean became a hero" (66).

In the story, Bachir and Dean shared the same role, both on Broadway and in the cultures that produced them; they both knew that they represented forbidden pleasure for the repressed citizens of prim, authoritarian cultures. They were desired for their forbidden beauty and simultaneously denounced, and they filled a void for the dissatisfied citizens of powerful, arrogant nations. For Ready, Bachir was James Dean's most subversive role, far more interesting than the three watered-down "rebel" roles in his Hollywood films, and also the role that provides the most insight into how Dean functioned for 1950s America. Ready writes that "Jimmy was a Bachir at heart" (64), and, to elaborate, "Bachir was James Dean gone evil, gone sexual, gone into the Western dream of the Arab, into the orchards, gone to Eden and come back with awful knowledge of just how little the keepers of the garden really understood about everything growing in it" (65–66). French colonial ideology and American late-capitalist ideology share a profound ignorance about human desires. Bachir and Dean each constitute a subversive presence within the ideologies that produced them.

Bachir and Dean both represent a highly sexualized Other. As Edward Said observes, "Just as the various colonial possessions—quite apart from their economic benefit to metropolitan Europe—were useful as places to send wayward sons, superfluous populations of delinquents, poor people, and other undesirables, so the Orient was a place where one could look for sexual experience unobtainable in Europe."[41] Jarrod Hayes, in *Queer Nations: Marginal Sexualities in the Maghreb*, explains that "the colonization of the 'Orient' not only provided a convenient vacation spot for Western tourists, it also provided a playground for the relief of tensions engendered by Western sexual normativity."[42] For Europeans, the "Orient" took on connotations of sexual openness in opposition to repressive European constraints, and European writers—Flaubert, Nerval, Burton, Lane, Conrad, Maugham, and, of course, Gide—colluded with the colonial paradigm by engaging in "sexual tourism in literary discourses" when they wrote about "Oriental sex."[43] In particular, European literature engaged in what Hayes calls "homo sexual tourism" by projecting homoeroticism onto the "Orient."[44] The "Oriental" man was cast in colonialist ideology and in its literary productions as an exotic and enticing seducer—just like the character James Dean played in *The Immoralist*.

Sexual tourism can only be understood in relation to European homophobia, and colonialism was in part an effort to export homegrown homophobia to all the corners of the Earth. As Hayes writes, "Colonialism . . . undertook several missions, the civilizing mission, missionary evangelization, and conversion of natives to the missionary position."[45] Hayes describes the policing of sexuality as "heterosexualization," and while it was the official colonial policy, it was accompanied in colonial discourses by its corollary: a desire for release from European sexual deprivation and a yearning for sexual freedom.[46] Desire and condemnation were two sides of the same coin in the colonial enterprise, and sexual tourism in literature invoked both.

L'Immoraliste is a thinly disguised account of André Gide's own experiences during a series of visits to North Africa, sometimes in the company of French male friends who shared his penchant for North African boys, and sometimes with his wife, Madeleine. In a biography of Gide, Alan Sheridan explains that the Gides' marriage was never consummated; it "remained a mariage blanc"[47]; he describes Madeleine as Gide's "poor, uncomprehending wife" during one of their first Algerian sojourns.[48] Gide made frequent visits to North Africa as a young man, but he eventually learned that there was no need to leave France to arrange encounters with "exotic" boys. Sheridan writes of the time period shortly after Gide published *L'Immoraliste*,

> Gide invented very little and usually spoke in the first person. Most of his fiction so far derived from his own life, his family, his marriage, his travels: that life was now riven in two. In *L'Immoraliste*, he had tried to bring the two parts together. But it was an uneven meeting: most of the book concerns Michel's public life (career, marriage); the secret life, though central, being the cause of the hero's downfall, is only hinted at. Gide had said as much as he dared. His new, secret life was no longer something that happened in North Africa, separable off in a circumscribed, exotic frame; it happened in the streets and baths of Paris, its imperious demands requiring daily excursions when he was there and frequent trips to the capital when he was in Cuverville. What had once been on the exotic margin of his life was now at its centre.[49]

Gide's new life in Paris was consistent with Edward Said's observation that "in time 'Oriental sex' was as standard a commodity as any other available in the mass culture, with the result that readers and writers could have it if they wished without necessarily going to the Orient." [50]

Robert Ready's story proposes that American men during the 1950s could fantasize about "Oriental sex" with James Dean without having to travel to the "Orient," for American dominant ideology of the fifties shared with colonial ideology an obsessive heterosexualization, and James Dean was the "Oriental" object of taboo desire. Dean was young and beautiful, and he held most social conventions, including compulsory heterosexuality, in disdain. Hayes writes that "the revolution against colonial rule had also always been sexual," [51] and Robert Ready might respond that Dean's rebellion against fifties conformity was also always sexual, and this aspect of his rebellion had its most public display in his short Broadway appearance in the role of Bachir. Even though many of Dean's fans in the fifties and beyond were unaware of, or unwilling to consider, Dean's sexuality in the context of his rebelliousness, his appeal cannot be separated from the fact that "marginal sexualities imply and/or create marginal subjectivities." [52]

Bachir in Ready's story has grown old and discovered that he is no more welcome in Algeria after independence than he was under French rule. The governments that replaced European colonial rulers after independence were sometimes not only neocolonial (in the sense that they perpetuated European colonialist policies), but also resolutely homophobic. Some Marxist and nationalist discourses upheld homophobia, condemning homosexuality as "bourgeois decadence, a Western evil imposed by colonialism." [53] Hayes points out that even Frantz Fanon's influential anticolonialist book *The Wretched of the Earth* implies that compulsory heterosexualization is a necessary aspect of the process of forging a nation, so that Fanon "actually reinforces the power of a national elite that he opposes in *The Wretched of the Earth*. The national bourgeoisie he wishes to eliminate thus finds itself strengthened in the very work that advocates its elimination." [54] Many of the new African nations' citizens, who had fought revolutions to end the European colonial system of inequity and exclusion, found themselves still being excluded on the basis of their sexual orientation in the postcolonial era.

In Ready's "Jimmy the Arab," Bachir's homosexuality is perceived as a threat by both of the ideologies competing for dominance in postcolonial Algerian politics: Marxism and Islamic fundamentalism. Despite their condemnation and his house arrest, Bachir perseveres, for he has a fictional character's immortality. The iconic Dean is immortal too and will never reach old age. Dean's alignment with Bachir in *The Immoralist* lasted only two weeks, and he apparently did not regret his sudden departure, for he was frustrated by the intense friction between him and Louis Jourdan as well as Daniel Mann. For Dean, it was not a satisfying experience. In a letter to a friend during rehearsals, he wrote, "I am now a colourful, thieving, blackmailing Arab boy played by James Dean. Don't know who the hell I am. They are rewriting a lot. In rehearsals I was working for the elements of tragedy. A real tragedian's role, pathos etc. I turn out to be the comic relief. The Leon Errol of the show. 'Balls.'"[55] Even though his performance had garnered positive reviews, Dean gave notice and left for a career kick-start in Hollywood.

After his rise to success, sudden death, and meteoric posthumous fame, Dean's legendary persona was based primarily on his nonthreatening film roles. Only die-hard Deaners and biographers are familiar with his pre-Hollywood roles, but Bachir argues in Ready's story that he could still detect himself underneath the glossy surfaces of Dean's more buffed and polished film roles; he evaluates the James Dean film oeuvre and concludes that Dean's challenge to social conventions persists, albeit submerged. What Bachir proudly shares with Dean is thievery, and what they both stole was their cultures' complacent belief in a heterosexual masculine norm. Ready's Bachir says about Dean:

> He was a thief. In '54 Jimmy was in *Philco TV Playhouse*'s "Run Like a Thief," and in '55 he was in *U.S. Steel Hour*'s "The Thief." In 1954, the year he began to rise, we began to take back our country from those who had stolen it from us. He stole manhood away to a different place in the fifties, turned it on men, the way Jim Stark steals Cal Trask's last name and turns it inside out. Like the multisexual Byron his mother middle named him after, he stole sex, fame, and death.
>
> Jimmy was a great thief, would have been greater, had not the fates used those same scissors to cut his Spyder's thread that day in Paso Robles. He was never what manly men had in mind, always what they had to fear—another thieving Arab in their midst, grudging even the fight he had no choice but to get into. (65)

With his characterization of Dean as a thief, Ready continues his appropriation of stereotypes to "turn them inside out," here evoking the stereotype of Arabs as thieves. Jarrod Hayes refers to this stereotype in his analysis of the writings of Jean Genet, who was, like Gide, a French sexual tourist in North Africa. Hayes quotes Genet as saying in an interview:

"In Arab countries, in Third World countries, a young boy, as soon as he meets a white guy who pays him a little attention, can only see in him a potential victim, a man to rob, and that's normal."[56] Hayes comments: "Thus the former colonized are exploiting the former colonizers. In Genet's view, even when Moroccan tricks are not stealing, they are still thieves. The cliché is complicated by Genet's lifelong career as a thief and his glorification of thieves in his poems, novels, and plays, but the stereotype of the Arab as thief by nature still stands."[57]

Robert Ready's story also reproduces the cliché of the Arab thief, but in Ready's tone, unlike Genet's, there is mockery of Orientalist discourses and a recognition that an effective strategy for the victims of stereotyping can be to embrace the stereotype and aggressively use its power to offend. For Ready, it is not a coincidence that Dean played the part of Bachir; it was a public acknowledgment of the part he was playing in his life. Jimmy the Arab lurks within the James Dean who scowls at us from the commemorative postage stamp: he is the defiant young man who drew attention like a magnet and reflected back the dreams, desires, and fears of a nation that would celebrate him but not accept him for what he was.

Postcolonial persecution takes many forms, from the Eurocentric racism in *Touki-Bouki* and the police brutality in *La Haine* to the homophobia denounced by "Jimmy the Arab." The rebel icon bequeathed by the fifties has become a cliché inadequate to new global complexities. While it can evoke nostalgia for an era of idealistic revolutionaries who led their countries to independence, it cannot effectively oppose the inequities imposed by colonial legacies and the contemporary reality of globalization. But as *Touki-Bouki, La Haine,* and "Jimmy the Arab" show, its international presence as a symbol of resistance is undeniable, and it can be appropriated and remade in limitless ways for situations far removed from its original mid-century American context.

CHAPTER 6

The Posthuman Rebel

Of all of the decades of the twentieth century, the one evoked most obsessively by American pop culture is the fifties. Films, fiction, television, comic books, and computer/video games are fixated by that decade and have enveloped it in a haze of mythology that obscures our view of the period's actual events. Fredric Jameson refers to the fifties as the "privileged lost object of desire" for Americans in his influential analysis of the postmodern nostalgia mode.[1] In Jameson's analysis, "the fifties" have become a mythical historical time through frequent cinematic recycling, and their ubiquity is evidence of our contemporary inability to imagine a future; we inhabit a world in which the past, the present, and the future are all subsumed by a pastiche of earlier styles and themes. Even some films acclaimed for their highly innovative visions of the future are actually indebted stylistically and thematically to the mid-twentieth century. Among the films that have consistently conjured up the fifties are science fiction films—perhaps not unexpectedly, since the genre experienced its Golden Age during that decade.

Nowhere is this more apparent than in *The Matrix*, released in 1999 and lauded for its dazzling, futuristic environment powered by innovative special effects. Its enormous success bathed it in an aura of novelty and tended to obscure its nostalgic ethos and its similarities to earlier films, for, despite its breathtaking effects, the film hearkens back to the fifties. Rebellious youth, technological thrills, loss of identity, and conflicted relationships with mother figures are themes transported from the century's middle to its end. *The Matrix* is immersed in fifties cultural beliefs and film conventions, and its two sequels continue the trend. Nowhere is the trilogy's evocation of the fifties more apparent than in its reenactment of young white Americans appropriating black cool in an effort to become rebels. It is a distinctly Hollywood conceit to suppose that a style produced during centuries of black suffering should be bequeathed to a young white man who alone has the ability to use its powers to save humankind from extinction.

The Matrix not only looks cool; it is also about the attainment of cool, about the transformation of a geek into an icon of incomparable cool. Thomas A. Anderson (Keanu Reeves) is a nondescript company drone, the nineties' version of the man in a gray flannel suit, indistinguishable—except for his dissatisfaction with his monotonous life—from the other clean-cut corporate employees who labor at identical desks in their office cubicles. Anderson is also a misfit computer hacker who spends his free time alone at home. But he is destined to escape geekdom and become Neo, an incomparably stylish and composed master of his surroundings. *The Matrix* follows the process of his transformation into a man who is impervious to pain, who can dodge bullets effortlessly, who struts through the city with supreme nonchalance clad in a black trench coat, and whose insouciance becomes transcendent as he soars upward through the sky, leaving the phony city below. Neo continues to perfect his imperturbable self-control over the course of the next two films in the trilogy. Anderson's transformation from computer geek to superhero reenacts the familiar scenario popularized by comic books but dating back to earlier *übermensch* aesthetics of an unexceptional person's metamorphosis into an undefeatable powerhouse, a well-worn but still attractive fantasy. The goal in the *Matrix* trilogy is to achieve that most stylish of fantasy roles: the über-rebel.

Thomas A. Anderson's transformation into Neo in *The Matrix* recalls the fifties' appropriation of black cool by whites, for the film relies on black characters to guide its white protagonist toward truth and fashion flair. Although Keanu Reeves is biracial—Asian and white—the film does not present him in those terms, and his role in relation to the film's black characters evokes the fifties paradigm of white malcontents learning from black trendsetters. It is the black characters who reveal the artificiality of what passes as the world, and they lead their white protégé to the last vestiges of reality, in the process imbuing him with the telltale signs of cool. Neo learns sartorial style and nonchalance from Morpheus (Laurence Fishburne), his hip black guide, who shares his name with the Greek god of dreams and proves he is a hipster by teaching Neo the difference between phoniness and the real thing. Morpheus leads Neo away from fakery and instructs him in living an enlightened life, in seeing clearly, and defending himself with lightning speed and dexterity against the forces of deception. When the computer-generated *Matrix* society is seen in this light, its artificiality is not so much the problem, but rather its utter lackluster conventionality. Tellingly, its defense force, the Agents, are dressed in identical black suits—the ultimate western conformist attire—and their uniformity is proven in *The Matrix Reloaded* when Agent Smith (Hugo Weaving) self-replicates into hundreds of identical copies. Morpheus is cast in the role of leading Neo out of his unfashionable doldrums to the latest style—the newest, hippest, most happening scene.

Ironically, it is the plain old real world that Morpheus strives to attain. The goal is mundane, but the style—the cool mystique—is compelling. Even in the face of staggering odds, Neo embodies the "relaxed intensity" at the heart of cool.[2] His demeanor epitomizes self-control, and his speech is terse and unemotional. Keanu Reeves brings his minimalist acting style to Neo's cool aura and also lends sexual ambiguity to the role, for Reeves has a history of refusing to pin down his own sexuality in interviews, and he accepts that his characters appeal to gay men. His enigmatic sexuality heightens the *Matrix* films' link to the fifties, for there are interesting parallels between Reeves and James Dean, including their difficult childhoods, their aloofness, and their mysterious sexualities, as Michael DeAngelis explains in *Gay Fandom and Crossover Stardom*.[3]

Neo's unruffled poise functions narratively as defiance in the face of the Agents, but its more important role is to impress the spectator. Neo and his partner in cool, Trinity (Carrie-Ann Moss), communicate in a clipped, telegraphic style, and their sexiest moments occur when they walk knowingly into danger with long, relaxed strides, their faces utterly composed and opaque, and their lean bodies, clad in black leather, held erect and defiant. When Neo loses his sight in *Matrix Revolutions*, he accepts his blindness stoically and even develops a sightless way of sensing his surroundings, the kind of sixth sense implied by cool's aloof detachment. Wrapped in science fiction futurism, the *Matrix* trilogy is actually a throwback to a time when bored young white men and women seized a black style to escape conformity and imagined themselves to be electrifyingly charismatic.

Norman Mailer analyzed the phenomenon in *The White Negro* (1957), and the *Matrix* trilogy is uncannily reminiscent of his swaggering macho version of cool's crossover into white America. The trilogy's drab, unsatisfying world is suggestive of Mailer's description of post–World War II life: "These have been the years of conformity and depression. A stench of fear has come out of every pore of American life, and we suffer from a collective failure of nerve."[4] In the films, as in fifties America, a postwar world has been cowed into submission by an overwhelming technological

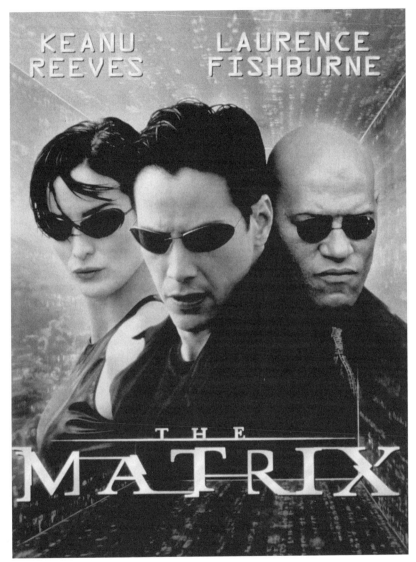

Trinity, Neo, and Morpheus exude cool in a poster for *The Matrix*.
(MovieGoods)

threat. Here the *Matrix* trilogy aligns itself with fifties science fiction fears of the bomb and the related threats of mutant life forms, alien invasion, and malevolent anti-human technology. The *Matrix* films' premise—that humans were defeated by machines in a devastating war—evokes the Second World War as the defining moment that drained vitality from

American society and spread the specter of death throughout a world stunned by the monumentally destructive power of atomic weaponry. The films' only hope is that a few individuals will resist conformity in the manner of the fifties hipster who adopted the role of the dissenting loner. "You can't interview a hipster," states a 1957 *Harper's Bazaar* article, "because his main goal is to keep out of a society which, he thinks, is trying to make everyone over in its own image."[5]

In the *Matrix* films, the AI regime has literally remade everyone in its own image of what a smoothly functioning human society would look like. The American hipster's distrust of the status quo might have seemed paranoid during the fifties, but paranoia is the only appropriate response in the trilogy, with its literal incarnation of the kind of bloodless society of drones that hipsters loathed. Mailer writes that for the hipster, "new kinds of victories increase one's power for new kinds of perception; and defeats, the wrong kind of defeats, attack the body and imprison one's energy until one is jailed in the prison air of other people's habits, other people's defeats, boredom, quiet desperation, and muted icy self-destroying rage."[6] In the *Matrix* scenario, human energy is literally imprisoned in vats, and Thomas A. Anderson leads an illusory life of boredom and quiet desperation until he is rescued by Morpheus, just as fifties hipsters imagined themselves rescued by the example set by black Americans, whose profound alienation from mainstream culture was long-standing.

> And in this wedding of the white and the black it was the Negro who brought the cultural dowry. Any Negro who wishes to live must live with danger from his first day, and no experience can ever be casual to him, no Negro can saunter down a street with any real certainty that violence will not visit him on his walk . . . The Negro has the simplest of alternatives: live a life of constant humility or ever-threatening danger.[7]

During the fifties when Jim Crow laws and lynchings were still common, black Americans did indeed face constant danger. Their marginalization from the American Dream success story made it possible for them to adopt a detached perspective on its ideology. Blues historian Paul Oliver writes that "in spite of the advances made during the post-war years, Blacks in the 1950s were still predominantly employed on unskilled or semi-skilled labor, and the educated intelligentsia represented a very small minority."[8] African Americans were for the most part excluded from the American Dream and faced continual racist harassment. They knew that it was a scary time and place to be alive and that daily life involved taking risks and weighing the consequences.

Morpheus and his band of outsiders in the *Matrix* trilogy also see the truth behind the artifice, but the films do not provide a historical context for Morpheus' acute perceptions. Instead, their premise is that black people are closer to reality than white people, are in fact "more real" than white people. This racist notion was widely disseminated in Eurocentric colonialist ideology and is dependent on a rigid classification of races based on supposed distinguishing traits, among them the contrast between white intellect and black physicality, between brain and body. Following from this is the essentializing myth that black people are less cerebral, closer to the earth, more natural, "more real." The *Matrix* films accept the colonialist paradigm by positing this as an inherent difference between black and white people, and there is no mention of their having had different historical experiences. This is what literature and film scholar James Snead means when he writes that "the history of black film stereotypes is the history of the denial of history in favor of an artificially constructed general truth about the unchanging black 'character.' We are being taken out of history into the realm of myth: things which never change, which were so at the beginning, are so now, and ever shall be."[9] Indeed, in *The Matrix*, Morpheus' small group includes both black and white rebels, but the black characters are coded as more "real." The vast majority of humans are seeded in vats; but two young black brothers, Tank and Dozer, were born from a human mother. Tank and Dozer also come from Zion, the last outpost of human civilization, located near the Earth's still-warm core—a heritage that only intensifies the impression of their "realness." Zion, we learn in *The Matrix Reloaded*, is populated predominantly by black people.

A racist paradigm associating black people with authenticity and life, and white people with artifice and death, runs throughout film history, as Richard Dyer has argued. He points out that in mainstream film, "white power secures its dominance by seeming not to be anything in particular, but also because, when whiteness *qua* whiteness does come into focus, it is often revealed as emptiness, absence, denial or even a kind of death."[10] "Life" is often associated with black film characters, and typically, he writes,

> tends to mean the body, the emotions, sensuality and spirituality; it is usually explicitly counterposed to the mind and the intellect, with the implication that white people's over-investment in the cerebral is cutting

them off from life and leading them to crush the life out of others and out of nature itself. The implicit counterposition is, of course, "death."[11]

This conventional cinematic opposition between "black life" and "white death," which has antecedents in literature and art, has created a situation in which

through the figure of the non-white person, whites can feel what being, physicality, presence, might be like, while also dissociating themselves from the non-whiteness of such things. This would work well were it not for the fact that it also constantly risks reminding whites of what they are relinquishing in their assumption of whiteness: fun, "life."[12]

Colonialism's ideological residue still permeates contemporary films, whether they are set in the distant past or the far-off future, with insidious ideas about what it means to be white or black through all time and in any conceivable place.

In *The Matrix*, the white predilection for artifice is on display both in Cypher, a white member of the rebel crew who chooses to betray his rebel colleagues in order to return to the comforts of the artificial Matrix, and in the trio of white Agents, with their icy demeanors, abhorrence for human smells, and desire to kill all humans. *The Matrix Reloaded* extends the white predilection for death, with its bleached-white twin killers, who periodically transform into eerie, swooping ghosts. This film also displays black "life" in a scene embarrassingly reminiscent of countless Hollywood "jungle melodramas"; the predominantly black population of Zion engages in frenzied dancing to the pounding rhythm of drums. In stereotypical Hollywood fashion, the war between artifice and reality is drawn along racial lines.

The circumstances of race relations are absent, even as a mythologized history of slavery is evoked when Morpheus reveals the hidden truth to Neo: "You are a slave, Neo. Like everyone else you were born into bondage, born into a prison that you cannot smell or taste or touch, a prison for your mind." He also asserts that "as long as the Matrix exists, the human race will never be free." His references to slavery and bondage and the struggle for freedom evoke African American history, as does the haven provided by his underground barge, which is reminiscent of the Underground Railroad's network of assistance for escaping slaves; yet the trilogy's hero is not black, but a white apprentice. Neo's role is highly overdetermined, not only evoking the second coming of Christ but also the freeing of the American slaves: the coming of "the One," says Morpheus, will "bring freedom to our people." In a common Hollywood pattern, black suffering and struggles are appropriated by a white protagonist. Neo, the white neophyte, is initially helpless—afraid of heights and, when released from his vat, weakened by atrophied muscles and never-before-used eyes—but eventually he surpasses his black mentor's bravery and combat skills, even having to rescue him in *The Matrix* and *The Matrix Reloaded*.

Neo's co-optation of black history and identity evokes Norman Mailer's claim that "the hipster had absorbed the existential synapses of the Negro, and for practical purposes could be considered a White Negro."[13] To hide the irony that a geeky young white guy is "the One," the savior who will lead "our people" out of bondage, *The Matrix* has Morpheus willingly choose to sacrifice himself to save Neo's life. As film scholar Linda Williams wryly observes about the continuing presence of the Uncle Tom figure in such films as *The Green Mile* and *Hurricane* (both also from 1999), "a reconfigured version of the Tom scenario still seems to be necessary to perform melodrama's moral legibility."[14] The fact that Neo saves Morpheus does not change the fact that the film appropriates African American history for a story about a young white man's heroism.

Neo's acquisition of cool—with its concomitant appropriation of black identity—accounts for some of the film's most breathtaking moments. With his brain plugged into a computer while his body reclines in a chair, Neo absorbs martial arts skills (which are appropriated from Asian cultures) directly from computer programs, and under Morpheus' tutelage he learns to become a first-rate fighter who understands the necessity of restraint and the power of efficiently directed movement. After some initial fumbling, he achieves an extraordinary level of control. This is cool. Richard Majors and Janet Mancini Billson emphasize the centrality of control:

> Being cool obviously means being in control and invulnerable in the face of crushing odds. It means weaving a web of insensitivity to pain and trouble that cannot be cut through by knives, clubs, guns, or words. The tough side of cool is that it involves risk-taking. To remain cool against well-armed police is to risk injury, imprisonment, or death. Lyman and Scott describe coolness as poise under pressure. The cool male can act and talk in a smoothly controlled fashion even in the tightest of corners. He can remain detached even in the face of emotionally charged situations. Playing it cool is a survival technique and a risky business.[15]

Neo dodges bullets with cool finesse in *The Matrix*. (MovieGoods)

In the martial arts sequences, Neo's body is inert, yet it is his remark-ably energetic martial arts combat with Morpheus that defines his meta-morphosis. These sequences are a cinematic tour de force, but behind the cutting-edge style lies Mailer's description of the hipster's cool mode: "the emphasis is on energy" because hipsters "are nothing without it since they do not have the protection of a position or a class to rely on . . . So the language of Hip is a language of energy, how it is found, how it is lost." [16] Hip vocabulary thus relies on words like "go," "make it," "with it," and "swing." "Movement is always to be preferred to inaction." [17] The *Matrix* trilogy makes good on Mailer's claim that movement is fundamental to the hipster creed; from the opening sequence of the first film, when Trin-ity defeats the Agents pursuing her by leaping and twirling and bouncing off walls and ceilings, the films are a swirl of energetic momentum. It is of course highly ironic that all of this movement occurs only in the minds of the participants while their bodies are motionless, but this irony is an es-tablished convention of the cyberpunk genre in films, fiction, and comic books. Phlegmatic computer nerds career mentally through cyberspace in sexy virtual bodies while their actual bodies remain immobile. In the *Matrix* films Neo's energy eventually surpasses everyone else's to the as-tounding degree that he can move faster than a speeding bullet in *The Matrix*, can fight off hundreds of Agent Smiths with lighting efficiency in

The Matrix Reloaded, and, even without the use of his eyes, can once and for all defeat the unyielding Agent Smith in *The Matrix Revolutions*. Neo is a model of Mailer's hipster, who "is seen more as a vector in a network of forces than as a static character in a crystallized field." [18]

The rebels of Zion are united in their desire to save humanity from imprisonment in the Matrix, but they are divided by their attitudes toward Neo, and the debate hinges on "faith." It requires faith to believe that Neo is "the One," and not everyone believes, as there is no objective proof. Instead, there is the Oracle (Gloria Foster in the first two films, Mary Alice in the third), a soothsayer who prophesies the rebels' future. Morpheus, the staunchest believer in Neo, takes Neo into the Matrix to meet her after building up his, and our, anticipation that she will be a mysterious figure. Instead, she is a familiar looking matronly black woman living in a graffiti-splattered, low-rent urban apartment building. Neo is ushered into her kitchen and finds her wearing an apron and baking cookies. She puts him at ease by speaking to him in a soothing voice and checking his throat and ears like a mother concerned about her little boy's health. The Oracle is a good mother who counteracts *The Matrix*'s acutely matriphobic depiction of human entrapment in womb-like containers from birth to death, bathed in pink amniotic fluid and penetrated by multiple metal tubes reminiscent of umbilical cords. The Oracle is different; not a possessive mother figure, she happily predicts the love between Neo

Neo faces off against Agent Smith in *The Matrix*. (MovieGoods)

and Trinity and sends Neo away with a freshly baked cookie and some oblique thoughts to ponder.

The Oracle becomes Neo's second black mentor. She rounds out his education by imparting wisdom, and in *The Matrix Revolutions* she indicates approval of the cool cat he has become by telling him that at first, "you were like a jittery June bug, and just look at you now!" However, her apron, ample figure, and kindhearted fussing over Neo are traits of a Hollywood mammy and perpetuate a longstanding stereotype associated with black women. Her patiently supportive role and mystical powers place her among similar black film characters who function to ensure a white protagonist's survival and success, what director Spike Lee calls "the magical mystical Negro"[19] and film scholar Krin Gabbard refers to as "black angels."[20] Spike Lee explains that several recent films feature "magical Negroes who appear out of nowhere and have these great powers but who can't use them to help themselves or their own people but only for the benefit of the white stars of the movies."[21] Even when they are not invested with magical powers, black characters in contemporary Hollywood films often have the same stereotypical Uncle Tom, Stepin Fetchit, and Mammy roles that date back a century to early shorts. Spike Lee points out that today, "they dress it up, they're slicker about it, it's much more sophisticated, but when you analyze it, it's the same old shit."[22]

James Snead identifies three cinematic tactics for perpetuating racial stereotypes: "mythification, marking, and omission."[23] Ahistorical stereotypes are disseminated through mythification; racial difference is unambiguously asserted when blackness is heightened through marking; and the infinite variety of black experiences is hidden through omission. The Oracle exemplifies the mythic figure. Krin Gabbard refers to her as "supernaturally nurturing" and deplores the tendency for white filmmakers to give us "a silly dream of black angels outside the everyday world but readily available when white characters need help."[24] He points out that these films are tapping into white guilt over slavery by promoting the classic fantasy that "the guilt for all those centuries of hatred and oppression can be wiped clean if the white man can find . . . the love and devotion of a powerful, dark-skinned man."[25] The *Matrix* trilogy joins other recent films with "black angels" in sending the message that "even if African-Americans *are* judging white people, they nevertheless find them to be worth saving."[26] Morpheus and the Oracle send that message, mobilizing all of their special powers to ensure Neo's survival, but their success can only be gauged by Neo's independence from them. In *The Matrix Reloaded*, they are still present to guide him, but their authority is now questioned, his level of cool having superseded theirs.

While Morpheus teaches Neo cool, the Oracle gives him faith, and the trilogy proceeds to evoke the world's religions with a grab bag of spiritual associations. The films' religious fervor might seem to contradict their commitment to the ethos of the fifties hipster; however, the hipster's sensibility connects with religious conviction via existentialism. Mailer observes,

> To be a real existentialist (Sartre admittedly to the contrary) one must be religious, one must have one's sense of the "purpose"—whatever the purpose may be—but a life which is directed by one's faith in the necessity of action is a life committed to the notion that the substratum of existence is the search, the end meaningful but mysterious; it is impossible to live such a life unless one's emotions provide their profound conviction.[27]

The *Matrix* trilogy includes existentialism in its religious and philosophical hodgepodge with an emphasis on individual choice, which in the second and third films is layered into the first film's spotlight on destiny. Neo learns he has to choose his fate and that this involves facing many dilemmas. The trilogy's existentialism culminates in the final rain-splattered showdown between Neo and Agent Smith in *The Matrix Revolutions* when Smith asks Neo why he perseveres, and Neo responds, "because I have a choice." Neo has become super-cool and proves he can integrate the lessons of Christianity, Buddhism, postmodernism, and existentialism passed on to him by the Oracle. But by making the Oracle the axis of their religious and philosophical content, the films play on "the well-established notion that black people are highly spiritual beings,"[28] a notion that derives from the same colonialist paradigm that associates black people with life and white people with death. Black spirituality, like black life, is an assumption based on the myth of an intuitive black connection with nature and the mysteries of the cosmos. Whites, in this opposition, are characterized as too rational to apprehend hidden truths.

Complimentary depictions of the myth of innate black spirituality are the other side of the coin of demeaning depictions, for stereotypes can be transmitted by "positive" representations of the Other as much as by "negative" representations. Edward Said supports this point in the context of Orientalism:

> Many of the earliest oriental amateurs began by welcoming the Orient as a salutary *dérangement* of their European habits of mind and spirit. The Orient was overvalued for its pantheism, its spirituality, its stability, its

longevity, its primitivism, and so forth . . . Yet almost without exception such overesteem was followed by a counter-response: the Orient suddenly appeared lamentably under-humanized, antidemocratic, backward, barbaric, and so forth.[29]

The name "Zion," given to the underground city of free humans populated primarily by black people, also evokes black spirituality by suggesting the dream of Christianized slaves finding a safe haven in "the promised land" and the Rastafarian belief in a utopian society. When we arrive in Zion in *The Matrix Reloaded*, we meet another black mentor, real-life African American philosophy professor Cornel West, in the role of a councilor. Additionally, a new black operator has been recruited for Neo. Predictably, the mostly black residents of Zion let loose with a Dionysian revel; their wild dancing is crosscut with Neo and Trinity making love, with the parallel editing suggesting that the white couple are caught up in the orgiastic excitement. The sequence perpetuates the colonialist European characterization of African dance as lewd and aphrodisiac. Unbridled black physicality is yet another embarrassing and essentializing cliché in the trilogy's version of a young white man's assumption of the mantle of cool.

Ironically, the trilogy obfuscates its appropriation of black history at the same time that it is about eliminating obfuscation from human lives. In the films, the Matrix functions as a concrete version of ideology, a false set of beliefs literally plugged into imprisoned brains, and it is remarkably successful in keeping the vast majority of humans, who do not know any better, satisfied. The AI regime unleashes its Agent Smith program only because Morpheus and his band of rebels are determined to free humanity from the Matrix's illusions. The Agents are the coercive branch of the AI regime, its police force, called upon to crush resisters when the illusory Matrix fails to placate them. Marxist theorist Louis Althusser, writing about the workings of modern capitalist societies, concludes that brute police and military force were usually not necessary to control subjects, who were kept adequately submissive by such ideological state apparatuses (ISAs) as schools, churches, the legal system, and the arts. As long as people accept the status quo version of reality disseminated by the ISAs, those in power need not fear. In the words of Althusser, "the vast majority of (good) subjects work all right 'all by themselves,' i.e., by ideology (whose concrete forms are realized in the ideological State Apparatuses). They are inserted into practices governed by the rituals of the ISAs."[30] While the *Matrix* trilogy exposes the ideological stranglehold imposed by its AI rulers over humans, it simultaneously inserts its spectators into its own ideology, for cinema is one of the most powerful of ISAs.

With its mythification and its reliance on essentializing racial oppositions, the *Matrix* trilogy inserts spectators into an ideology of race that has perpetuated racist injustice for centuries. The trilogy gives major roles to black actors who play "positive" roles, but it does not evince knowledge about the historical and cultural contexts for its representations, thereby locating itself within a racial discourse that erases the specifics of black history and assumes the presence of innate black traits. As such, it is part of the powerful system governing contemporary race relations, for, as Michel Foucault—who rejects Althusser's version of ideology—explains, power does not emanate from a nefarious ruling elite; rather, it is produced at all levels and circulates throughout the social order. He writes,

> The omnipresence of power: not because it has the privilege of consolidating everything under its invincible unity, but because it is produced from one moment to the next, at every point, or rather in every relation from one point to another. Power is everywhere; not because it embraces everything, but because it comes from everywhere. And "Power," insofar as it is permanent, repetitious, inert, and self-reproducing, is simply the over-all effect that emerges from all these mobilities, the concatenation that rests on each of them and seeks in turn to arrest their movement."[31]

Foucault's model would suggest that the trilogy's resolution—when Neo travels to Machine City, the center of AI power, and strikes a deal that authorizes him to annihilate the rogue program Agent Smith—is an unlikely scenario for emancipation. It is a utopian dream in which power instantly dissolves and is replaced by a new liberated era made possible by Agent Smith's demise and portrayed as green and grassy, a visual release from the films' previous gray dystopian palette. History, however, suggests that power and its attendant discourses are threaded far too intricately throughout society for this sort of instantaneous freedom.

In the fifties, hipsters fancied that their cool mystique provided an escape from the tainted commercial world. Their dream was short-lived, for by the beginning of the sixties the advertising industry was already embracing the language of cool. Thomas Frank explains in *The Conquest of Cool* that by the late fifties, advertisers were chafing against the decade's stale and unimaginative commercial strategies. Frank argues that the advertising industry did not so much cynically co-opt the sixties counterculture as anticipate it in their attempts to find more creative ways to appeal to consumers. Hip consumerism was the answer, a consumerism "driven by disgust with mass society itself."[32] Advertisers were "drawn to the counterculture because it made sense to them, because they saw a reflection of the new values of consuming and managing to which they had been ministering for several years."[33] Counterculture youth in the sixties defined themselves in part by their shared styles in clothing, music, art, and other "lifestyle" symbols. Their goal was to distinguish themselves from their parents, and consequently they comprised a market ready and willing to buy fashionably defiant accoutrements. Corporate capitalism received a boost from this eager new market and from the discourse of hip that opened up new advertising approaches. Americans were exhorted to "be different," to "buck the trend," to "be themselves," to "be a rebel" by purchasing a particular car or cigarette brand or soft drink or beer or chewing gum. It helped that cool exalts the new and disdains the old, an attitude conveniently consistent with corporate capitalism's strategy of planned obsolescence. Cool had been conquered, and it continues to provide much of the imagery and language of advertising to this day, when, determined to be at cool's cutting edge, corporations employ market researchers to "cool hunt" by scouring the world's youth cultures for the next exploitable trend.

It should therefore come as no surprise that the *Matrix* trilogy's commitment to cool is itself a marketing strategy. The first film was a phenomenal success for Time Warner, and although the two sequels were less of a sensation, the trilogy as a whole has been hugely profitable. The irony, as *New York Times* columnist Frank Rich points out, is that Time Warner—"the powerful machine behind the films"—accomplished the equivalent of the AI regime's deceptive manipulation of human brains while it drained human energy as a power source.[34] Time Warner "pulled off a comparable feat by plugging the country into its merchandising program for *Matrix Reloaded* to loot our wallets."[35] Media giants like Time Warner continue to consolidate their ownership of the entertainment industry with FCC approval, eliminating competition while seizing monopoly control. They are today's ruling powers, with immense influence over what we see, hear, know, and think. We live in their matrix. What better device to obscure their power than the figure of Neo, the underdog hero who fights the forces of omnipotent control, all the while embodying unsurpassable cool. With the *Matrix* trilogy, a media giant wrapped itself in cool like a fifties hipster, only corporate hipsters do not fight the power. They are the power.

CHAPTER 7

The Virtual Rebel

On the World Wide Web, you can enter your birth date and, on the basis of biorhythms, learn your compatibility with James Dean. After performing nearly instantaneous calculations on my date, the Web site informed me that I am 38% compatible with Dean, and it detailed the precise nature of our compatibility: physical 91%, emotional 0%, and intellectual 23%.[1] Elsewhere on the Web are the results of a poll that had asked, "What's your favorite James Dean feature?" The 793 votes are divided this way:

Eyes (347)	44%
Hair (142)	18%
Lips (141)	18%
Body (71)	9%
Other (92)	12%[2]

On another Web site, someone ponders the irony that "it's strange that some people try so hard to be like James Dean, when he didn't even want to be himself throughout his life."[3]

There are hundreds of James Dean Web sites, including the self-proclaimed "official" one belonging to CMG Worldwide, the company that owns the rights to James Dean merchandising and endorsements after winning a high-profile 1992 lawsuit against Warner Bros., which had also claimed to own those rights. CMG's site can be viewed in Spanish, French, Chinese, German, Japanese, English, Portuguese, Korean, and Malay.[4] On the many Dean-related Web sites, people express their devotion to Dean and reveal the extraordinarily diverse responses he evokes.

Magazines promise to reveal the truth about James Dean. (The David Loehr Collection)

Indeed, James Dean is continually reinvented on the Internet; galleries of online portraits have been created that have only a tenuous connection to the actual person who died in 1955. The Deans found online are "copies of copies," not quite constituting Baudrillard's simulacra, in which copies are generated without the existence of an original.[5] Virtual James Deans retain a connection to the actual James Dean, and the knowledge that there was once an authentic Dean animates the enterprise. Online manifestations of Dean may stray wildly from his life story, yet they are rooted in an awareness that there was once a flesh-and-blood James Dean who can be revered, idolized, imitated, or mocked. Authenticity is a crucial and intense element of the James Dean mystique; it does not, however, impose the expectation that all evocations of Dean will be constrained by accuracy.

It is tempting to assume that over time and through electronic mediation, the actual James Dean has become more remote and our access more limited, but in truth, access to him was already severely restricted during his lifetime and immediately after his death. Warner Bros. and Hollywood's star machinery in the form of gossip columns and fan magazines manufactured an inaccurate portrait of Dean during his brief career, and the posthumous stories that circulated were mostly frenzied fantasies. Despite magazines' claims that they would divulge "the truth" about the "real" James Dean, stories were either carefully constructed

James Dean adorns magazine covers internationally. (The David Loehr Collection)

by the Warner Bros. publicity department or, after his death, were the projections of fans with lively imaginations who claimed that they had been romantically involved with him or that he was still alive. One story printed after his death declares in its headline: "Jimmy Dean's Alive!" and continues,

> Now it can be told: JIMMY DEAN WAS NEVER KILLED! Based on information from authoritative sources, the editors of PRIVATE LIVES believe that Jimmy is really secretly hiding somewhere in NEW YORK CITY. A reward of $50,000 is offered for information leading to the actual person of Jimmy Dean! Informed sources, whose names we cannot disclose, say that Jimmy was horribly mangled by that "fatal" accident last year. He is said to be afraid for the world to see his now-marred face. So to you, Jimmy, we write this open letter: Come out of hiding. Your fans love you—will always love you—no matter what you look like! Remember, the face doesn't make the man. Besides, today plastic surgery is easy and simple and relatively painless. It is better to have scars on your face than scars on your soul! So please come back, Jimmy—if only for the sake of your loving fans.[6]

Getting at "the truth" of the elusive Dean was usually the goal. Alice Packard's 1956 "The Real Jimmy Dean" begins, "For Jim, life was a quest and his goal was to find himself. How well did he succeed?"[7] The 1956 "Melancholy Genius" exclaims, "He Carried His Doom Like a Banner," and promises "The Life Story of James Dean."[8] A magazine cover story from 1956 announces, "JIMMY DEAN RETURNS! Read His Own Words from the Beyond." The following words extend from the lips of a ghostly pale Dean: "How I found a new life beyond death through one girl's love."[9]

While he was still actually alive (as opposed to being posthumously declared alive), tabloids published stories that variously characterized him as tortured, demonic, strange, or heartbroken. One article, titled "Demon Dean," declares, "Out of the corner of his eyes he's daring Hollywood to change him. And telling the world in his bebop lingo, he means to act, not charm!"[10] Another article starts, "Take a good look at James Dean. He dresses—and behaves—like Brando. He admits he's a 'devil' and can't see how people manage to stay in the same room with him. Yet You Can't Ignore the New Scowl Boy."[11] Fan magazines published articles about Dean titled "Lone Wolf," "Tough Guy or Big Bluff?" and "Genius or Jerk?"[12] After his death, Dean stories and biographies were published in a variety of languages. A posthumous French biography is titled *James Dean, ou Le Mal de Vivre* (*James Dean, or the Uneasiness of Living*); the cover, underneath a drawing of a particularly tortured Dean visage, reads, *"Le vrai James Dean, épris d'absolu, avide de tendresse et amoreux de la vie"* (The true James Dean, caught up with the absolute, avid for tenderness, and in love with life).[13]

The virtual James Deans circulating on the World Wide Web decades after his death are no more ludicrous or bizarre than the fantasies that circled the globe during the 1950s. They are often thoughtful, funny, and creative. Their diversity reveals conflicting perspectives on how to remember Dean, polarized between the "official" site that keeps a lid on speculations about his bisexuality and on creative leaps of imagination that use Dean as inspiration for free-ranging riffs. In the official site and others like it, Dean tends to be associated with homespun virtues and a media-driven nostalgia for the fifties, from which he emerges as an emblem of bobby socks, rock 'n' roll, and vintage cars. (Dean himself is quoted as having said, "I'm not the bobby-sox type."[14]) In the "unofficial" sites, Dean is anything anyone might want him to be. Since the advent of the World Wide Web, the dissemination of James Dean musings is no longer controlled by official channels; fans—and detractors—can circulate their thoughts without access to a magazine or book publishing deal or a multi-million-dollar film budget. Communication between fans has become easier with the Internet, and interest in Dean is flourishing as a result.

The virtual James Deans who thrive on the Internet are symptoms of a digital age characterized by contradictory urges. We desire both hypermediation, or the desire for a proliferation of media effects, and immediacy, or the desire to erase all traces of mediation and achieve a direct experience of unmediated reality. Virtual reality, for example, strives to duplicate our experience of "the real" by using increasingly sophisticated technology. This "double logic," write media scholars Jay David Bolter and Richard Grusin, wants "ideally . . . to erase its media in the very act of multiplying them,"[15] dictating that "the medium itself should disappear and leave us in the presence of the thing represented: sitting in the race car or standing on a mountaintop."[16]

Illusionism is not new; it has motivated developments in realist aesthetics for centuries, for example, in seventeenth-century paintings that use linear perspective and careful lighting techniques to achieve verisimilitude. In certain media, such as film, the aesthetic of illusionism has reigned supreme, pushing other approaches to the margins, where experimental work resides until it is noticed and devoured by the center, which typically subordinates it to the well-established pursuit of illusionistic immediacy. Many, if not most, applications of digital media have pursued the same objective: the erasure of their own presence as they attempt to produce a "real" experience. However, as Bolter and Grusin explain, hypermedia and transparent media "are not striving for the real in any metaphysical sense. Instead, the real is defined in terms of the viewer's experience; it is that which would evoke an immediate (and therefore authentic) emotional response."[17] Our experience of "the real" is complex, for it has already been subsumed by previous exposure to media conventions, so that when we evaluate the "reality" of a media presentation, we compare it to our accumulation of other media experiences more than to our knowledge of "actual" reality. Our previous exposure to screens determines how we respond to new screened material.

The phenomenon of immediacy/hypermediacy can be likened to the project of celebrity worship: both are fueled by the desire to transport people into what promises to be a more satisfying reality. Stars, like the media, embody a double logic: they are actual people who live everyday lives, and they are also perceived as celestial beings, beyond human, who live life with a vigor the rest of us can only dream about. When stars shimmer on the pages of glossy magazines or shine down from a bright, sparkling screen, they radiate pure energy and inhabit their bodies with carefree ease. They appear to transcend human weaknesses, especially when they're closely associated with the witty lines that roll effortlessly from their lips in films and on television. The demands placed on stars by the public are not unlike the contradictory impulses of immediacy and hypermediacy: give us an image of your perfect lives, but also provide us with direct, unmediated access to your flaws and misfortunes; erect the barriers of star mythology, but simultaneously break them down to reveal the sophisticated machinery behind them.

When star mythology and electronic technology join forces on the Internet, they illustrate their double logics and the various ways that people negotiate them. The Net has made fandom more visible and less regulated, creating an easily accessible forum for all kinds of star worship. Although there are hundreds of Web sites that express devotion to James Dean—originating in France, Germany, Italy, England, Spain, Argentina, Brazil, Japan, the United States, and elsewhere—not all Web references to Dean are adulatory. Fiction writer Robert Brady published a satirical treatise on the phenomenon of the James Dean look-alike in the online magazine *Eclectica* in 1998. It is titled "The James Dean Parameters," and with the breathless pace of a protracted tongue-twister, it submits the existence of look-alikeness to minute scrutiny. It begins like this:

> We're all more or less aware of the parade of James Dean look-alikes that Hollywood has trotted out over the years since James Dean finally gave us all a precise idea of what a James Dean look-alike should look like. But how many of us are aware of the privilege we enjoy in this regard? It wasn't always this way. People in 1912, to pinpoint just one example, hadn't the slightest idea what a James Dean look-alike should look like, since James Dean hadn't been born yet, so there was no one to resemble, a palpable deficiency that stretched from the mid-1950's all the way back to the beginning of the human race! But even though nobody knows for sure who was the very first guy to look like James Dean, it's certain there were quite a number of pre-James Dean James Dean look-alikes, before the person we now know and accept as exemplifying authentic James Deanicity came along and established once and for all what all subsequent James Dean look-alikes would have to look like. As for the Deanless millennia, although via the movies we can't look very far back, historical detective work has led James Dean look-alike experts to conclude that the earliest verifiable example of a pre-James Dean James Dean look-alike lived in northern Russia early in the seventh century A.D., but of course that individual was quite a bit ahead of his time, as were the many previous, and subsequent, pre-James Dean James Dean look-alikes all the way through history, until James Dean came along and at last gave them all somebody to look like.[18]

The pleasure of Brady's piece is the detailed nature of its mock-serious analysis, which goes on to explain the ironies inherent in the fact that James Dean only looked like James Dean for a short period of his life, since the infant, child, and adolescent Dean cannot be said to look like James Dean. Brady punctures the Dean mystique with his satirical scrutiny and shows a canny awareness of the double logic of Dean: he existed in the form of an actual person, but he also exists in mythology that has its own strange assumptions, which, taken to their logical extreme, make possible pre-James Dean James Dean look-alikes.

At the other end of the spectrum is the "official" Dean site (www.james dean.com) owned by CMG Worldwide, which owns the James Dean name and image.[19] Its corporate ownership and its proclamation of officialdom set it up as the center of efforts to safeguard the sanitized James Dean. This site promotes the type of Dean resurrected in *The Love Bug* and commemorated on the 1996 U.S. postage stamp: a wholesome Dean appropriate for the whole family who personifies "simpler times" and small-town Midwestern American virtues. He is a good-natured farm boy, loyal to his friends and family, blessed with talent that is intrinsically linked to Fairmount and has also manifested itself in Fairmount's other notable natives. It is a reassuring portrait, one that imposes clarity on a life that, according to most accounts, was marked by confusion. Clarity is evident in the site's style as well as its content, with a clear, uncomplicated layout and straightforward links. Its home page features a paragraph written by Marcus Winslow, Dean's cousin, who succinctly summarizes the small-town Dean:

> I'm Jimmy's cousin and I grew up with Jimmy on our farm in Fairmount, Indiana. Growing up Jimmy appeared to be just another Grant County boy growing up in a small Indiana town. Jimmy played on the school basketball and baseball team and was, of course, Adeline Nall's favorite acting student in the drama club. When he went away to be an actor, we had no way of knowing how much he would affect the world. To the world, James Dean is loved and revered as an American Icon—to me, he's just "Jimmy."[20]

This text is accompanied by a photograph of Winslow as a young boy straining to pull a little red wagon in which the adolescent Jimmy is sitting. Needless to say, the restless, strung-out James Dean who resided in cheap hotels in New York and seedy low-rent apartments in Los Angeles is not in evidence at JamesDean.com.

The rest of the site features information about Dean, including a biography, filmography, quotes, photos, racing career, trivia, and, perhaps most importantly, James Dean collectibles (books, videos, DVDs, and "special offers"). CMG Worldwide is after all a commercial enterprise, and its self-description on JamesDean.com boasts of being "among the most prestigious in the licensing industry." CMG has its headquarters in Indianapolis, Indiana, with additional offices in Hollywood and Rio de Janeiro; the company "secured its position during the 1970s as the premier company for representing the families and estates of deceased celebrities. Today, CMG Worldwide represents over 200 diverse personalities and corporate clients in the sports, entertainment, and music fields." Its list of other clients' sites includes celebrities who are alive (Sophia Loren, Bill Elliott) as well as deceased (Marilyn Monroe, Babe Ruth), and the company's own Web site announces that this week's "featured site" is "The Official Jascha Heifetz Site."[21] Jascha Heifetz, James Dean, Babe Ruth,

Marilyn Monroe: the specifics of their lives and accomplishments blur into an amalgam of homogenous celebrity.

The "official" Dean site is designed in part to generate excitement around the annual "Museum Days / Remembering James Dean" festival in Dean's hometown in late September, commemorating his September 30 death. The festival is an economic godsend to tiny Fairmount, which for these few days every year is overrun by thousands of visitors from all over the world who drop money on lodgings, food, carnival rides, and all manner of Dean souvenirs and gifts. Fairmount shines every year in late September and takes the opportunity to boast of its distinguished progeny. The Web site declares:

> It's no wonder Fairmount, Indiana, adopted as its motto "Fairmount—Home of Distinguished People." From this tiny Midwestern town have come numerous notables, including cartoonist and creator of "Garfield," Jim Davis; CBS National News commentator, Phil Jones; Director of the National Hurricane Center, Robert C. Sheets; famed military historian/author, Dr. James A. Huston; and Mary Jane Ward, author of the award-winning novel, *Snake Pit*.[22]

Not included is the text of a poem James Dean wrote about Fairmount when he was living in New York:

> My town likes industrial impotence
> My town's small, loves its diffidence
> My town thrives on dangerous bigotry
> My town's big in the sense of idolatry
> My town believes in God and his crew
> My town hates the Catholic and Jew
> My town's innocent, selfistic caper
> My town's diligent, reads the newspaper
> My town's sweet, I was born bare
> My town is not what I am, I am here.[23]

Dean's biographers agree that he eagerly left Fairmount as soon as he graduated from high school: Fairmount High's commencement exercises took place on May 16, 1949, and Dean departed for California by train on June 14.[24] Val Holley titles a chapter in his Dean biography, "The Recovering Hoosier," writing that "the remarkable thing about James Dean's Indiana background is that he rose above it. He threw off aspects that were limiting—racist and homophobic bigotry, small-mindedness—and retained only those that were charming and natural."[25] Holley describes Indiana's "dark past," explaining that the state was settled not from the east, but primarily from the south, "so its attitudes were largely southern."[26] Thus it became a Ku Klux Klan stronghold during the 1920s, and racist attitudes lingered there during Dean's lifetime and beyond. Dean's attempt at poetry was a condemnation of Fairmount's Klan-tainted racist past and its homophobia. He was repulsed by bigotry and by arbitrary constraints imposed by narrow-minded authorities.

Nevertheless, Dean's feelings for Fairmount were complicated, since despite its provincialism, it was nonetheless the home of people to whom he was close, among them the aunt and uncle who raised him (Marcus and Ortense Winslow); his two cousins, Joan and Marcus Jr.; his high school acting teacher, Adeline Nall; and his mentor, Reverend James DeWeerd. Dean returned to Fairmount several times after his 1949 departure, once in the fall of 1952. On a late-night whim in New York, he announced to friends Dizzy (Liz) Sheridan and Bill Bast that the best place to get a good meal was from his Aunt Ortense in Fairmount, so they packed up and hitchhiked there for a weeklong stay.[27] His last visit to Fairmount was in February of 1955, when he traveled there with photographer Dennis Stock and posed for him in down-home settings, including a cattle pen, where, surrounded by cows and observed by a curious pig, he knelt on the frozen ground and beat on a bongo drum. Stock's photo essay, titled "Moody New Star," was published in *Life* magazine the following month.[28]

One of Stock's Fairmount photos was the inspiration for "James Dean & the Pig," a poem by Joseph Like; it compares Dean's stance "leaning casual against the pig" to that of King Charles II in an oil painting showing him in bewigged finery standing beside his horse "back home again in England/bringing French plays and baroque/fashion . . . /And this is exactly how James Dean/is standing. In the center of the sty—/the dung & mud-splashed boards . . . /Ready to become anyone else but Jimmy Dean/from Gas City, from a long line/of farmers rising at 5 o'clock/& slopping the hogs."[29] Dean's regal bearing transcends the pig sty in Like's poem, which also asserts that true royalty is not a product of aristocratic heritage and can emerge instead from a long line of farmers. Such true aristocrats are refined even among pigs and mud.

A poem by Reuben Jackson takes a less sanguine view of Fairmount: "indiana is no place to be colored./(eyes on your every swagger.)/no homies to embrace/like sal mineo upside/griffith planetarium's darkness,/james dean's rose red lips/and jacket."[30] Jackson's poem is closer to Dean's own, but in all three—Dean's, Like's, and Jackson's—the idea is that James Dean had to bust out of Fairmount to live the life he chose.

Ironically, the town Dean chafed at now capitalizes on him. He is probably one of Fairmount's most lucrative commodities, and his appropriation by commercial enterprises is on full display there. The commercial aspect of Fairmount's James Dean enterprise is mentioned in a piece written for CBS News "Sunday Morning" by political correspondent and Fairmount native Phil Jones, who was assigned to cover the twenty-fifth "Museum Days/Remembering James Dean" festival in September 2000. In his article, titled "Going Home for James Dean: A Hometown Boy Reports on a Hometown Boy," Jones reports on the enormity of profits derived from Dean posthumously:

> Mark Roesler manages the multimillion-dollar-a-year licensing of James Dean for the family. About 1,400 products use his name and likeness, including Rebel cologne that comes with a pair of sunglasses. He says that a James Dean collectible doll will be unveiled by Mattel within the next few months.[31]

Jones' piece moves immediately from this observation to Fairmount residents' concern about safeguarding a wholesome image of Dean:

> Those in Jim Dean's high school class of 1949 don't appreciate the way some outsiders characterize their classmate. They remember him as a good student, straight as they come, popular with the girls, a terrific athlete, a star in basketball and baseball, a regular guy. "I know these people are always saying that Jim was kind of weird and all this, but there's nothing weird about him. He was just like the rest of us," says Phyllis Cox, who was Dean's friend.[32]

Jones and the Fairmount residents enthusiastically signify Dean's heterosexuality by describing him as "straight as they come, popular with the girls, a terrific athlete, a star in basketball and baseball, a regular guy, just like the rest of us." The terse phrase "kind of weird" suffices to elide Dean's bisexuality and other "irregularities." Jones doesn't comment on the connection between the multi-million-dollar-a-year industry and residents' fears that their version of Dean might be dislodged by revelations about his sexuality. Presumably the profitable Dean industry might suffer if a less conventional version of Dean were to supplant the image of a small-town "nothing-weird-about-him" hero.

Fairmount's promotion of Dean as a small-town hero is longstanding. Val Holley cites a 1956 quote from an Indiana resident who was a Dean family friend: "The stories Hollywood inspired about him made good reading for many, but they sickened those closest to him . . . If people could know how Jimmy grew up, there would be no mystery . . . The folks who knew him best in Fairmount will never believe that he was anything but the fine, sensitive, quiet lad they remember, both before and after he became the rage of Hollywood."[33] Holley astutely analyzes these remarks as

> far more revealing of Fairmount than of the actor. The town that gave the world James Dean has always refused to acknowledge things about him that, in spite of being "un-Indianan," were true. Some of its residents condition their cooperation with biographers on a promise not to write about any of his homosexual experiences. Willful blindness to Dean's bohemian life in New York and Hollywood—the surly moodiness, promiscuity, and noteworthy ability to mislead—became a hallmark of Fairmount life. This was due in part to another of Dean's cover-ups: his letters home avoided references to Rogers Brackett, Alec Wilder, girlfriends, and boyfriends, leading his family to believe he remained untainted by the tents of wickedness. "Hell, I've said it until I'm sick of sayin' it," droned Dean's uncle, Marcus Winslow, to a reporter in 1973. "Jim Dean was just like any other kid who grew up in this town. But Hollywood and the rest of the world refuse to believe any of that." In brief, for Fairmount, the authentic Dean remained in stasis after he left town in May 1949 for southern California.[34]

Some Fairmount residents with a distaste for eccentricity of any kind have criticized some of the thousands of fans that arrive each September, especially the "weird" ones. Biographer Paul Alexander quotes a resident as saying,

> The people who come to Museum Days are not the kind of people we know around here . . . One year I saw this guy who had his hair shaved on both sides and sticking straight up in the air. Looked like he had a spike in his head. Had on a great big old wool overcoat. Why do you need that sort of stuff in Fairmount? There are a lot of weird people who come here. I would guess that they come from the East some place. Him and the three that were with him. Half of them you couldn't tell whether they were male or female. Simple-looking people, but not us country folks.[35]

The event that attracts "a lot of weird people," Fairmount's "Museum Days/Remembering James Dean" celebration, is a loud and nostalgic affair, with fifties and sixties oldies blaring, live bands and dancing, the Fussgängers Volksmarch 10K Walk, Garfield's Great Race, the Children's Pet Parade, the Kiddie Tractor Pull, the Grand Parade, the James Dean Run of Vintage Cars, the James Dean Rock Lasso Contest, the World Famous James Dean Look-Alike Contest, the James Dean Bicycle Tour, the Gospel Music Fest, the crowning of a Senior Citizens King and Queen, a fifties dance contest, the Garfield the Cat Photo and Art Contest, and free screenings of Dean's films. A carnival contributes bright lights and dizzying motion, while a large field is set aside for a display of vintage cars and booths selling loads of Dean memorabilia. It is a decidedly raucous event for a young man remembered by many for his moody introspection. But it does indeed bring together young and old, gray-haired and spike-haired, gay and straight, black and white. Fairmount residents mingle with "weirdos" from the East. And there is yet more irony in the fact that if James Dean had survived, he could no longer win the James Dean look-alike contest, but might have a shot at the title of Senior Citizens King.

For people who choose not to attend the festivities in Fairmount, the official James Dean Web site is offered as a substitute. The Web site illustrates contemporary western culture's complex and contradictory ways of thinking about the concept of authenticity. A frenzied search for authenticity characterizes western technological culture, for we live during a time when corporate mass production obliterates uniqueness. When everything is (re)created in minute detail—eighteenth-century villages populated by actors in period garb, new furniture that is "distressed" to make it appear antique, "international bazaars" in the food courts of countless malls, "ye olde video shoppes"—the idea of originality is laden with value but is simultaneously usurped by its copies. The prevalence of simulacra provokes a quest for something that is "really," not just cosmetically, authentic. Deceased celebrities are high on the list of valuable originals, because direct access to them is barred; a premium is thus placed on proximity to something or someone that came into contact with them before they died.

Reverence for proximity to the deceased James Dean is cleverly satirized in William Kotzwinkle's coming-of-age novel *Book of Love*, set in the fifties replete with greased-back ducktails, black leather jackets, and a red Buick convertible salvaged from the junkyard with imitation leopard skin on the steering wheel and seats.[36] Teen protagonist Jack Twiller and his buddy Leo Bodell devote themselves to mumbling, slouching imitations of James Dean after watching *Rebel Without a Cause* and resolve to meet the author of the book *My Friend, James Dean* to get "the whole story" about their idol. The boys hitchhike to New York City, where the

Vintage cars on display at the "Museum Days/Remembering James Dean" festival in Fairmount.

author invites Leo in and sends Jack away to wander the streets all night. The next morning Jack quizzes Leo for information about Dean, but Leo is withdrawn and uncooperative, and finally spits out the only thing he was told about Dean: "Jimmy would have liked you."[37] He reveals only that he and the author listened to records, with the implication that the author was intent on, and perhaps succeeded in, seducing him. So much for getting close to James Dean.

JamesDean.com relies on the premise that proximity to the town where Dean lived will bring fans closer to the actual Dean and reveal something authentic about him. In this way, the site participates in the aesthetic of immediacy, in the promise of unmediated access to the "real" James Dean. There are many ironies in this promise, such as the fact that most "visitors" to the Web site are not present in Fairmount; they are miles and miles away, perhaps on the other side of the planet, in front of their computers. The Web site is only possible because of technological mediation, rendering immediacy an illusion. Additionally, the Dean preserved by Fairmount is unreliable, telling us more about a small town's wistful adherence to its dreams than about the actual actor. Individuals cannot be reduced to the influence of one location, even if they spent their entire lives there. It is fun to visit Fairmount and speculate about how it may have changed since Dean's years there, stop by his grave and the house where he lived, and fantasize about his strolling these same streets. The attempt to apprehend the "authentic" Dean through immersion in Fairmount or the "official" Web site, though, is problematic.

Dean fans definitely find each other in Fairmount, and there is a strong communal bond at the annual festival. Immediacy may be an illusion; community is not. Fans of all ages, races, nationalities, and sexualities can share their fascination with Dean in the festive streets of Fairmount in late September. Likewise, the CMG Web site creates the Internet's pseudo-community: fans do not share the same physical space, but even though they are separated by thousands of miles, they jack into an implicitly communal experience. Visiting the Web site is an activity Dean fans share; the information they acquire there is shared information, and it serves to strengthen a sense of themselves as part of a group and not simply isolated individuals.

A scan of the Internet reveals that virtual James Deans are by no means confined to the locations once inhabited by the actual James Dean. One particularly exotic virtual Dean exists in the form of a gay James Dean Bar and Guest House in Patong, on Phuket Island, Thailand, a region struck by the tsunami of December 2004. Here is an unofficial Dean, one who probably won't find his way into the official CMG Worldwide site. The Web site tells us that the James Dean Bar and Guest House is a gay-owned lodging "right in the heart of Phuket's gay nightlife—the Paradise Complex."[38] A photograph depicts a bright and cheerful structure with blue columns, white walls, and a pagoda-inspired orange-tiled roof. This virtual Dean is out of the closet and not only comfortable, but blissfully untroubled in a warm tropical "paradise." The actual James Dean never left North America (he visited Mexico several times when he and producer Rogers Brackett, at the time his lover, spent time in Tijuana for the bullfights), and only flew in an airplane for the first time when he traveled from New York to Los Angeles with Elia Kazan on March 8, 1954, with his clothes in a brown paper bag.[39] Now, years after his death, he leads a virtual life as a tropical bar and guest house, sheltering other young men in a place unlike anything he saw when he was alive.

Ironically, one of Hollywood's heirs to the James Dean mystique—Leonardo DiCaprio—spent time in South Thailand on Phi Phi Leh Island just southeast of Phuket when he starred in the big-budget film *The Beach* (Danny Boyle, 2000). In 1999, before the film's release, the patong .com Web site predicted that the film would be good for tourism in South Thailand, asserting that "Phuket will remain the most desirable and attractive area for tourism, and Patong is the fun zone." One outcome predicted by the site was increased tolerance for gays: "So, the gay area will grow and change. For now, the Paradise is the focus, but places like the Andaman Queen on Soi Bangla are being more open about attracting gays."[40]

The Beach did in fact shine a global spotlight on South Thailand, for it provoked heated controversy over environmental damage sustained during filming. The clash between a massively wealthy American film studio (Rupert Murdoch's 20th Century Fox) and local Thai forces revealed the destructive side of celebrity culture. While not as cataclysmic as a tidal wave, celebrity culture can leave its own path of destruction. As Pennapa Hongthong writes, "They came, they saw, they filmed—and completely ruined a stunningly beautiful beach."[41] The filmmakers bulldozed the beach at Maya Bay on Phi Phi Leh Island to widen it, uprooting plants and leveling dunes, causing major erosion and leaving the beach severely damaged. Warnings were issued about beach erosion even before 20th Century Fox obtained permission from the Thai Royal Forestry Department (RFD), but, according to Hongthong, the RFD approved the project after Fox paid a large sum of money and promised to restore the beach after filming was completed. Environmentalists and local observers complained that Fox caused irreparable damage to the beach and failed in a feeble attempt to restore it. An environmentalist is quoted as saying that "this is exactly what we feared would happen. Leonardo's celebrity has been used to kill the park law."[42] Environmental groups filed a lawsuit against Fox, a Thai production company, and the RFD, and also protested at the film's opening, urging viewers to boycott it. Even before the trial ended, the Tourism Authority of Thailand (TAT) was launching a campaign to promote tourism to the area, setting up "Leonardo's Island" tours of the film's locations, which prompted an outcry from Thai citizens who felt that the area was already suffering from the effects of rampant tourism.[43] Their concern was heightened by their knowledge of an earlier Thai debacle involving a film studio, a movie star, and a beach. After the release of *The Man with the Golden Gun* in 1974, the island where it was filmed became known even by locals as "James Bond Island," and was visited by thousands of tourists who ravaged the site with their litter. Ever since then, few residents even remember the original name of the island.[44]

James Dean, James Bond, Leonardo DiCaprio—all have left their mark on the islands of South Thailand, erasing the difference between fictional characters and actors and showing how the phenomena of immediacy and hypermediacy can create actual changes in the physical and social world. In the case of *The Man with the Golden Gun* and *The Beach*, film crews equipped with mountains of technological paraphernalia came to remote locations to "capture" them for worldwide transmission, but first they altered them to fit their technological needs and preconceived notion of what a pristine paradise should look like. After they had trampled them and abandoned them, the locations were descended on by tourists in search of authenticity—looking for an aura left behind by the presence of Leonardo DiCaprio or "James Bond" (Roger Moore at the time)—and they too transformed the land. The irony is that the locations' remote and unspoiled nature was what initially attracted the filmmakers and is what they emphasized in their fictions, but in the process of creating the illusion of immediacy, they eliminated those very qualities.

Tourist culture, media culture, and celebrity culture collided in Phuket, and the result is the typically stratified resort economy. The enormous gap in income between foreign tourists and local Thais on Phuket is observed by author Chang-Rae Lee in an article titled "The Spicy Pleasures of Phuket." Lee writes that he and his wife stopped to have a drink at one of Phuket's most expensive resorts, the Amanpuri:

> Here the very rich cloister themselves in 360-count sateen sheets and aromatherapy baths of fenugreek and eucalyptus. In the high season

(mid-October to mid-May) the studio villas start at $490 a night, with the largest—six bedrooms with a live-in cook and maid and an ocean view—going for a cool $6,000. It is, of course, an exceedingly beautiful place, with unbroken vistas of the Andaman Sea from the central pool and reception *sala*, the traditional open-sided wooden pavilion, where the hostesses pad around in their bare feet, silent as owls. But this is serious cash anywhere, and in a developing country like Thailand, a week's stay at Amanpuri could easily equal a local laborer's lifetime earnings.[45]

Although not all tourists plunk down $6,000 a night at the Amanpuri, Phuket is nonetheless characterized by the contrast between obscene wealth and extreme poverty that is also found in many other popular tourist sites around the world. Tellingly, within days of the 2004 tsunami, wealthy foreign tourists were back on Phuket's beaches, soaking up the sun, oblivious to the indignation of residents and relief workers cleaning up the debris nearby.[46]

Far from both Fairmount and Phuket, intoning lyrics filled with pain and confusion, there is another James Dean, an actual James Dean: James Dean Bradfield, lead singer for the British band Manic Street Preachers. Here is James Dean as a Brit-pop singer for the 1990s and beyond. This Dean has kept up with musical developments and grown beyond the bobby sox and golden oldies exalted in Fairmount. James Dean Bradfield was born in 1969 and grew up in Blackwood, South Wales. A Web site devoted to him explains that he was almost named "Clint Eastwood Bradfield" by his biker father, but his mother intervened and they compromised on "James Dean." Accompanying this explanation is a photograph of a slouching James Dean Bradfield wearing a red *Rebel* jacket and holding a cigarette.[47] Bradfield has inherited more than just Dean's name, taste in clothing, and posture; he has something of his identity as well, for his band is surrounded by an aura of Dean-like despair. In February of 1995, the Manic Street Preachers' guitarist and lyricist Richey Edwards sped away from a London hotel in his silver Vauxhall Cavalier and was never seen again.[48] Authorities suspect suicide, but there has been no trace of Edwards, and the band members were left with the troubling enigma of their bandmate's disappearance.

Dean is also associated with sorrow in a French Web site from which he emerges as a tragic and misunderstood figure. The site provides a standard account of Dean's life with an emphasis on heartbreak involving the death of his mother and his breakup with Pier Angeli *dont il ne guerira jamais totalement* (from which he'll never totally recover). The pitfalls of translation are on display when Dean's original statement—"I'm not the bobby-sox type"—is translated as *Je ne suis pas un dragueur*, meaning "I'm not a pick-up artist." For the most part the site romanticizes his tragic isolation:

> *James Dean était-il capable de trouver le bonheur? De l'accepter? Ou était-il destiné à souffrir comme les personnages de fiction qu'il incarnait? Où, en effet, s'arrête la légende et où commence la vie?*[49]
>
> (Was James Dean capable of finding happiness? Of accepting it? Or was he destined to suffer like the fictional characters he embodied? Where, in fact, does the legend stop and the life begin?)

This sad and lonely Dean is perhaps the most durable one, the one who persists as an instant emblem of heartbreak and despair. Sadness crosses over into morbidity on the "graveside scenes" link at the deaners.net fan site, which takes us to a page of photographs of tributes left at Dean's gravestone in Fairmount.[50] The morbid aspect of the site is alleviated by its bright and cheerful presentation and by the colorful flowers adorning the grave. One photo identifies a beautifully elaborate tribute as "Naomi Yamada's Thousand Crane tribute," a reference to the traditional Japanese notion that your wish will come true if you fold a thousand origami paper cranes.[51]

But the tragic, morbid Dean is not the only Dean. Another virtual Dean has been capable of finding and accepting happiness: a James Dean impersonator named Mark Gruetzman, winner in 1999 and 2000 of the James Dean look-alike contest at Fairmount's annual James Dean festival. His Web site's tone eschews tragic romanticism and gets right to the point:

> That's right folks!
>
> What could liven up a party or event more than your very own James Dean impersonator? Two time National James Dean contest winner Mark Gruetzman. Available at very reasonable rates.[52]

Photographs of Gruetzman as Dean on the Web site bear an uncanny resemblance to photos of the actual Dean. After marveling at the remarkable likeness, I e-mailed Gruetzman with questions: Does he get hired often? For what sorts of events? What does he do when he is on the job as a James Dean impersonator? Does he perform, or does he mingle in the guise of Dean? Gruetzman sent a gracious response explaining that "impersonation work is usually one of two things: a meet and greet, which for someone who is a JD fan can be a huge surprise, or a walk around character at a party or business event. I've also had a few parts in independent films as James Dean." He also explained that in the look-alike contests in Fairmount, "a lot of people enter the contest, but there are usually 3–5 that are competitive."[53]

The impersonation phenomenon is another twist on our cultural obsession with simulacra, for it requires a major suspension of disbelief no matter how closely the impersonator resembles the original. Since people are not duped by impersonators, there are other reasons for the impersonator's appeal. For one thing, there is the incredible moment of recognition when a fan sees his or her idol "in the flesh"; even though fans know they are in the presence of an impersonator, they can experience an uncanny disruption of their equilibrium. It is also significant that impersonators typically appear when groups are present, for, just like the diverse community of fans who visit Fairmount in late September, this is primarily a communal experience. An impersonator can provide a group of fans a focus for their shared fandom, and the playful tension between belief and disbelief can unify the group. Even when an impersonator is met with ironic distance, there is still a communal element, for the shared expression of irony can provide a cohesive group identity. There is also a ritualistic aspect to the presence of an impersonator. Repetition is a cornerstone of any devotion, and fandom entails devoted loyalty. Watching an effective impersonator, or interacting with one, is a way of ritualistically repeating one's devotion.

Some fans have elevated the ritualistic aspect of fandom to quasi-religious status, as Gilbert Rodman points out in his study of Elvis culture. Rodman explains,

> A performance by an Elvis impersonator is . . . much more than just another concert or nightclub act; it's a spiritual revival: a ritualized ceremony that brings the Elvis faithful together in order to make a public expression (and reaffirmation) of their devotion.[54]

There can be a powerful connection between an impersonator and an audience of fans, and the devotional experience can elevate both. James Dean fandom does not have the gargantuan proportions of Elvis fandom, or the same level of quasi-religious fervor, but there is nonetheless a palpable ritualistic and communal spirit underlying the impersonation phenomenon. At the 1996 festival in Fairmount, the look-alike contest took place outdoors on a hot autumn night, the culmination of the day's many events. A stage where the contestants slouched and sneered in their best

Dean poses was lit by festive lights, and a carnival mood prevailed, with audience members cheering their favorite look-alike contestants. There was a feeling of good-natured camaraderie, of pleasure in the electrified moment. Contestants were not required to perform in any way, just to "be" James Dean. This was a comparatively low-key event, albeit the stakes were high for the contestants, for whom winning the contest could mean a boost in their marketability as Dean impersonators. Mark Gruetzman, winner in 1999 and 2000, was joined in 2000 by Lyndon Biegas, the winner of the first annual "Little Jimmy Dean Look-Alike Contest." Biegas had competed unsuccessfully against adults and against his little brother (who appears in a photo to have been about five years old) for several years before the "Little Jimmy Dean" prize was inaugurated.[55] There have also been women as well as Japanese contestants in past years.

A past winner of the Dean look-alike contest, archivist David Loehr, has a Web site for his James Dean Gallery. One link leads to a virtual tour of the gallery and depicts each room's floor plan, allowing the virtual visitor to click on each room to see photos of its contents. The gallery displays

> literally thousands of items, including clothing worn by Dean in films and in his private life, high school yearbooks, school papers from his early years, snapshots, signed photos, and the lease to Dean's last place of residence which is signed, initialed and dated July, 1955 . . . As you tour the exhibit, you'll see several dozen original movie posters in over twenty different languages from around the world which show the actor's international impact. There are hundreds of books and magazines dedicated to Dean dating from the mid-fifties to the present, also from many different countries. There are showcases full of tribute and novelty items that have been produced since the '50s, such as souvenir plates, mugs, ceramic busts, puzzles, gum cards, scarves, and much more.[56]

One of the rooms in the gallery is named the Kenneth Kendall room, and during the annual festival, sculptor Kenneth Kendall, who sculpted a bust of Dean at Dean's request, can be found there holding court and meeting fans. The gallery also has a well-stocked gift shop, and visitors to the Web site can purchase items there almost as easily as if they were present in the flesh.

Every Dean Web site is the product of human agency, and David Loehr makes his presence known with a quick-time movie of himself introducing the virtual visitor to his gallery. In general those who create and maintain

Dean Web sites keep themselves in the background. But in some cases the Webmaster's identity is a central element of the site. Such is the case with John Seger's site, where Seger begins by identifying himself and explaining that he is related to Dean.

> My name is John Seger. My mother was James Dean's 1st cousin, making me his cousin, first generation removed. My mother's father was Albert Wilson, and his sister was Mildred Marie Wilson, James Dean's mother. The following pictures are some of my faves.[57]

Like most other Dean fan sites, Seger's displays carefully chosen photographs of Dean. From the beginning of his career, part of Dean's appeal was his extraordinary value as an image: he was far more than merely photogenic; his photographs were a visual magnet for people's projections of their own complicated internal lives. Biographer David Dalton writes that Dean was "like an anti-matter star, his core was a vacuum that sucked in everything indiscriminately and converted it into his image. This image, in turn, exerted a gravitational pull of equal magnitude on his generation."[58] There were breathtaking numbers of photographs taken of Dean as he molded and modeled his composite persona, and these photographs are still treasured on the World Wide Web a half-century after his death. Dean is a consummately visual icon—ideal for our visually oriented age—still exerting his tremendous ability to provide a form for inchoate feelings of anxiety and disillusionment.

Dean's image may signify the torment of inexpressible solitude, but the Internet is providing a way for those who identify with his alienation to find each other across geographic barriers and share their loneliness. Several Web sites make it possible for fans to chat about Dean online, heightening the communal nature of electronic Dean fandom. It may appear ironic that Dean's studied solitude is an avenue leading to community, but implicit in Dean imagery is Dean's own awareness of his inability to fit in and his resulting anguish. David Dalton explains that when Dean, the misunderstood outsider, became the consummate symbol for the American teen, "it was as if the only way he could become one of them was to make them one of him; if he couldn't get into their club, they would have to join his!"[59] The World Wide Web has made it possible for anyone anywhere to join his club.

Dean's club has long been global, and the Internet reveals the extent of his worldwide dissemination. A Hungarian man's story testifies to Dean's power to inspire:

My friends called me Abbey.

It was 1969, behind the iron curtain of communist Hungary and during a difficult period in my life, I learned, from the German Bravo magazine, about James Dean, his short life and his tragic death. From that point on, my life changed forever. I felt at peace with inner found strength. I was 16 year old, and I made a promise to myself that if I ever reached freedom, that I would take a bouquet of flowers to the grave of James Dean.

While fighting for my freedom in any way I could, they did everything to break me down. After 11 years, in the summer of 1980, I escaped within 48 hours by crossing two communist borders by foot.

I arrived in New York in the Fall of 1980 and I didn't realize that the greatest challenge of my life was just beginning.

Deadly accidents, alcohol and drugs, even Hurricane Andrew, tried to detour my way, but in the end I overcame all of these difficulties.

Now, 30 years later, I kept my promise, so my MISSION IS COMPLETE. Abbey.[60]

Dean's influence can be seen in Abbey's hipster garb and hairstyle in photos showing him beside Dean's grave, the site that symbolized his goal during years of struggle.

Virtual fandom provides easy access to foreign-language Web sites, even making it possible to obtain instant translations performed mechanically by a computer program. I requested a translation of a German site and learned that the software has a few bugs, resulting in an English text that makes a surreal contribution to the continual reinvention of James Dean:

James Dean: The classical author under the Sexgoettern. Young, wildly and sexy he erspielte himself in only three films Unsterblichkeit. To admire dozens from fans have themselves it made to the function and in such a way find one in the InterNet a large number of Fanpages. The most extensive and most complex is the official James Dean Fanpage. On it one finds a Biographie, a Filmographie, picture galleries, information about the annual James Dean Festival and much more besides. The page is in German and English callable. The James Dean gallery shows all stations of the life of the rebel in a time border. With numerous photos from child legs and affectionately investigated texts answer this page to the fans almost each response. Besides become here in a Shop numerous fan articles offered and visitors can undertake a virtual route by the James Dean Memorial Gallery. Who "would like" to see Jimmy in dreamed moments on its display, the James Dean Bildschirmschoner can down-loaden itself here.[61]

Fans also have a prominent place on the deaners.net site, created and maintained by Sandra Weinhardt; this site is "for and about James Dean fans, and some of the content is contributed by them." Its motto is "Dean-ers: James Dean Fans Speak Out." Weinhardt has modestly written at the bottom of one page, "The whole Deaners website is made by a lone, individual, self-taught webmistress with no background in anything. (There are occasional sections by talented guest authors)."[62] In fact, the site is well designed and displays a playful sense of humor; it is a testament to one person's ability to use the Internet effectively.

This site—in addition to comprehensive information about Fairmount's festivals from years past, photo galleries of classic and custom cars, reviews of recent films about Dean, photographs from the look-alike contests, and a gallery of Dean drawings made by fans—also has a link to "interesting Deaner people." Here we meet Magdalin Leonardo, a Dean fan and documenter of Dean fandom. She has a Web site linked to the deaners.net site on the town of Marfa, Texas, where *Giant* was filmed; she describes Marfa as "a very special place, the last surviving link to the late star's film legacy." There are photographs of Marfa, and Leonardo encourages fans to visit:

> Here, in this tiny Texas town (est. population: 2500), you can walk the streets Jimmy wandered, visit the places he made famous, talk to the fans who met him, and visit the roadside ruins of Reata—still standing after 43 years in the desert sun . . . Getting there won't be easy. And for most of you, it won't be fast. But for Dean fans, it is most definitely a trip worth taking. I had been to all the familiar Dean sites in New York, California and Indiana. I had met countless fans. But nothing could prepare me for the precious experience of Marfa. It is truly a great Dean adventure, one I highly recommend. So put on your cowboy hat, kick up your spurs, and join me now. Take a journey into the past and relive the magic of James Dean's Marfa.[63]

Leonardo skillfully blurs the distinction between an actual visit (which she acknowledges won't be easy or fast) and a virtual visit ("put on your cowboy hat, kick up your spurs, and join me now") to Marfa. She facilitates the slippage between actual and virtual, suggesting that either one will provide an experience of immediacy, of access to the authentic Dean. The site is divided into pages devoted to particular locations in Marfa: The Arcon Inn, Reata Ruins, El Paisano Hotel, Borunda's Bar and Grill, and so forth. But even more than places, Leonardo values people and has undertaken a long-term project of collecting people's James Dean stories. Her Web site states: "Magdalin's just mad about Marfa. She's also mad about Dean fans—in fact, she's writing a book about them! So if you're a Dean fan with an interesting story to tell—or if you're just plain interesting—send her email."[64] Although her Marfa Web site stresses access to the authentic Dean via actual and virtual travel, her deeper commitment is to the communal experience of fandom.

Leonardo likes to document some of fandom's more bizarre manifestations. On her Marfa Web site she writes about "Jimmy Beans: A Candy-Coated Tribute." This, it turns out, is a jelly bean mural of Dean. She writes, "This marvelous work of art was made from 10,000 jelly beans and measured a massive 4 ft. × 4 ft. It was created by artist Peter Rocha for The Jelly Belly Company of Illinois. Rocha has created many other murals for the Jelly Belly Company too, including ones of Elvis, Laurel & Hardy, Johnny Carson, President Ronald Reagan, even the Statue of Liberty!"[65] Leonardo traveled to "Tom's Patio and Country Cottage, an adorable little pit stop on West Highway 90" in Texas to see the mural, but unfortunately it was no longer there and she had to settle for photos of it. Leonardo's pleasure in Dean fandom and fans is palpable, and not surprisingly she has started a "new fan club for a new Century" called "James Dean Remembered."

James Dean *is* remembered on the Net; there are traces of him in all sorts of virtual locations. While Magdalin Leonardo's "James Dean Remembered" club is designed to provide a shared forum for fans to keep Dean's memory "alive," a mock newspaper story written by author Joe Middleton is about a successful attempt to make James Dean actually come alive.[66] The piece perceptively satirizes the contemporary cultural obsession with literalizing memory. Given current cloning experiments, as well as Hollywood's preoccupation with using computer-generated imagery to bring dead celebrities back to the screen, Middleton's piece does not seem entirely far-fetched. He begins by establishing that science and entertainment have collaborated in the Dean cloning venture:

Time Warner announced this morning that they had successfully cloned the late James Dean using the latest scientific techniques. Rapid growth enhancement (RGE) treatments mean that the clone has a physical age of 21 despite a real age of under a month. Since James Dean (2) as he will be known was hatched he has also been undergoing computer stimulated learning on all known information about the late film star.[67]

It is only a slight science fiction stretch to imagine entertainment mega-corporation Time Warner in the business of cloning celebrities. In the story, science no longer maintains the pretense that it operates free of corporate control; scientists are employed by powerful companies, owners of sports teams, and politicians, all in the interests of increased profits. In this fictional near-future, human cloning was launched by scientists working for businessman and ex-politician Ross Perot before his death: "Perot's clone was the first success story, taking over the ailing ex-presidential candidate's business and political interests just before the original died." Competing interests, though, have complicated the profitability of the cloning enterprise. Dean 2 is the first clone from a dead host, and in his case "surviving relatives and lack of finance have barred some of the most obviously commercial prospects for the industry," but "the studio is hopeful that its multi-million dollar investment will bear fruit." They are heartened by the clone's progress so far:

> Studio sources claim that Dean 2's developing personality is remarkably similar to the late star's and he is already showing burgeoning acting talent. Some speculative tabloid reports have claimed that Dean is already smoking sixty cigarettes a day and annoying partygoers with his bongo playing.[68]

Middleton astutely acknowledges that when Dean is evoked, sex is not far behind:

> The world media are most interested however in investigating the cloned star's sexuality. Despite his sex symbol status while alive, after his death Dean has been the subject of frenzied speculation that he was in fact a closet homosexual or at least bi-sexual. Studio executive Jack Hawks commented "No one knows the truth about the late James Dean's sexuality." But with a wink he added, "our lad has certainly been showing a more than healthy interest in his nurses."[69]

The fictional studio executive doesn't specify whether these nurses are male or female, leaving it to our imaginations.

Like the satirical piece by Robert Brady on pre–James Dean James Dean look-alikes, Middleton's story uses Dean to hold a funhouse mirror up to our culture and catch its most peculiar reflections. And Middleton's Dean, who is not actually James Dean at all but the clone Dean 2, is an effective metaphor for all of the virtual Deans residing on the Internet. They are copies fashioned from a mix of iconographic detritus and cultural fantasies and desires. These virtual Deans are variously humorous, beautiful, instructive, poignant, and tragic, and they carry with them a nostalgic view back to the middle of the twentieth century and, simultaneously, a speculative peek forward into the uncertainty of the new one.

From the time he became a celebrity and then a legend, James Dean has been mediated: in print, in photographs, in theatre, in films, on television, in video, in sculpture, in paints (and paint-on-velvet, not to mention jelly bean murals), and now on the computer's World Wide Web. Every medium creates a new spin on Dean, but also implicitly refers back to older media. The Internet incorporates the visual nature of paintings, photographs, theatre, film, and video, as well as the narrative capabilities of print, theatre, film, and video; it also allows greater freedom of expression than the earlier media. In addition, it extends each medium's promise to provide unmediated access to the authentic Dean. New media are billed as offering the ultimate in "reality," but their limitations are soon revealed, and, in the meantime, the entertainment conglomerates have been busy creating the next new medium. As Joe Middleton suggests in his cloning metaphor, the entertainment industry is voracious in its pursuit of immediacy and transparency.[70] But no medium—even cloning—will succeed in rendering James Dean present. He is gone, and, besides, he was notoriously remote and inaccessible during his lifetime, even to his best friends. His mysterious inaccessibility has contributed to making him a favorite subject of remediation, with each medium picking up where the others left off. The virtual Deans who populate the Internet will be incorporated into the next medium's manifestations of Dean. Just as James Dean himself was a charismatic composite of his era's styles, so virtual Deans are an amalgam of all of the fantasies that have been powerfully drawn to the spinning vortex of his image.

Although James Dean has been gone for half a century, his transfigured selves still circulate and produce new offspring, some of them predictable clones and others unexpected variations. His legacy, the rebel icon, is surprisingly ubiquitous. Its manifestations tell us how far we have come from the fifties, but also how little progress has been made in addressing the social and political problems that afflict adolescent rebels around the world. Unemployment, racism, sexism, homophobia, poverty, violence, and inadequate education leave young people beleaguered, and adolescents are also subjected to tirades of blame for the very social ills that trap them. Their attempts to express themselves in unique ways are immediately co-opted by advertisers and the corporate empire and sold back to them in bland mass-marketed forms, consigning them to the status of easily manipulated consumers. Jim Stark's wail of distress in *Rebel Without a Cause*—"You're tearing me apart!"—still rings true in the twenty-first century and is a continual reminder that the film's original young audience members failed when they grew up to change the intolerable conditions they had chafed against. Instead they created a suffocating global trap in which the rebel icon is simultaneously up for sale and an enduring protest.

Notes

Introduction: The Rebel Icon

1. Jon Lewis, *The Road to Romance and Ruin: Teen Films and Youth Culture* (New York: Routledge, 1992), 20.

2. Dick Hebdige, *Subculture: The Meaning of Style* (London: Methuen, 1979).

3. John Fiske, *Understanding Popular Culture* (Boston: Unwin Hyman, 1989).

4. Tricia Rose, "Flow, Layering, and Rupture in Postindustrial New York," in *Signifyin(g), Sanctifyin', and Slam Dunking: A Reader in African American Expressive Culture*, ed. Gena Dagel Caponi (Amherst: University of Massachussetts Press, 1999), 214.

5. Ibid., 216.

6. Dell deChant, "The Economy as Religion: The Dynamics of Consumer Culture," *The Civic Arts Review* 16, no. 2 (summer/fall 2003): 6, http://car.owu .edu/Vol.%2016%20No.%202html.

Chapter 1: Birth of an Icon

1. Robert Ready, "Jimmy the Arab," in *Mondo James Dean: A Collection of Stories and Poems about James Dean*, ed. Lucinda Ebersole and Richard Peabody (New York: St. Martin's Griffin, 1996), 63.

2. The James Dean Gallery has been open for seventeen years and has had over sixty thousand visitors (James Dean Gallery Web site, http://www.jamesdean gallery.com). However, the Gallery was unable to meet its expenses in its new location, and David Loehr announced that it would close to the public on December 31, 2005. After his announcement, he received sufficient donations to avoid having to close. When this book was going to press, it was unclear how long he would be able to keep the gallery open. Loehr continues to maintain the gallery's Web site and conduct online business. "Announcing Closure Might Let James Dean Museum Stay Open," *Houston Chronicle* online, http://www.chron.com/disp/story .mpl/ent/celebrities/3605779.html.

3. Philippe Defechereux and Jean Graton, *James Dean: The Untold Story of a Passion for Speed*, trans. Intex Translations (Los Angeles: Mediavision Publications, 1996 [originally published in Brussels: Graton Editeur, 1995]), 50.

4. Martin Sheen, quoted in David Hofstede, *James Dean: A Bio-Bibliography* (Westport, Conn.: Greenwood Press, 1996), 19.

5. Jon Savage, "Sex, Rock, and Identity: The Enemy Within," in *Facing the Music*, ed. Simon Frith (New York: Pantheon Books, 1988), 143.

6. Marshall Fishwick, "Entrance," in *Icons of Popular Culture*, ed. Marshall Fishwick and Ray B. Browne (Bowling Green, Ohio: Bowling Green University Popular Press, 1970), 2.

7. Marshall Fishwick, "Introduction," in *Icons of America*, ed. Ray B. Browne and Marshall Fishwick (Bowling Green, Ohio: Bowling Green University Popular Press, 1978), 3.

8. Ralph Brauer, "Iconic Modes: The Beatles," in Browne and Fishwick, 117.

9. David Dalton, *James Dean: American Icon* (New York: St. Martin's Press, 1984), 237.

10. Ibid.

11. Andy Warhol, quoted in Randall Riese, *The Unabridged James Dean: His Life and Legacy from A to Z* (Chicago: Contemporary Books, 1991), 546.

12. Joan Mellen, *Big Bad Wolves: Masculinity in the American Film* (New York: Pantheon Books, 1977), 192.

13. Ibid., 190.

14. Stuart Ewen, *Captains of Consciousness: Advertising and the Social Roots of the Consumer Culture* (New York: McGraw-Hill, 1976), 214–215.

15. Estes Kefauver, quoted in Seth Cagin and Philip Dray, *Born to Be Wild: Hollywood and the Sixties Generation* (Boca Raton: Coyote, 1994), 41.

16. Graham McCann, *Rebel Males: Clift, Brando and Dean* (New Brunswick, N.J.: Rutgers University Press, 1991), 12.

17. Dick Pountain and David Robins, *Cool Rules: Anatomy of an Attitude* (London: Reaktion, 2000), 42.

18. Robert Farris Thompson, quoted in Pountain and Robins, 36.

19. Ibid.

20. Pountain and Robins, 38.

21. Ibid., 41.

22. Nelson George, quoted in Joel Dinerstein, "Lester Young and the Birth of Cool," in *Signifyin(g), Sanctifyin', & Slam Dunking: A Reader in African American Expressive Culture*, ed. Gena Caponi (Amherst: UMass Press, 1999), 241.

23. Pountain and Robins, 42.

24. Ibid., 64.

25. Ibid., 26.

26. Ibid.

27. Ibid.

28. Ibid., 28.

29. Paul Rudnick, "Everybody's a Rebel," *Spy Magazine*, March 1992, 55.

30. McCann, 6–7.

31. Richard Dyer, *Heavenly Bodies: Film Stars and Society* (New York: St. Martin's Press, 1986), 4.

32. Ibid.

33. Paul Alexander, *Boulevard of Broken Dreams: The Life, Times, and Legend of James Dean* (New York: Viking, 1994), 269.

34. Hofstede, 19.

35. Rudnick, 55.

36. Timothy Shary, *Generation Multiplex: The Image of Youth in Contemporary American Cinema* (Austin: University of Texas Press, 2002), 104.

37. Jon Lewis, *The Road to Romance and Ruin: Teen Films and Youth Culture* (New York: Routledge, 1992), 20.

38. Richard Schickel, *Brando: A Life in Our Times* (New York: Atheneum, 1991), 82–83.

39. Peter Manso, *Brando: The Biography* (New York: Hyperion, 1994), 347.

40. Tino Villanueva, *Scene from the Movie Giant* (Willimantic, Conn.: Curbstone Press, 1993), 27.

41. Ibid., 29.

42. Ibid., 42.

43. Ibid., 50.

44. Ibid., 15.

45. Ibid., 16.

46. Lucy Garcia, quoted in Simon Romero, "A Texas Town Holds Fast to Its Ties to a Classic," *The New York Times*, June 9, 2003, A18.

47. Mellen, 192.

48. Alexander, 209–210.

49. Richard Dyer, *The Matter of Images: Essays on Representation* (London: Routledge, 1993), 42.

50. Richard Dyer, "Rock—The Last Guy You'd Have Figured?" in *You Tarzan: Masculinity, Movies and Men*, ed. Pat Kinkham and Janet Thumin (New York: St. Martin's Press, 1993), 28.

51. Savage, 143–144.

52. Ibid., 143.

53. Alexander, 162.

54. Dalton, 7–8.

55. "The Girls in James Dean's Life," quoted in Dalton, 58.

56. Savage, 136.

57. Michael DeAngelis, *Gay Fandom and Crossover Stardom: James Dean, Mel Gibson, and Keanu Reeves* (Durham, N.C.: Duke University Press, 2001), 108.

58. Liz Sheridan, *Dizzy and Jimmy: My Life with James Dean, A Love Story* (New York: Regan Books, 2000).

59. John Gilmore, *Live Fast—Die Young: My Life With James Dean* (New York: Thunder's Mouth Press, 1997).

60. DeAngelis, 108–109.

61. David Considine, *The Cinema of Adolescence* (Jefferson, N.C.: McFarland, 1985). In addition to *Rebel Without a Cause*, films with monstrous moms include *Peyton Place* (Mark Robson, 1957), *The Restless Years* (Helmut Käutner, 1958), and *Five Finger Exercise* (Daniel Mann, 1962).

62. Nina Leibman, *Living Room Lectures* (Austin: University of Texas Press, 1995), 30.

63. Deb Schwartz, "Dean of Style," *Out*, September 1996, 147.

64. Lucinda Ebersole and Richard Peabody, eds., *Mondo James Dean: A Collection of Stories and Poems about James Dean* (New York: St. Martin's Griffin, 1996).

65. Bentley Little, "The Idol," in Ebersole and Peabody, 20–32.

66. Lewis Shiner, "Kings of the Afternoon," in Ebersole and Peabody, 68–79.

67. Stephanie Hart, "Who Killed Jimmy Dean?" in Ebersole and Peabody, 80–88.

68. Janice Eidus, "Jimmy Dean: My Kind of Guy," in Ebersole and Peabody, 16–19.

69. Louisa Ermelino, "No-Man's Land," in Ebersole and Peabody, 110–115.

70. Jack C. Haldeman II, "South of Eden, Somewhere near Salinas," in Ebersole and Peabody, 89–107.

71. Edwin Corley, excerpt from *Farewell My Slightly Tarnished Hero*, in Ebersole and Peabody, 35–62.

72. Ai, "James Dean," in Ebersole and Peabody, 5–7.

73. Ed Graczyk, excerpt from *Come Back to the Five and Dime, Jimmy Dean, Jimmy Dean*, in Ebersole and Peabody, 127–135.

74. Erika Doss, *Elvis Culture: Fans, Faith, and Image* (Lawrence: University Press of Kansas, 1999), 134.

75. Savage, 140.

76. Ibid.

77. Andy Medhurst, quoted in Savage, 144.

78. David Aberbach, *Surviving Trauma: Loss, Literature, and Psychoanalysis* (New Haven, Conn.: Yale University Press, 1989), 124. In this fascinating examination of loss, professor of Jewish studies and scholar of trauma David Aberbach cites the examples of Winston Churchill, Adolf Hitler, Jiddu Krishnamurti, Marilyn Monroe, and John Lennon, all of whom suffered profoundly as children due to the loss of one or both parents and who grew up to exude tremendous charisma while struggling with depression and deep self-doubt, and all of whom compensated for a sense of disconnection and emptiness by reaching for unity with the public and beyond, belonging "not to a secure family but 'to the ocean and the sky and the whole world'" (141). Aberbach explains that

> the charismatic often appears to create a "new identity," a semi-mythic persona, out of a character split and distorted by unresolved childhood griefs, and to incorporate this persona into a wider social or political entity. In this way, the charismatic may master grief, by transforming it into a creative motivation. Charismatic "appeal" may be understood in both senses of the word: as a powerful aesthetic attraction to the public, and as a cry for help artfully disguised or transcended. The response to charismatic appeal might involve not merely a reaction to an aesthetic phenomenon but also, at the same time, a simple human reply to the appeal for help. (125)

John Lennon's case most closely resembles James Dean's in that Lennon's mother died and he was also abandoned by his father, resulting in a search for, and inevitable rejection of, parent figures, and an intense anti-authoritarianism. Aberbach states that "his anti-authoritarianism was an important facet of his appeal to the young during the 1960s and 1970s. For him as for the other charismatics, independence and originality were bound up with unresolved grief, depression and hostility towards parental authority" (141). Dean, like Lennon, exuded a charismatic appeal bound up with anti-authoritarian anger that transcended personal wounds to become a social stance. Dean and Lennon each came to represent an abstract idea of resistance to authority, and in both cases people were drawn to the unknowable mystery that lay behind their angry exteriors.

79. Mercedes McCambridge, quoted in Joseph Humphreys, ed., *Jimmy Dean on Jimmy Dean* (London: Plexus Publishing, 1990), 115.

80. George Stevens, quoted in Humphreys, 125.

81. Alexandra Marshall, "Born to be Mild," in "Men's Fashions of the Times," supplement to *The New York Times*, September 21, 2003, 65.

82. Ibid., 68.

83. James William Gibson, *Warrior Dreams: Paramilitary Culture in Post-Vietnam America* (New York: Hill and Wang, 1994), 44.

84. Rudnick, 55.

85. Thomas Frank, "Why Johnny Can't Dissent," in *Commodify Your Dissent: Salvos from The Baffler*, ed. Thomas Frank and Matt Weiland (New York: W. W. Norton, 1997), 34.

86. Ibid.

87. Ibid., 41.

88. Advertisement for Adobe Software, *Rolling Stone* 825, November 11, 1999, 2–3.

89. Thomas Frank and Dave Mulcahey, "Consolidated Deviance, Inc.," in Frank and Weiland, 73.

90. MDI Entertainment, Inc., Licensed Brands, http://www.mediaentertainment.com/cmp/jd_about.html.

91. Nancy Hass, "I Seek Dead People," in the "Home Design" supplement to *The New York Times*, October 12, 2003, 38.

92. Dennis Hopper, quoted in Riese, 144–145.

93. Kenneth Anger, quoted in Alexander, 102.

94. The Dean icon has merged with the icon we know as a postage stamp. As military historian David Curtis Skaggs writes in "Postage Stamps as Icons," "When paper is so imprinted as to become currency or postage stamps, it becomes iconic. At that moment, the paper takes on value—both economically and symbolically—which it could not have had before" (198). However recognizable James Dean's image was before 1996, it has gained incomparable international exposure by virtue of its placement on a stamp. As Skaggs writes, "For years postage stamps were dominated by portraits of culture-heroes. In many instances . . . they were like classical busts of Roman emperors and generals . . . people who belonged on Olympus as well as on letters. And what power they had: the authority to take documents across the land, indeed around the world" (198). David Curtis Skaggs, "Postage Stamps as Icons," in Browne and Fishwick.

95. "Year's Favorite Stamp Features James Dean," *The Providence Journal*, December 30, 1996, A2.

96. Fredric Jameson, *Postmodernism, or, The Cultural Logic of Late Capitalism* (Durham, N.C.: Duke University Press, 1991), 286.

97. Jon Lewis writes, "Brando and Dean, who in our collective memory have come to represent youth in the 1950s, were, at the very least, very serious. But as they have been re-represented in such nostalgic works as *American Graffiti* (George Lucas, 1973) and the TV series *Happy Days*, they appear hopelessly romantic, emblems of a lost machismo that seems by now fairly humorous and anachronistic" (32).

98. Fishwick, "Introduction," 11.

Chapter 2: Disney's Dean

1. James Dean wrote a poem titled "My Town" in which he attacked Fairmount's bigotry, quoted in David Dalton, *James Dean: The Mutant King* (New York: St. Martin's Press, 1974), 85.

2. Paul Alexander, *Boulevard of Broken Dreams: The Life, Times, and Legend of James Dean* (New York: Viking, 1994), 283.

3. Elroy Hamilton, quoted in Alexander, 283–284.

4. Richard Schickel writes, "Taking advantage of the nation's sudden infatuation with basic transportation that had a lovably cute air about it, the picture [*The Love Bug*] was a huge, surprise success. It was 1969's top grossing film, ultimately returning over $23 million to the studio in domestic rentals, more than any non-animated feature other than *Mary Poppins*," in Richard Schickel, *The Disney Version* (New York: Touchstone, 1985), 382.

5. Ibid., 400–403.

6. *The Love Bug* is loosely based on a book titled *Car-Boy-Girl*, written by Gordon Buford in 1961.

7. Dean Jones, *Under Running Laughter* (Grand Rapids, Mich.: Chosen Books, 1982), 29.

8. Karal Ann Marling, *As Seen on TV: The Visual Culture of Everyday Life in the 1950s* (Cambridge, Mass.: Harvard University Press, 1994), 130.

9. Eric Smoodin, *Animating Culture* (New Brunswick, N.J.: Rutgers University Press, 1993), 111.

10. Ibid.

11. Ibid.

12. Schickel, 352.

13. Marling, 158.

14. Patricia Leigh Brown, "Drag Racing 21st-Century Style," *The New York Times*, July 22, 2001, 12.

15. Andrew Weiner, "Seek, Destroy, Enjoy!" *The Providence Phoenix*, July 21, 2000, 16.

16. Ibid.

17. Ibid.

18. James Dean, quoted in Graham McCann, *Rebel Males: Clift, Brando and Dean* (New Brunswick, N.J.: Rutgers University Press, 1991), 157.

19. Ibid.

20. Donald Spoto, *Rebel: The Life and Legend of James Dean* (New York: Harper Paperbacks, 1996), 292.

21. Ibid.

22. Ibid.

23. Ibid., 293.

24. J. P. Rupp, "The Love Bug," in *Car Crash Culture*, ed. Mikita Brottman (New York: Palgrave, 2001 [originally published in *Journal of Forensic Sciences*, July 1973]), 77–81.

25. "Editor's note," in Brottman, 81.

26. John Keats, *The Insolent Chariots* (Philadelphia: J. B. Lippincott, 1958), 10–13.

27. Phil Patton, *Bug: The Strange Mutations of the World's Most Famous Automobile* (New York: Simon and Schuster, 2002), 31.

28. Philippe Defechereux and Jean Graton, *James Dean: The Untold Story of a Passion for Speed*, trans. Intex Translations (Los Angeles: Mediavision Publications, 1996 [originally published in Brussels: Graton Editeur, 1995]), 51.

29. Thomas Frank, *The Conquest of Cool: Business Culture, Counterculture, and the Rise of Hip Consumerism* (Chicago: University of Chicago Press, 1997), 67–68.

30. Jones, 33.

31. R. W. Connell, *Masculinities* (Berkeley: University of California Press, 1995), 77.

32. Eve Kosofsky Sedgwick, *Between Men: English Literature and Male Homosocial Desire* (New York: Columbia University Press, 1985), 38.

33. Steven Cohan, *Masked Men: Masculinity and the Movies in the Fifties* (Bloomington: Indiana University Press, 1997), 84.

34. John Wayne, quoted in Cohan, 202.

35. McCann, 27.

36. Dean's and Brando's public hints of homosexuality and the new stars' non-traditional visual treatment in films were contained, points out Steven Cohan, by the assumption that their "deviations from hegemonic masculinity" could be explained by their boyishness, by their "impersonation of manhood." As adult "boyish" men, they "challenged the conflation of 'gender' and 'sexuality' traditionally assumed in American culture." Cohan concludes that "the new stars could not dismantle the dualism that upheld the period's hegemonic masculinity, but their popularity testifies to the ways in which audiences did indeed sense if not fully articulate the category crisis they personified as boys who are not men." In Cohan, 203, 263.

37. David Savran, *Taking It Like A Man: White Masculinity, Masochism, and Contemporary American Culture* (Princeton N.J.: Princeton University Press, 1998), 133.

38. Stuart Hall, quoted in Elizabeth Bell et al., *From Mouse to Mermaid* (Bloomington: Indiana University Press, 1995), 86.

39. Patton, 110.

40. Schickel, 383.

41. Steven Watts, *The Magic Kingdom: Walt Disney and the American Way of Life* (Boston: Houghton Mifflin, 1997), 358.

42. Ibid., 360.

43. Ibid., 23.

44. Carl Hiaasen, *Team Rodent: How Disney Devours the World* (New York: Library of Contemporary Thought, 1998), 10–11.

45. The realities of life in Celebration are carefully documented in Andrew Ross, *The Celebration Chronicles: Life, Liberty, and the Pursuit of Property Value in Disney's New Town* (New York: Ballantine Books, 1999).

46. Watts, 36.

47. Frank, 26–33.

48. Ibid., 28.

49. Ruth La Ferla, "Seattle-born Grunge Look Is Back as a Backlash to Glamour," *The New York Times News Service*, in *The Providence Journal*, October 1, 2003, G8.

50. Schickel, 319.

51. Ibid., 306.

52. Ibid., 318.

53. Disneyland, Jean Baudrillard explains, creates the illusion that it is a self-contained sanctuary of fantasy and fun detached from the serious real world surrounding it, but actually the whole U.S. has embraced Disneyesque artifice in the form of antiseptic malls and idealized re-creations of small-town ambience. In Jean Baudrillard, *Simulations*, trans. Paul Foss, Paul Patton, and Phillip Beitchman (New York: Semiotext(e), 1983), 23–26.

54. Henry Giroux, education and cultural studies scholar, succinctly identifies Disney's role in creating an America where youth are "growing up corporate" when he writes that "Disney's view of children as consumers has little to do with innocence and a great deal to do with corporate greed and the realization that behind the vocabulary of family fun and wholesome entertainment is the opportunity for teaching children that critical thinking and civic action in society are far less important to them than the role of passive consumers." In Henry Giroux, *The Mouse that Roared: Disney and the End of Innocence* (Lanham, Md.: Rowman and Littlefield, 1999), 158.

55. Julian Halevy, quoted in Schickel, 327–328.

56. Schickel, 306.

57. Ibid., 301.

58. Ibid., 344.

59. Eleanor Harris, "Rock Hudson: Why He's Number 1," *Look*, March 18, 1958, 48, quoted in Richard Meyer, "Rock Hudson's Body," in *Inside/Out: Lesbian Theories, Gay Theories*, ed. Diana Fuss (New York: Routledge, 1991), 265.

60. Meyer, 265.

61. Schickel, 282.

62. Ibid., 345.

63. Ibid., 383.

64. Ibid., 356.

65. Dean Jones, "Commentary," *The Love Bug*, special ed. DVD. Directed by Robert Stevenson (Burbank, CA: Buena Vista Home Entertainment, 2002).

66. Giroux, 158.

67. Patton, 110–111.

68. Michelle Lee, "Commentary," *The Love Bug*, special ed. DVD.

69. "Germany to Pay Nazi-era Laborers," *The Providence Journal*, May 31, 2001, A10.

70. Defechereux and Graton, 48.

71. Dean Jones, "Why Hollywood Makes Dirty Movies," Christianity.com, http://www.christianity.com...3,PTID1000/CHID102634/CIID111125,00.html.

72. Dean Jones, "The Great Divorce," Christianity.com, http://www.christianity.com...3,PTID1000/CHID102634/CIID199976,00.html.

73. J. G. Ballard, interview by Iain Sinclair. In Iain Sinclair, *Crash: David Cronenberg's Post-mortem on J. G. Ballard's "Trajectory of Fate"* (London: BFI Publishing, 1999), 97.

74. Ibid.

75. Patton, 113–114.

76. Michael Joseph Gross, "The Second Time as Comedy," *The New York Times*, March 13, 2005: 17.

77. Ibid.

Chapter 3: Rebel Wrecks

1. J. G. Ballard, *Crash* (New York: Noonday Press, 1994 [1973]), 50.

2. Ibid.

3. Ibid., 83.

4. Ibid., 84.

5. Ibid., 64.

6. Ibid., 117.

7. Ibid., 201.

8. Ibid., 203.

9. Ibid., 48–49.

10. Ibid., 49.

11. Jean Baudrillard, *The Ecstasy of Communication*, trans. Bernard Schutze and Caroline Schutze, ed. Sylvère Lotringer (New York: Semiotext(e), 1988), 22.

12. Ibid., 12.

13. Ibid., 13–14.

14. Jean Baudrillard, "Ballard's *Crash*," *Science-Fiction Studies* 18, no. 55, part 3 (November 1991): 315.

15. Ibid., 319.

16. Jean Baudrillard, quoted in Bradley Butterfield, "Ethical Value and Negative Aesthetics: Reconsidering the Baudrillard-Ballard Connections," *PMLA* 114, no. 1 (January 1999): 69.

17. Butterfield, 69.

18. Ballard, 17.

19. Elizabeth Taylor became close to James Dean during the filming of *Giant;* she was one of his only confidants on the set and they both had a strained relationship with director George Stevens. As a token of her friendship with Dean, Taylor gave him a kitten, whom he named Marcus after his young cousin Marcus

Winslow, in Fairmount (who now manages the James Dean Estate). In the days after Dean's death, Taylor, whom George Stevens forced to return to the *Giant* set, became ill and suffered a collapse for which she required hospitalization. Vaughan's desire in *Crash* to plunge into Elizabeth Taylor's limousine with his car and annihilate himself and her can be interpreted as a desire to become James Dean, to get close to Taylor and go out in an apocalyptic car wreck, only Vaughan, unlike Dean, wants to take her with him.

20. Ballard, 64.

21. Ibid.

22. Ronald Martinetti, *The James Dean Story: A Myth-Shattering Biography of a Hollywood Legend* (Seacaucus, N.J.: Citadel Stars, 1995), 8.

23. Maurice Zolotov, quoted in Joseph Humphreys, ed., *Jimmy Dean on Jimmy Dean* (London: Plexus Publishing, 1990), 122–123.

24. Leonard Spiegelglass, quoted in Martinetti, 40.

25. James Dean, quoted in Humphreys, 124.

26. Ballard, 88.

27. Wheeler Winston Dixon, *Disaster and Memory: Celebrity Culture and the Crisis of Hollywood Cinema* (New York: Columbia University Press, 1999), 50.

28. Ibid., 49.

29. Ballard, 16.

30. Barbara Creed, "The *Crash* Debate: Anal Wounds, Metallic Kisses," *Screen* 39, no. 2 (Summer 1998): 177.

31. Ballard, 85.

32. Ibid., 109.

33. Ibid., 111.

34. Mark Seltzer, "Wound Culture: Trauma in the Pathological Public Sphere," *October* 80 (Spring 1997): 3, quoted in Creed, 177.

35. Salman Rushdie, "Crash," *The New Yorker* (September 15, 1997): 68.

36. Ibid., 69.

37. J. G. Ballard, quoted in Iain Sinclair, *Crash: David Cronenberg's Post-mortem on J. G. Ballard's "Trajectory of Fate"* (London: BFI Publishing, 1999), 117.

38. Sinclair, 116.

39. Jonathan D. Rockoff, "Photographer Whose Gun Was Linked to Crime Dies," *The Providence Journal*, July 6, 2000, A1.

40. Ibid., A15.

41. Fred Botting and Scott Wilson, "Automatic Lover," *Screen* 39, no. 2 (Summer 1998): 190.

42. Dixon, 129.

43. J. G. Ballard, "Introduction to the French Edition," in *Crash* (New York: Vintage, 1985 [originally published in French ed., Paris: Calmann-Levy, 1974; English translation first appeared in *Foundation* 9 (November 1975)], 4–5.

44. Ibid., 6.

45. Botting and Wilson, 190.

46. Ballard, *Crash* (1994 edition), 102.

47. Ibid., 116.

48. Creed, 176.

49. Ibid., 175.

50. Ibid., 179.
51. Mark Dery, "Sex Drive: Interviews with David Cronenberg and J. G. Ballard," *21C: The Magazine of Culture, Technology and Science* 24 (1997): 51.
52. Ibid.
53. Sinclair, 122.
54. Art Simon, quoted in Associated Press, "It Kind of Seems Like Princess Diana All Over Again," *The Providence Journal*, July 19, 1999, A5.
55. Associated Press, A5.
56. Mikita Brottman and Christopher Sharrett, "The End of the Road: David Cronenberg's *Crash* and the Fading of the West," *Car Crash Culture*, ed. Mikita Brottman (New York: Palgrave, 2001), 207.
57. Ibid., 209.

Chapter 4: The Teen Rebel

1. David Dalton, *James Dean: American Icon* (New York: St. Martin's Press, 1984), 193.
2. John Dos Passos, "The Sinister Adolescents," in *Mid-century* (Boston: Houghton Mifflin, 1960), 479–486. The profile of James Dean was originally published in *Esquire* magazine, October 1958.
3. Paul Goodman, *Growing Up Absurd: Problems of Youth in the Organized System* (New York: Random House, 1960), 29, quoted in Douglas T. Miller and Marion Nowak, *The Fifties: The Way We Really Were* (New York: Doubleday, 1977), 286.
4. Mike A. Males, *The Scapegoat Generation: America's War on Adolescents* (Monroe, Me.: Common Courage Press, 1996), 3.
5. Ibid., 30.
6. Ibid., 16.
7. John J. Di Iulio, quoted in James Traub, "The Criminals of Tomorrow," *The New Yorker*, November 4, 1996, 52.
8. Mark Dery, "Deadly Childhood: Kids, Alienation, and Amorality," *gettingit .com*, a webzine, http://www.gettingit.com/article/32.
9. Thomas Hine, quoted in Kathleen Megan, "Rethinking the Curse of the Teenager Label," *The Providence Journal*, January 6, 2000, G2.
10. Megan, G2.
11. Somini Sengupta, "Innocence of Youth is Victim of Congo War," *The New York Times*, June 23, 2003, A1.
12. *New York Times* News Service, "Thai Forces Storm Hospital, Free Hostages," *The Providence Journal*, January 25, 2000, A3.
13. Marie Smyth, "The Militarization of Youth in Violently Divided Societies: Observations on Northern Ireland, the Middle East, and South Africa," in *Georgetown Journal of International Affairs* (Summer/Fall 2003): 88.
14. Fredric Jameson, *Postmodernism, or, The Cultural Logic of Late Capitalism* (Durham, N.C.: Duke University Press, 1991).
15. Jon Lewis, *The Road to Romance and Ruin: Teen Films and Youth Culture* (New York: Routledge, 1992), 150–151.
16. Males, 274.

17. Michele Aaron, "Pass/Fail," *Screen* 42, no. 1 (Spring 2001): 93.

18. Ibid., 92.

19. Ibid., 94.

20. Graham McCann, *Rebel Males: Clift, Brando and Dean* (New Brunswick, N.J.: Rutgers University Press, 1991), 27–28.

21. Julianne Pidduck, "Risk and Queer Spectatorship," *Screen* 42, no. 1 (Spring 2001): 97.

22. Aaron, 96.

23. Stacey D'Erasmo, "Boy Interrupted," *Out* magazine, October 1999, 126.

24. Hilary Swank, quoted in D'Erasmo, 69.

25. McCann, 156.

26. Aaron, 94.

27. Pidduck, 100.

28. Rachel Swan, "Boys Don't Cry," *Film Quarterly* 54, no. 3 (Spring 2001): 47.

29. Ibid., 49.

30. Ibid., 48.

31. Jacques Lacan, "The Mirror Stage as Formative of the Function of the I as Revealed in Psychoanalytic Experience," in *Écrits: A Selection*, trans. Alan Sheridan (New York: W. W. Norton: 1977), 1–7.

32. D'Erasmo, 126.

33. Scott Heller, ad for *Boys Don't Cry*, *The New York Times*, April 9, 2000, AR27.

34. Cover of *Out* magazine, October 1999.

35. Cover of *InStyle* magazine, August 2001.

36. Johanna Schneller, "A Woman in Full," *InStyle* magazine, August 2001, 242.

37. Ibid., 240.

38. Chang Ta-chun, "Wild Child," *Wild Kids: Two Novels about Growing Up*, trans. Michael Berry (New York: Columbia University Press, 2000). Page numbers are given parenthetically in the text.

39. Alan M. Wachman, "Competing Identities in Taiwan," in *The Other Taiwan: 1945 to the Present*, ed. Murray A. Rubenstein (Armonk, N.Y.: M. E. Sharpe, 1994), 21.

40. Ibid., 18.

41. Ibid., 17.

42. Chu Yen, "Sociocultural Change in Taiwan as Reflected in Short Fiction, 1979–1989," in *Cultural Change in Postwar Taiwan*, ed. Stevan Harrell and Huang Chün-chieh (Boulder, Colo.: Westview Press, 1994), 212.

43. Ibid., 217.

44. Dick Pountain and David Robins, *Cool Rules: Anatomy of an Attitude* (London: Reaktion Books, 2000), 22.

45. Ibid.

46. Stephen Holden, *The New York Times* News Service, "Heartbreaking Tale Captures the Plight of Desperate Teens," *The Providence Journal*, September 5, 2003, E2.

47. Bryan MacWilliams, "Forced into Prostitution," in *The Chronicle of Higher Education* 50, no. 6 (3 October 2003): A34.

48. *Pixote*, in turn, was the inspiration for a more recent Brazilian film, *City of God* (Fernando Meirelles and Katia Lund, 2003), about the desperate lives of young *favela* dwellers.

Chapter 5: The Postcolonial Rebel

1. This process is captured in *Ça Twiste à Popenguine*, a 1993 Senegalese film directed by Moussa Sene Absa, in which Senegalese youth in 1964 adopt the names and styles of French pop stars and American rhythm and blues performers while growing up in a small Senegalese fishing village where the reign of strict Christian and Islamic elders and the rigid schooling in French language and history are experienced as stifling.

2. Kwame Anthony Appiah, "The Postcolonial and the Postmodern," in *The Post-Colonial Studies Reader*, ed. Bill Ashcroft, Gareth Griffiths, and Helen Tiffin (London: Routledge, 1995), 124.

3. Naomi Klein, *No Logo* (New York: Picador USA, 2000), 195–229.

4. Robert Sklar, "Anarchic Visions," *Film Comment* 36, no. 3 (May–June 2000): 41.

5. Ibid., 42.

6. Frantz Fanon, *The Wretched of the Earth* (New York: Grove Press, 1963), 178.

7. Ibid., 179.

8. Nwachukwu Frank Ukadike, *Black African Cinema* (Berkeley: University of California Press, 1994), 221.

9. Ibid., 176.

10. François Pfaff, *Twenty-Five Black African Filmmakers* (Westport, Conn.: Greenwood Press, 1988), 220, quoted in Ukadike, 176.

11. Djibril Diop Mambety, "The Hyena's Last Laugh: A Conversation with Djibril Diop Mambety," an interview by Nwachukwu Frank Ukadike, California Newsreel Library of African Cinema, www.newsreel.org/articles/mambety.htm [Originally published in *Transition 78* 8, no. 2 (1999): 136–153].

12. Hybrid postcolonial subjectivity is theorized by Homi Bhabha, "Signs Taken for Wonders," in *The Location of Culture* (London: Routledge, 1994), 102–122.

13. Ukadike, 173.

14. Ella Shohat and Robert Stam, *Unthinking Eurocentrism: Multiculturalism and the Media* (New York: Routledge, 1994), 294.

15. John Akomfrah, "Dream Aloud: John Akomfrah, the Ghanaian-British Director, on the Exhilaration of African Cinemas," an interview by June Givanni, *Sight and Sound* 5, no. 9 (September 1995): 38.

16. Mambety, 3.

17. Mambety, quoted in Sklar, 42.

18. Djibril Diop Mambety, "African Conversations: An Interview with Djibril Diop Mambety," an interview by June Givanni, *Sight and Sound* 5, no. 9 (September 1995): 38.

19. Kevin Elstob, "Review of *Hate* (*La Haine*)," *Film Quarterly* 51, no. 2 (Winter 1997–98): 45.

20. Alec G. Hargreaves and Mark McKinney, "Introduction: The Post-Colonial Problematic in Contemporary France," in *Post-Colonial Cultures in France*, ed. Alec G. Hargreaves and Mark McKinney (London: Routledge, 1997), 4.

21. Ibid., 19.

22. Ibid., 12.

23. Ibid.

24. Elstob, 44.

25. Hargreaves and McKinney, 12.

26. Elstob, 45.

27. Hargreaves and McKinney, 13.

28. Ibid.

29. Ibid., 11.

30. Ruth Goodman Goetz and Augustus Goetz, *The Immoralist: A Drama in Three Acts by Ruth and Augustus Goetz, Based on the Novel by André Gide* (New York: Dramatists Play Service, 1954).

31. André Gide, *The Immoralist*, trans. Dorothy Bussy (New York: Alfred A. Knopf, 1954 [Paris: Mercure de France, 1921]).

32. Ibid., 22.

33. Ibid., 52.

34. Donald Spoto, *Rebel: The Life and Legend of James Dean* (New York: Harper Paperbacks, 1996), 169.

35. Robert Ready, "Jimmy the Arab," in *Mondo James Dean: A Collection of Stories and Poems about James Dean*, ed. Lucinda Ebersole and Richard Peabody, 63–66 (New York: St. Martin's Griffin, 1996).

36. Edward Said, *Orientalism* (New York: Pantheon Books, 1978), 3.

37. Ibid.

38. Ibid., 286–287.

39. The following quotations from the short story are from Robert Ready, "Jimmy the Arab." Page numbers are given parenthetically in the text.

40. Shohat and Stam, 108.

41. Edward Said, quoted in Jarrod Hayes, *Queer Nations: Marginal Sexualities in the Maghreb* (Chicago: University of Chicago Press, 2000), 23.

42. Hayes, 23.

43. Edward Said, quoted in Hayes, 24.

44. Hayes, 26. Hayes uses the term "homo sexual tourism" as shorthand for "homosexual sexual tourism" to distinguish it from "homosexual tourism." The latter refers to homosexual tourists traveling abroad, while the former indicates tourists having sexual relations with the local population. Clearly homosexual tourists are not necessarily sexual tourists. Jarrod Hayes, e-mail message to author, January 24, 2006.

45. Ibid., 34.

46. Ibid.

47. Alan Sheridan, *André Gide: A Life in the Present* (Cambridge, Mass.: Harvard University Press, 1999), 128.

48. Ibid., 167.

49. Ibid., 197.

50. Said, quoted in Hayes, 24.

51. Hayes, 136.

52. Ibid., 66.

53. Ibid.

54. Ibid., 146.

55. James Dean, quoted in Joseph Humphreys, ed., *Jimmy Dean on Jimmy Dean* (London: Plexus Publishing, 1990), 57.

56. Genet, quoted in Hayes, 42.

57. Hayes, 42.

Chapter 6: The Posthuman Rebel

1. Fredric Jameson, *Postmodernism, or, The Cultural Logic of Late Capitalism* (Durham, N.C.: Duke University Press, 1991), 19.

2. Joel Dinerstein, "Lester Young and the Birth of Cool," in *Signifyin(g), Sanctifyin', & Slam Dunking: A Reader in African American Expressive Culture*, ed. Gena Dagel Caponi (Amherst: University of Massachusetts Press, 1999), 241.

3. Michael DeAngelis, *Gay Fandom and Crossover Stardom: James Dean, Mel Gibson, and Keanu Reeves* (Durham, N.C.: Duke University Press, 2001).

4. Norman Mailer, *The White Negro* (San Francisco: City Lights, 1957), 2.

5. Caroline Bird, quoted in Mailer, 1.

6. Mailer, 3.

7. Ibid., 4.

8. Paul Oliver, *Blues Fell This Morning: Meaning in the Blues* (Cambridge: Cambridge University Press, 1990 [1960]), 283.

9. James Snead, *White Screens, Black Images: Hollywood from the Dark Side* (New York: Routledge, 1994), 139.

10. Richard Dyer, "White," *Screen* 29 no. 4 (Autumn 1988): 44.

11. Ibid., 56. Dyer analyzes the association of white characters with death and black characters with life in the films *Jezebel* (William Wyler, 1938), *Simba* (Brian Desmond Hurst, 1955), and *Night of the Living Dead* (George A. Romero, 1969).

12. Richard Dyer, *White* (London and New York: Routledge, 1997), 80.

13. Mailer, 4.

14. Linda Williams, *Playing the Race Card: Melodramas of Black and White from Uncle Tom to O. J. Simpson* (Princeton, N.J.: Princeton University Press, 2001), 303.

15. Richard Majors and Janet Mancini Billson, *Cool Pose: The Dilemmas of Black Manhood in America* (New York: Lexington Books, 1992), 30.

16. Mailer, 11.

17. Ibid.

18. Ibid., 10.

19. Spike Lee, quoted in Alex Kuffner, "Do The Right Thing: Be Wary of Movie Stereotypes, Spike Lee Says," *The Providence Journal*, April 5, 2001, B1.

20. Krin Gabbard, "Black Angels," *The Chronicle of Higher Education* 49, no. 39 (June 6, 2003): B15.

21. Spike Lee, "Thinking about the Power of Images: An Interview with Spike Lee," *Cineaste* 26, no. 2 (March 2001): 5.

22. Ibid.
23. Snead, 143.
24. Gabbard, B16.
25. Ibid. Films in this category include *The Hudsucker Proxy* (Joel Coen, 1994), *What Dreams May Come* (Vincent Ward, 1998), *The Green Mile* (Frank Darabont, 1999), and *The Legend of Bagger Vance* (Robert Redford, 2000).
26. Ibid.
27. Mailer, 4.
28. Gabbard, B16.
29. Edward Said, *Orientalism* (New York: Pantheon Books, 1978), 150.
30. Louis Althusser, *Lenin and Philosophy and Other Essays*, trans. Ben Brewster (New York: Monthly Review, 1971), 181.
31. Michel Foucault, *The History of Sexuality Volume 1: An Introduction*, trans. Robert Hurley (New York: Vintage Books, 1980), 93.
32. Thomas Frank, *The Conquest of Cool: Business Culture, Counterculture, and the Rise of Hip Consumerism* (Chicago: Chicago University Press, 1997), 28.
33. Ibid., 26.
34. Frank Rich, "There's No Exit from the Matrix," *The New York Times*, May 25, 2003, Sec. 2, 1.
35. Ibid.

Chapter 7: The Virtual Rebel

1. "Your Compatibility," http://celebmatch.com.birthdayform.php?category id=387&celebrity=JamesDean.
2. "James Dean Is Not Dead," http://www.geocities.com.
3. "James Dean: The Icon of Cool," http://www.geocities.com.
4. "JamesDean.com The Official Web Site," http://www.jamesdean.com/index2.php.
5. Jean Baudrillard, *Simulations*, trans. Paul Foss, Paul Patton, and Phillip Beitchman (New York: Semiotext(e), 1983), 11.
6. David Dalton, *James Dean Revealed: James Dean's Sexsational Lurid Afterlife in the Fan Magazines* (New York: Delta Books, 1991), 146.
7. Alice Packard, quoted in Joseph Humphreys, ed., *Jimmy Dean on Jimmy Dean* (London: Plexus Publishing, 1990), 66.
8. *James Dean Anniversary Book* (Dell, 1956), quoted in Humphreys, 69.
9. Dalton, 154.
10. Humphreys, 70.
11. Ibid.
12. Dalton, 55, 51, 60.
13. Humphreys, 55.
14. Ibid., 33.
15. Jay David Bolter and Richard Grusin, *Remediation: Understanding New Media* (Cambridge, Mass.: MIT Press, 1999), 5.
16. Ibid., 8–9.
17. Ibid., 53.

18. Robert Brady, "The James Dean Parameters," *Eclectica* magazine (June/July 1998), http://www.eclectica.org/v2n4/brady.html.

19. "JamesDean.com."

20. Ibid. This paragraph appeared on an earlier version of JamesDean.com's home page. The Web site was recently redesigned. Its home page is now a dense combination of links, photographs, and an audio clip. The site still features biographical information about Dean, photographs, and information about Fairmount and the festivals honoring Dean. It also still sells merchandise and explains its licensing policies for James Dean's name/image/likenesses.

21. "CMG Worldwide," http://www.cmgww.com/.

22. "JamesDean.com."

23. James Dean, "My Town," quoted in David Dalton, *James Dean: The Mutant King* (New York: St. Martin's Press, 1974), 85.

24. Donald Spoto, *Rebel: The Life and Legend of James Dean* (New York: Harper, 1996), 61, 63.

25. Val Holley, *James Dean: The Biography* (New York: St. Martin's Griffin, 1995), 14.

26. Ibid.

27. Spoto, *Rebel*, 133–134.

28. David Dalton, *James Dean: American Icon* (New York: St. Martin's Press, 1984), 282.

29. Joseph Like, "James Dean & the Pig," in *Real Things: An Anthology of Popular Culture in American Poetry*, ed. Jim Elledge and Susan Swartwout (Bloomington: Indiana University Press, 1999), 44–46.

30. Reuben Jackson, "James Dean," in *Mondo James Dean: A Collection of Stories and Poems about James Dean*, ed. Lucinda Ebersole and Richard Peabody (New York: St. Martin's Griffin, 1996), 67.

31. Phil Jones, "Going Home for James Dean: A Hometown Boy Reports on a Hometown Boy," http://www.wfor.cbsnow.com.

32. Ibid.

33. Holley, 7.

34. Ibid.

35. Fairmount resident, quoted in Paul Alexander, *Boulevard of Broken Dreams: The Life, Times, and Legend of James Dean* (New York: Viking, 1994), 291.

36. William Kotzwinkle, *Book of Love* (Boston: Houghton Mifflin, 1980).

37. Ibid., 233.

38. "James Dean Bar and Guest House," http://www.patong.com/jamesdean/home.html.

39. Dalton, *James Dean: American Icon*, 281.

40. "Welcome to Gay Patong," http://www.beachpatong.com/gaypatong/.

41. Pennapa Hongthong, "Storms Complete the Destruction of Maya Beach," *The Nation*, November 14, 1999, http://www.thaistudents.com/thebeach/archives.html.

42. James East, "Beach's Role in Tourism Push Angers Greens," *South China Morning Post*, December 11, 1999, http://www.thaistudents.com/thebeach/archives.html.

43. Bruce Cheesman, "Greens Cheer at Thai Tourism Blue," http://www.thaistudents.com/thebeach/archives.html.

44. Ibid.

45. Chang-Rae Lee, "The Spicy Pleasures of Phuket," *The New York Times Magazine*, "The Sophisticated Traveler" supplement, May 14, 2000, 72.

46. "Foreign Visitors Returning to Beaches on Thai Island." *The Seattle Times*, January 2, 2005, http://seattletimes.newsource.com/html/nationworld/2002138146_quakenotes02.html.

47. Andy Gardner, "James Dean Bradfield," http://www.personal.dundee.ac.uk/~agardner/james.html.

48. "Manic Street Preachers," http://web.ukonline.co.uk/maniks.

49. "La Vie de James Dean," http://www.blue.fr/dean/jdvie.htm.

50. "Deaners: James Dean Fans Speak Out," http://www.deaners.net.

51. "1998 James Dean Memorial Service Flower Photos," http://ourtentativetimes.net/99memorial/grave99.html/.

52. "Rent Dean," http://lavender.fortunecity.com/clockwork/326/rentdean.html.

53. Mark Gruetzman, e-mail message to author, June 27, 2001.

54. Gilbert B. Rodman, *Elvis after Elvis: The Posthumous Career of a Living Legend* (London: Routledge, 1996), 114.

55. "Deaners: James Dean Fans Speak Out."

56. "The James Dean Memorial Gallery," http://www.jamesdeangallery.com.

57. John Seger, "James Dean Picture Page." http://community—1.webtv.net/rockalittle/JAMESDEANpicturepage/.

58. Dalton, *James Dean: American Icon*, 245.

59. Ibid., 237.

60. Abbey, "Fairmount, Indiana, September 30, 1999," http://www.deaners.com.

61. "James Dean, the Classical Author under the Sexgoettern," http://www.com-online.de/freizeit/sexgoetter/dean.html&prev=/s.

62. "Deaners: James Dean Fans Speak Out."

63. Magdalin Leonardo, "Marfa," http://www.ourtentativetimes.net/marfa/index.html.

64. Ibid.

65. "Jimmy Beans: A Candy-Coated Tribute," in Leonardo, http://www.ourtentativetimes.net/marfa/index.html.

66. Joe Middleton, "Future Fantastic," http://www.philipkdick.com/articles/clone.html.

67. Ibid.

68. Ibid.

69. Ibid.

70. Ibid.

Bibliography

Publications

Aaron, Michele. "Pass/Fail." *Screen* 42, no. 1 (Spring 2001): 92–96.

Aberbach, David. *Surviving Trauma: Loss, Literature, and Psychoanalysis*. New Haven, Conn.: Yale University Press, 1989.

Advertisement for Adobe Software, *Rolling Stone* 825, November 11, 1999.

Ai. "James Dean." In *Mondo James Dean: A Collection of Stories and Poems about James Dean*, ed. Lucinda Ebersole and Richard Peabody, 5–7. New York: St. Martin's Griffin, 1996.

Akomfrah, John. "Dream Aloud: John Akomfrah, the Ghanaian-British Director, on the Exhilaration of African Cinemas." Interview by June Givanni. *Sight and Sound* 5, no. 9 (September 1995): 37–39.

Alexander, Paul. *Boulevard of Broken Dreams: The Life, Times, and Legend of James Dean*. New York: Viking, 1994.

Althusser, Louis. *Lenin and Philosophy and Other Essays*, trans. Ben Brewster. New York: Monthly Review, 1971.

Appiah, Kwame Anthony. "The Postcolonial and the Postmodern." In *The Post-Colonial Studies Reader*, ed. Bill Ashcroft, Gareth Griffiths, and Helen Tiffin, 119–124. London: Routledge, 1995. Originally published in Kwame Anthony Appiah, *In My Father's House: Africa in the Philosophy of Culture*, 137–157. Oxford: Oxford University Press, 1993.

Associated Press. "It Kind of Seems Like Princess Diana All Over Again." *The Providence Journal*, July 19, 1999, A5.

Ballard, J. G. *Crash*. New York: Noonday Press, 1994 [1973].

———. "Introduction to the French Edition." In *Crash*, 1–6. New York: Vintage, 1985. Originally published in French ed., Paris: Calmann-Levy, 1974. English translation first appeared in *Foundation* 9 (November 1975).

Baudrillard, Jean. "Ballard's *Crash*." *Science-Fiction Studies* 18, no. 55, part 3 (November 1991): 313–320.

———. *The Ecstasy of Communication*, trans. Bernard Schutze and Caroline Schutze, ed. Sylvère Lotringer. New York: Semiotext(e), 1988.

————. *Simulations*, trans. Paul Foss, Paul Patton, and Phillip Beitchman. New York: Semiotext(e), 1983.

Bell, Elizabeth, et al., eds. *From Mouse to Mermaid*. Bloomington: Indiana University Press, 1995.

Bhabha, Homi. "Signs Taken for Wonders." In *The Location of Culture*, 102–122. London: Routledge, 1994.

Bolter, Jay David, and Richard Grusin. *Remediation: Understanding New Media*. Cambridge, Mass.: MIT Press, 1999.

Botting, Fred, and Scott Wilson. "Automatic Lover." *Screen* 39, no. 2 (Summer 1998): 186–192.

Brauer, Ralph. "Iconic Modes: The Beatles." In *Icons of America*, ed. Ray B. Browne and Marshall Fishwick, 112–123. Bowling Green, Ohio: Bowling Green University Popular Press, 1978.

Brottman, Mikita, ed. *Car Crash Culture*. New York: Palgrave, 2001.

Brottman, Mikita, and Christopher Sharrett. "The End of the Road: David Cronenberg's *Crash* and the Fading of the West." In *Car Crash Culture*, ed. Mikita Brottman, 199–213. New York: Palgrave, 2001.

Brown, Patricia Leigh. "Drag Racing 21st-Century Style." *The New York Times*, July 22, 2001, 12.

Butterfield, Bradley. "Ethical Value and Negative Aesthetics: Reconsidering the Baudrillard-Ballard Connections." *PMLA* 114, no. 1 (January 1999): 64–77.

Cagin, Seth, and Philip Dray. *Born to Be Wild: Hollywood and the Sixties Generation*. Boca Raton: Coyote, 1994.

Chang, Ta-chun. "Wild Child." In *Wild Kids: Two Novels about Growing Up*, trans. Michael Berry, 129–257. New York: Columbia University Press, 2000.

Chu, Yen. "Sociocultural Change in Taiwan as Reflected in Short Fiction, 1979–1989." In *Cultural Change in Postwar Taiwan*, ed. Stevan Harrell and Huang Chün-chieh. Boulder, Colo.: Westview Press, 1994.

Cohan, Steven. *Masked Men: Masculinity and the Movies in the Fifties*. Bloomington: Indiana University Press, 1997.

Connell, R. W. *Masculinities*. Berkeley: University of California Press, 1995.

Considine, David. *The Cinema of Adolescence*. Jefferson, N.C.: McFarland, 1985.

Corley, Edwin. "Excerpt from *Farewell My Slightly Tarnished Hero*." In *Mondo James Dean: A Collection of Stories and Poems about James Dean*, ed. Lucinda Ebersole and Richard Peabody, 35–62. New York: St. Martin's Griffin, 1996.

Creed, Barbara. "The *Crash* Debate: Anal Wounds, Metallic Kisses." *Screen* 39, no. 2 (Summer 1998): 175–179.

Dalton, David. *James Dean: American Icon*. New York: St. Martin's Press, 1984.

————. *James Dean Revealed: James Dean's Sexsational Lurid Afterlife in the Fan Magazines*. New York: Delta Books, 1991.

————. *James Dean: The Mutant King*. New York: St. Martin's Press, 1974.

DeAngelis, Michael. *Gay Fandom and Crossover Stardom: James Dean, Mel Gibson, and Keanu Reeves*. Durham, N.C.: Duke University Press, 2001.

Defechereux, Philippe, and Jean Graton. *James Dean: The Untold Story of a Passion for Speed*, trans. Intex Translations. Los Angeles: Mediavision Publications, 1996. Originally published in Brussels: Graton Editeur, 1995.

D'Erasmo, Stacey. "Boy Interrupted." *Out* magazine, October 1999, 65–69, 126.

Dery, Mark. "Sex Drive: Interviews with David Cronenberg and J. G. Ballard." *21C: The Magazine of Culture, Technology and Science* 24 (1997): 40–51.

Dinerstein, Joel. "Lester Young and the Birth of Cool." In *Signifyin(g), Sanctifyin', & Slam Dunking: A Reader in African American Expressive Culture*, ed. Gena Dagel Caponi, 239–276. Amherst: University of Massachusetts Press, 1999.

Dixon, Wheeler Winston. *Disaster and Memory: Celebrity Culture and the Crisis of Hollywood Cinema*. New York: Columbia University Press, 1999.

Dos Passos, John. "The Sinister Adolescents." In *Mid-century*, 479–486. Boston: Houghton Mifflin, 1960.

Doss, Erika. *Elvis Culture: Fans, Faith, and Image*. Lawrence: University Press of Kansas, 1999.

Dyer, Richard. *Heavenly Bodies: Film Stars and Society*. New York: St. Martin's Press, 1986.

———. *The Matter of Images: Essays on Representation*. London: Routledge, 1993.

———. "Rock—The Last Guy You'd Have Figured?" In *You Tarzan: Masculinity, Movies and Men*, ed. Pat Kinkham and Janet Thumin, 27–34. New York: St. Martin's Press, 1993.

———. *White*. London and New York: Routledge, 1997.

———. "White." *Screen* 29 no. 4 (Autumn 1988): 44–64.

Ebersole, Lucinda, and Richard Peabody, eds. *Mondo James Dean: A Collection of Stories and Poems about James Dean*. New York: St. Martin's Griffin, 1996.

Eidus, Janice. "Jimmy Dean: My Kind of Guy." In *Mondo James Dean: A Collection of Stories and Poems about James Dean*, ed. Lucinda Ebersole and Richard Peabody, 16–19. New York: St. Martin's Griffin, 1996.

Elstob, Kevin. "Review of *Hate* (*La Haine*)." *Film Quarterly* 51, no. 2 (Winter 1997–98): 44–49.

Ermelino, Louisa. "No-Man's Land." In *Mondo James Dean: A Collection of Stories and Poems about James Dean*, ed. Lucinda Ebersole and Richard Peabody, 110–115. New York: St. Martin's Griffin, 1996.

Ewen, Stuart. *Captains of Consciousness: Advertising and the Social Roots of the Consumer Culture*. New York: McGraw-Hill, 1976.

Fanon, Frantz. *The Wretched of the Earth*. New York: Grove Press, 1963.

Fishwick, Marshall. "Entrance." In *Icons of Popular Culture*, ed. Marshall Fishwick and Ray B. Browne, 1–12. Bowling Green, Ohio: Bowling Green University Popular Press, 1970.

———. "Introduction." In *Icons of America*, ed. Ray B. Browne and Marshall Fishwick, 3–12. Bowling Green, Ohio: Bowling Green University Popular Press, 1978.

Fiske, John. *Understanding Popular Culture*. Boston: Unwin Hyman, 1989.

Foucault, Michel. *The History of Sexuality Volume 1: An Introduction*, trans. Robert Hurley. New York: Vintage Books, 1980.

Frank, Thomas. *The Conquest of Cool: Business Culture, Counterculture, and the Rise of Hip Consumerism*. Chicago: University of Chicago Press, 1997.

———. "Why Johnny Can't Dissent." In *Commodify Your Dissent: Salvos from The Baffler*, ed. Thomas Frank and Matt Weiland, 31–45. New York: W. W. Norton, 1997.

Frank, Thomas, and Dave Mulcahey. "Consolidated Deviance, Inc." In *Commodify Your Dissent: Salvos from The Baffler*, ed. Thomas Frank and Matt Weiland, 72–78. New York: W. W. Norton, 1997.

Fuss, Diana, ed. *Inside/Out: Lesbian Theories, Gay Theories*. New York: Routledge, 1991.

Gabbard, Krin. "Black Angels." *The Chronicle of Higher Education* 49, no. 39 (June 6, 2003): B15–B16.

"Germany to Pay Nazi-era Laborers." *The Providence Journal*, May 31, 2001, A10.

Gibson, James William. *Warrior Dreams: Paramilitary Culture in Post-Vietnam America*. New York: Hill and Wang, 1994.

Gide, André. *The Immoralist*, trans. Dorothy Bussy. New York: Alfred A. Knopf, 1954 [Paris: Mercure de France, 1921].

Gilmore, John. *Live Fast—Die Young: My Life with James Dean*. New York: Thunder's Mouth Press, 1997.

Giroux, Henry. *The Mouse That Roared: Disney and the End of Innocence*. Lanham, Md.: Rowman and Littlefield, 1999.

Goetz, Ruth Goodman, and Augustus Goetz. *The Immoralist: A Drama in Three Acts by Ruth and Augustus Goetz, Based on the Novel by André Gide*. New York: Dramatists Play Service, 1954.

Goodman, Paul. *Growing Up Absurd: Problems of Youth in the Organized System*. New York: Random House, 1960.

Graczyk, Ed. "Excerpt from *Come Back to the Five and Dime, Jimmy Dean, Jimmy Dean*." In *Mondo James Dean: A Collection of Stories and Poems about James Dean*, ed. Lucinda Ebersole and Richard Peabody, 127–135. New York: St. Martin's Griffin, 1996.

Gross, Michael Joseph. "The Second Time as Comedy." *The New York Times*, "Arts and Leisure," March 13, 2005, 15, 17.

Haldeman II, Jack C. "South of Eden, Somewhere near Salinas." In *Mondo James Dean: A Collection of Stories and Poems about James Dean*, ed. Lucinda Ebersole and Richard Peabody, 89–107. New York: St. Martin's Griffin, 1996.

Hargreaves, Alec G., and Mark McKinney. "Introduction: The Post-Colonial Problematic in Contemporary France." In *Post-Colonial Cultures in France*, ed. Alec G. Hargreaves and Mark McKinney, 3–25. London: Routledge, 1997.

Hart, Stephanie. "Who Killed Jimmy Dean?" In *Mondo James Dean: A Collection of Stories and Poems about James Dean*, ed. Lucinda Ebersole and Richard Peabody, 80–88. New York: St. Martin's Griffin, 1996.

Hass, Nancy. "I Seek Dead People." In the "Home Design" supplement to *The New York Times*, October 12, 2003, 38.

Hayes, Jarrod. *Queer Nations: Marginal Sexualities in the Maghreb*. Chicago: University of Chicago Press, 2000.

Hebdige, Dick. *Subculture: The Meaning of Style*. London: Methuen, 1979.

Heller, Scott. Ad for *Boys Don't Cry*, *The New York Times*, April 9, 2000, AR27.

Hiaasen, Carl. *Team Rodent: How Disney Devours the World*. New York: Library of Contemporary Thought, 1998.

Hofstede, David. *James Dean: A Bio-Bibliography*. Westport, Conn.: Greenwood Press, 1996.

Holden, Stephen. *The New York Times* News Service. "Heartbreaking Tale Captures the Plight of Desperate Teens." *The Providence Journal*, September 5, 2003, E1–E2.

Holley, Val. *James Dean: The Biography*. New York: St. Martin's Griffin, 1995.

Howlett, John. *James Dean: A Biography*. London: Plexus, 1997.

Humphreys, Joseph, ed. *Jimmy Dean on Jimmy Dean*. London: Plexus Publishing, 1990.

InStyle magazine. Cover. August 2001.

Jackson, Reuben. "James Dean." In *Mondo James Dean: A Collection of Stories and Poems about James Dean*, ed. Lucinda Ebersole and Richard Peabody, 67. New York: St. Martin's Griffin, 1996.

Jameson, Fredric. *Postmodernism, or, The Cultural Logic of Late Capitalism*. Durham, N.C.: Duke University Press, 1991.

Jones, Dean. "Commentary." *The Love Bug*. Special ed. DVD. Directed by Robert Stevenson. Burbank, Calif.: Buena Vista Home Entertainment, 2002.

———. *Under Running Laughter*. Grand Rapids, Mich.: Chosen Books, 1982.

Keats, John. *The Insolent Chariots*. Philadelphia: J. B. Lippincott, 1958.

Klein, Naomi. *No Logo*. New York: Picador USA, 2000.

Kotzwinkle, William. *Book of Love*. Boston: Houghton Mifflin, 1980.

Kuffner, Alex. "Do the Right Thing: Be Wary of Movie Stereotypes, Spike Lee Says." *The Providence Journal*, April 5, 2001, B1, B4.

Lacan, Jacques. *Écrits: A Selection*, trans. Alan Sheridan. New York: W. W. Norton, 1977.

La Ferla, Ruth. "Seattle-Born Grunge Look Is Back as a Backlash to Glamour." *The New York Times News Service*. *The Providence Journal*, October 1, 2003, G8.

Lee, Michelle. "Commentary." *The Love Bug*. Special Ed. DVD. Directed by Robert Stevenson. Burbank, Calif.: Buena Vista Home Entertainment, 2002.

Lee, Spike. "Thinking about the Power of Images: An Interview with Spike Lee." *Cineaste* 26, no. 2 (March 2001): 4–9.

Leibman, Nina. *Living Room Lectures*. Austin: University of Texas Press, 1995.

Lewis, Jon. *The Road to Romance and Ruin: Teen Films and Youth Culture*. New York: Routledge, 1992.

Like, Joseph. "James Dean & the Pig." In *Real Things: An Anthology of Popular Culture in American Poetry*, ed. Jim Elledge and Susan Swartwout, 44–46. Bloomington: Indiana University Press, 1999.

Little, Bentley. "The Idol." In *Mondo James Dean: A Collection of Stories and Poems about James Dean*, ed. Lucinda Ebersole and Richard Peabody, 20–32. New York: St. Martin's Griffin, 1996.

MacWilliams, Bryon. "Forced into Prostitution." *The Chronicle of Higher Education* 50, no. 6 (3 October 2003): A34–A36.

Mailer, Norman. *The White Negro*. San Francisco: City Lights, 1957.

Majors, Richard, and Janet Mancini Billson. *Cool Pose: The Dilemmas of Black Manhood in America*. New York: Lexington Books, 1992.

Males, Mike A. *Framing Youth: 10 Myths about the Next Generation*. Monroe, Me.: Common Courage Press, 1999.

———. *The Scapegoat Generation: America's War on Adolescents*. Monroe, Me.: Common Courage Press, 1996.

Mambety, Djibril Diop. "African Conversations: An Interview with Djibril Diop Mambety." Interview by June Givanni. *Sight and Sound* 5, no. 9 (September 1995): 30–31.

———. "The Hyena's Last Laugh: A Conversation with Djibril Diop Mambety." Interview by Nwachukwu Frank Ukadike. California Newsreel Library of African Cinema. www.newsreel.org/articles/mambety.htm. Originally published in *Transition* 78 8, no. 2 (1999): 136–153.

Manso, Peter. *Brando: The Biography*. New York: Hyperion, 1994.

Marling, Karal Ann. *As Seen on TV: The Visual Culture of Everyday Life in the 1950s*. Cambridge, Mass.: Harvard University Press, 1994.

Marshall, Alexandra. "Born to be Mild." "Men's Fashions of the Times." Supplement to *The New York Times*, September 21, 2003, 65–68.

Martinetti, Ronald. *The James Dean Story: A Myth-Shattering Biography of a Hollywood Legend*. Seacaucus, N.J.: Citadel Stars, 1995.

McCann, Graham. *Rebel Males: Clift, Brando and Dean*. New Brunswick, N.J.: Rutgers University Press, 1991.

Megan, Kathleen. "Rethinking the Curse of the Teenager Label." *The Providence Journal*, January 6, 2000, G2.

Mellen, Joan. *Big Bad Wolves: Masculinity in the American Film*. New York: Pantheon Books, 1977.

Meyer, Richard. "Rock Hudson's Body." In *Inside/Out: Lesbian Theories, Gay Theories*, ed. Diana Fuss, 259–288. New York: Routledge, 1991.

Miller, Douglas T., and Marion Nowak. *The Fifties: The Way We Really Were*. New York: Doubleday, 1977.

New York Times News Service. "Thai Forces Storm Hospital, Free Hostages." *The Providence Journal*, January 25, 2000, A3.

Oliver, Paul. *Blues Fell This Morning: Meaning in the Blues*. Cambridge: Cambridge University Press, 1990 [1960].

Orr, David Gerald. "The Icon in the Time Tunnel." In *Icons of America*, ed. Ray B. Browne and Marshall Fishwick, 13–23. Bowling Green, Ohio: Bowling Green University Popular Press, 1978.

Out magazine. Cover. October 1999.

Patton, Phil. *Bug: The Strange Mutations of the World's Most Famous Automobile*. New York: Simon and Schuster, 2002.

Perry, George. *James Dean*. London: DK Adult, 2005.

Pfaff, François. *Twenty-Five Black African Filmmakers*. Westport, Conn.: Greenwood Press, 1988.

Pidduck, Julianne. "Risk and Queer Spectatorship." *Screen* 42, no. 1 (Spring 2001): 97–102.

Pountain, Dick, and David Robins. *Cool Rules: Anatomy of an Attitude*. London: Reaktion, 2000.

Ready, Robert. "Jimmy the Arab." In *Mondo James Dean: A Collection of Stories and Poems about James Dean*, ed. Lucinda Ebersole and Richard Peabody, 63–66. New York: St. Martin's Griffin, 1996.

Rich, Frank. "There's No Exit from *The Matrix*." *The New York Times* May 25, 2003, Sec. 2, 1, 22.

Riese, Randall. *The Unabridged James Dean: His Life and Legacy from A to Z.* Chicago: Contemporary Books, 1991.

Rockoff, Jonathan D. "Photographer Whose Gun Was Linked to Crime Dies." *The Providence Journal,* July 6, 2000, A1, A15.

Rodman, Gilbert B. *Elvis after Elvis: The Posthumous Career of a Living Legend.* London: Routledge, 1996.

Romero, Simon. "A Texas Town Holds Fast to Its Ties to a Classic." *The New York Times,* June 9, 2003, A8.

Rose, Tricia. "Flow, Layering, and Rupture in Postindustrial New York." In *Signifyin(g), Sanctifyin', and Slam Dunking: A Reader in African American Expressive Culture,* ed. Gena Dagel Caponi, 191–221. Amherst: University of Massachusetts Press, 1999.

Ross, Andrew. *The Celebration Chronicles: Life, Liberty, and the Pursuit of Property Value in Disney's New Town.* New York: Ballantine Books, 1999.

Rudnick, Paul. "Everybody's a Rebel." *Spy Magazine,* March 1992, 52–58.

Rupp, J. P. "The Love Bug." In *Car Crash Culture,* ed. Mikita Brottman, 77–81. New York: Palgrave, 2001. Originally published in *Journal of Forensic Sciences* (July 1973).

Rushdie, Salman. "Crash." *The New Yorker,* September 15, 1997, 68–69.

Said, Edward. *Orientalism.* New York: Pantheon Books, 1978.

Savage, Jon. "Sex, Rock, and Identity: The Enemy Within." In *Facing the Music,* ed. Simon Frith, 131–172. New York: Pantheon Books, 1988.

Savran, David. *Taking It like a Man: White Masculinity, Masochism, and Contemporary American Culture.* Princeton, N.J.: Princeton University Press, 1998.

Schickel, Richard. *Brando: A Life in Our Times.* New York: Atheneum, 1991.

———. *The Disney Version.* New York: Touchstone, 1985.

Schneller, Johanna. "A Woman in Full." *InStyle* magazine, August 2001, 238–244.

Schwartz, Deb. "Dean of Style," *Out* magazine, September 1996, 99, 147.

Sedgwick, Eve Kosofsky. *Between Men: English Literature and Male Homosocial Desire.* New York: Columbia University Press, 1985.

Seltzer, Mark. "Wound Culture: Trauma in the Pathological Public Sphere." *October* 80 (Spring 1997): 3–26.

Sengupta, Somini. "Innocence of Youth Is Victim of Congo War." *The New York Times,* June 23, 2003, A1, A11.

Shary, Timothy. *Generation Multiplex: The Image of Youth in Contemporary American Cinema.* Austin: University of Texas Press, 2002.

Sheridan, Alan. *André Gide: A Life in the Present.* Cambridge, Mass.: Harvard University Press, 1999.

Sheridan, Liz. *Dizzy and Jimmy: My Life with James Dean, A Love Story.* New York: Regan Books, 2000.

Shiner, Lewis. "Kings of the Afternoon." In *Mondo James Dean: A Collection of Stories and Poems about James Dean,* ed. Lucinda Ebersole and Richard Peabody, 68–79. New York: St. Martin's Griffin, 1996.

Shohat, Ella, and Robert Stam. *Unthinking Eurocentrism: Multiculturalism and the Media.* New York: Routledge, 1994.

Sinclair, Iain. *Crash: David Cronenberg's Post-Mortem on J. G. Ballard's "Trajectory of Fate."* London: BFI Publishing, 1999.

Skaggs, David Curtis. "Postage Stamps as Icons." In *Icons of America*, ed. Ray B. Browne and Marshall Fishwick, 198–208. Bowling Green, Ohio: Bowling Green University Popular Press, 1978.

Sklar, Robert. "Anarchic Visions." *Film Comment* 36, no. 3 (May–June 2000): 41–43.

Smoodin, Eric. *Animating Culture*. New Brunswick, N.J.: Rutgers University Press, 1993.

Smyth, Marie. "The Militarization of Youth in Violently Divided Societies: Observations on Northern Ireland, the Middle East, and South Africa." *Georgetown Journal of International Affairs* (Summer/Fall 2003): 83–90.

Snead, James. *White Screens, Black Images: Hollywood from the Dark Side*. New York: Routledge, 1994.

Spoto, Donald. *Rebel: The Life and Legend of James Dean*. New York: Harper Paperbacks, 1996.

Swan, Rachel. "Boys Don't Cry." *Film Quarterly* 54, no. 3 (Spring 2001): 47–52.

Traub, James. "The Criminals of Tomorrow." *The New Yorker*, November 4, 1996, 50–52.

Ukadike, Nwachukwu Frank. *Black African Cinema*. Berkeley: University of California Press, 1994.

Villanueva, Tino. *Scene from the Movie Giant*. Willimantic, Conn.: Curbstone Press, 1993.

Wachman, Alan M. "Competing Identities in Taiwan." In *The Other Taiwan: 1945 to the Present*, ed. Murray A. Rubenstein, 17–80. Armonk, N.Y.: M. E. Sharpe, 1994.

Watts, Steven. The *Magic Kingdom: Walt Disney and the American Way of Life*. Boston: Houghton Mifflin, 1997.

Weiner, Andrew. "Seek, Destroy, Enjoy!" *The Providence Phoenix*, July 21, 2000, 16.

Williams, Linda. *Playing the Race Card: Melodramas of Black and White from Uncle Tom to O. J. Simpson*. Princeton, N.J.: Princeton University Press, 2001.

"Year's Favorite Stamp Features James Dean." *The Providence Journal*, December 30, 1996, A2.

Electronic Documents

Abbey. "Fairmount, Indiana, September 30, 1999." http://www.deaners.com.

Brady, Robert. "The James Dean Parameters." *Eclectica* magazine (June/July 1998). http://www.eclectica.org/v2n4/brady.html.

Cheesman, Bruce. "Greens Cheer at Thai Tourism Blue." http://www.thaistudents.com/thebeach/archives.html.

"CMG Worldwide." http://www.cmgww.com/.

"Deaners: James Dean Fans Speak Out." http://www.deaners.net.

deChant, Dell. "The Economy as Religion: The Dynamics of Consumer Culture." *The Civic Arts Review* 16, no. 2 (Summer/Fall 2003): 1–9. http://car.owu.edu/Vol.%2016%20No.%202html.

Dery, Mark. "Deadly Childhood: Kids, Alienation, and Amorality." *gettingit.com*, a webzine. http://www.gettingit.com/article/32.

East, James. "Beach's Role in Tourism Push Angers Greens." *South China Morning Post*, December 11, 1999. http://www.thaistudents.com/thebeach/archives.html.

"Foreign Visitors Returning to Beaches on Thai Island." *The Seattle Times*, January 2, 2005. http://seattletimes.newsource.com/html/nationworld/2002138146_quakenotes02.html.

Gardner, Andy. "James Dean Bradfield." http://www.personal.dundee.ac.uk/~agardner/james.html.

Hongthong, Pennapa. "Storms Complete the Destruction of Maya Beach." *The Nation*, November 14, 1999. http://www.thaistudents.com/thebeach/archives.html.

"James Dean Bar and Guest House." http://www.patong.com/jamesdean/home.html.

"JamesDean.com The Official Web Site." http://www.jamesdean.com/index.php.

"James Dean Is Not Dead." http://www.geocities.com.

"James Dean, the Classical Author under the Sexgoettern." http://www.com-online.de/freizeit/sexgoetter/dean.html&prev=/s.

"James Dean: The Icon of Cool." http://www.geocities.com.

"Jimmy Beans: A Candy-Coated Tribute." In "Marfa," by Magdalin Leonardo. http://www.ourtentativetimes.net/marfa/index.html.

Jones, Dean. "The Great Divorce." *Christianity.com* http://www.christianity.com...3,PTID1000/CHID102634/CIID199976,00.html.

———. "Why Hollywood Makes Dirty Movies." Christianity.com http://www.christianity.com...3,PTID1000/CHID 102634/CIID111125,00.html.

Jones, Phil. "Going Home for James Dean: A Hometown Boy Reports on a Hometown Boy." http://www.wfor.cbsnow.com.

Lee, Chang-Rae. "The Spicy Pleasures of Phuket." *The New York Times Magazine*. "The Sophisticated Traveler." Supplement, May 14, 2000, 72.

Leonardo, Magdalin. "Marfa." http://www.ourtentativetimes.net/marfa/index.html.

"Manic Street Preachers." http://web.ukonline.co.uk/maniks.

MDI Entertainment, Inc. "Licensed Brands." http://www.mediaentertainment.com/cmp/jd_about.html.

Middleton, Joe. "Future Fantastic." http://www.philipkdick.com/articles/clone.html.

"1998 James Dean Memorial Service Flower Photos." http://ourtentativetimes.net/99memorial/grave99.html/.

"Rebel.com." http://www.rebel.com.

"Rent Dean." http://lavender.fortunecity.com/clockwork/326/rentdean.html.

Seger, John. "James Dean Picture Page." http://community1.webtv.net/rockalittle/JAMESDEANpicturepage/.

"The James Dean Memorial Gallery." http://www.jamesdeangallery.com.

"La Vie de James Dean." http://www.blue.fr/dean/jdvie.htm.

"Welcome to Gay Patong." http://www.beachpatong.com/gaypatong/.

"Your Compatibility." http://celebmatch.com.birthdayform.php?categoryid=387&celebrity=JamesDean.

Index

Page numbers in *italics* indicate illustrations.